D0565394

VELVET
BEFORE THE
LIVING END

IMAGE COMICS, INC.
Robert Kirkman – Chief Operating Officer
Erik Larsen – Chief Financial Officer
Todd McFarlane – President
Marc Silvestri – Chief Executive Officer
Jim Valentino – Vice-President

Eric Stephenson – Publisher
Ron Richards – Director of Business Development
Jennifer de Guzman – Director of Trade Book Sales
Kat Salazar – Director of PR & Marketing
Jeremy Sullivan – Director of Digital Sales
Emilio Bautista – Sales Assistant
Branwyn Bigglestone – Senior Accounts Manager
Emily Miller – Accounts Manager
Jessica Ambriz – Administrative Assistant
Tyler Shainline – Events Coordinator
David Brothers – Content Manager
Jonathan Chan – Production Manager
Drew Gill – Art Director
Meredith Wallace – Print Manager
Monica Garcia – Senior Production Artist
Jenna Savage – Production Artist
Addison Duke – Production Artist
Tricia Ramos – Production Assistant
IMAGECOMICS.COM

ED BRUBAKER
WRITER

STEVE EPTING
ARTIST

ELIZABETH BREITWEISER
COLORS

CHRIS ELIOPOULOS
LETTERS

DAVID BROTHERS
EDITS

DREW GILL
PRODUCTION

SPECIAL THANKS TO SIDNEY STONE

A NOTE ON FOREIGN LANGUAGES:
Dialogue in an italic font should be read as a foreign language.

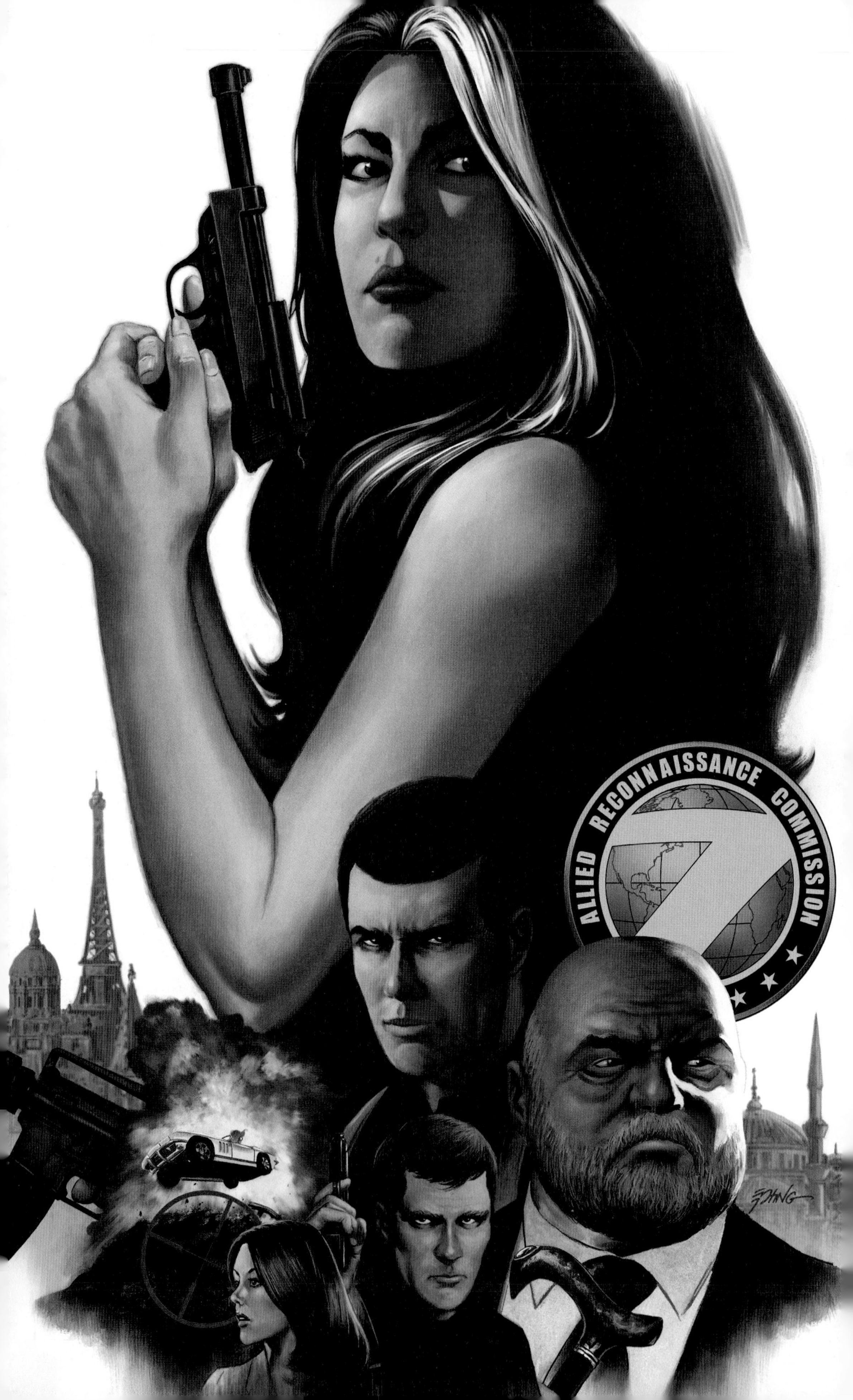
ALLIED RECONNAISSANCE COMMISSION

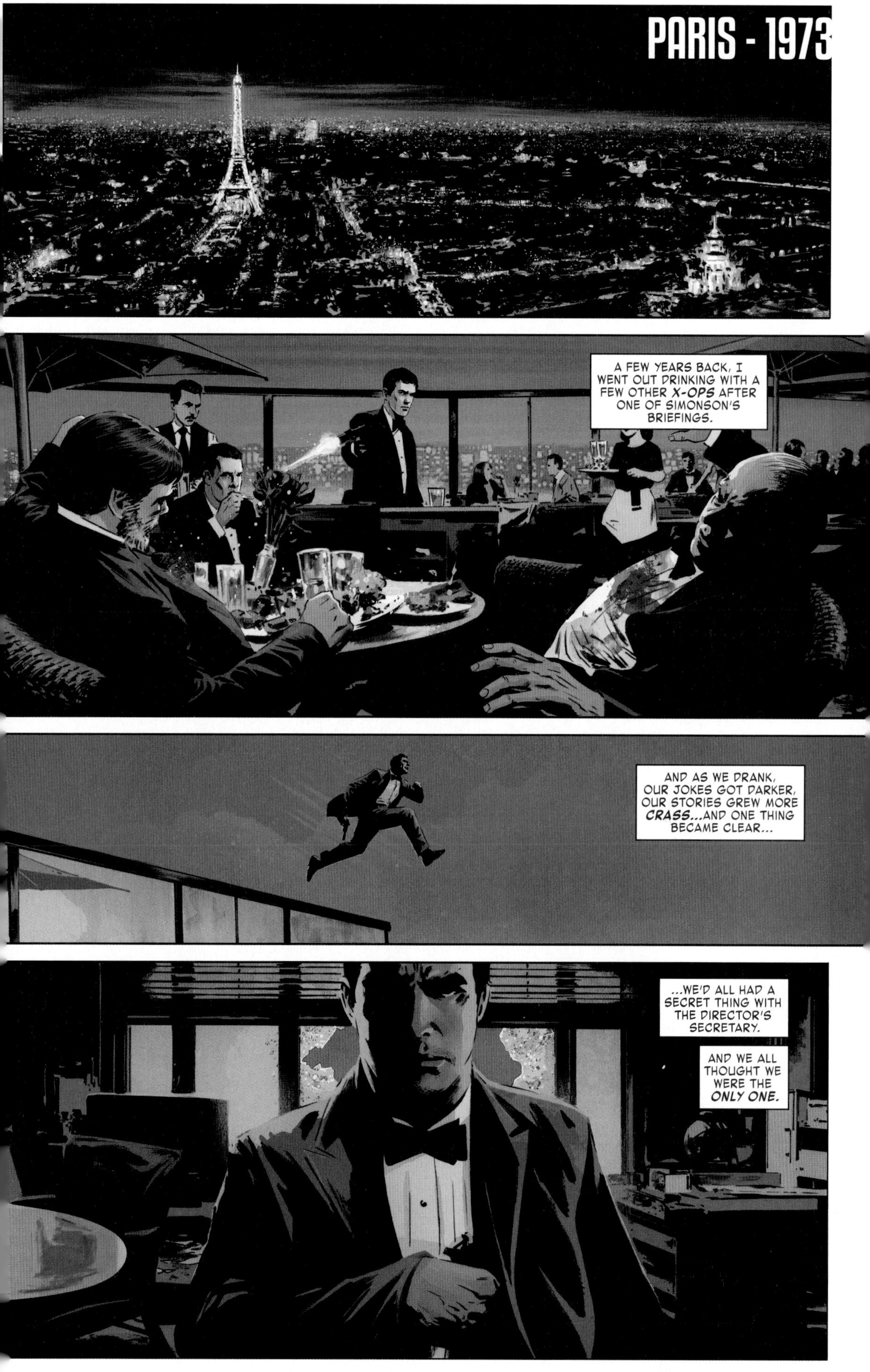
PARIS - 1973
A FEW YEARS BACK, I WENT OUT DRINKING WITH A FEW OTHER X-OPS AFTER ONE OF SIMONSON'S BRIEFINGS.
AND AS WE DRANK, OUR JOKES GOT DARKER, OUR STORIES GREW MORE CRASS...AND ONE THING BECAME CLEAR...
...WE'D ALL HAD A SECRET THING WITH THE DIRECTOR'S SECRETARY.
AND WE ALL THOUGHT WE WERE THE ONLY ONE.

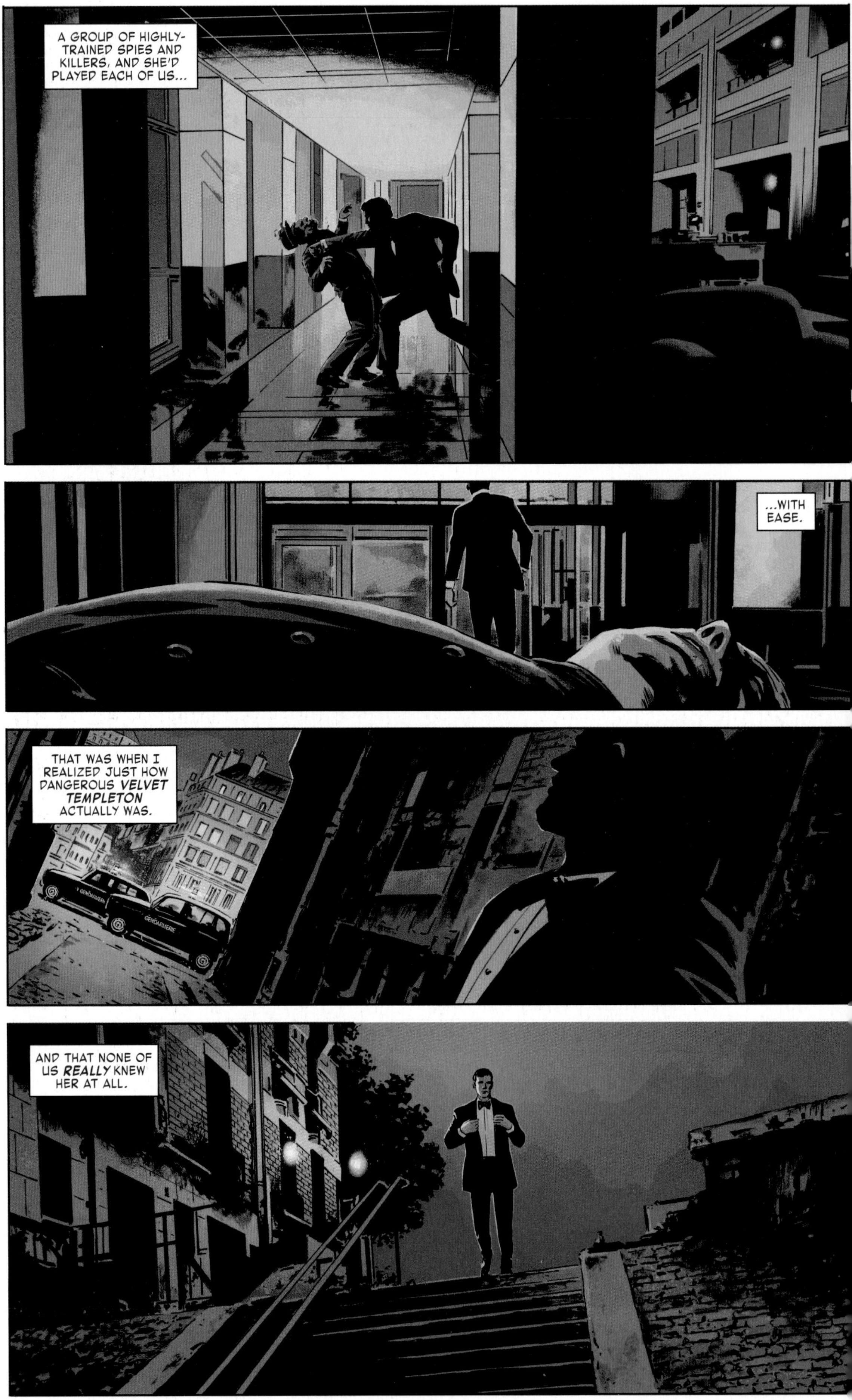

A GROUP OF HIGHLY-TRAINED SPIES AND KILLERS, AND SHE'D PLAYED EACH OF US...
...WITH EASE.
THAT WAS WHEN I REALIZED JUST HOW DANGEROUS *VELVET TEMPLETON* ACTUALLY WAS.
GENDARMERIE
GENDARMERIE
AND THAT NONE OF US *REALLY* KNEW HER AT ALL.

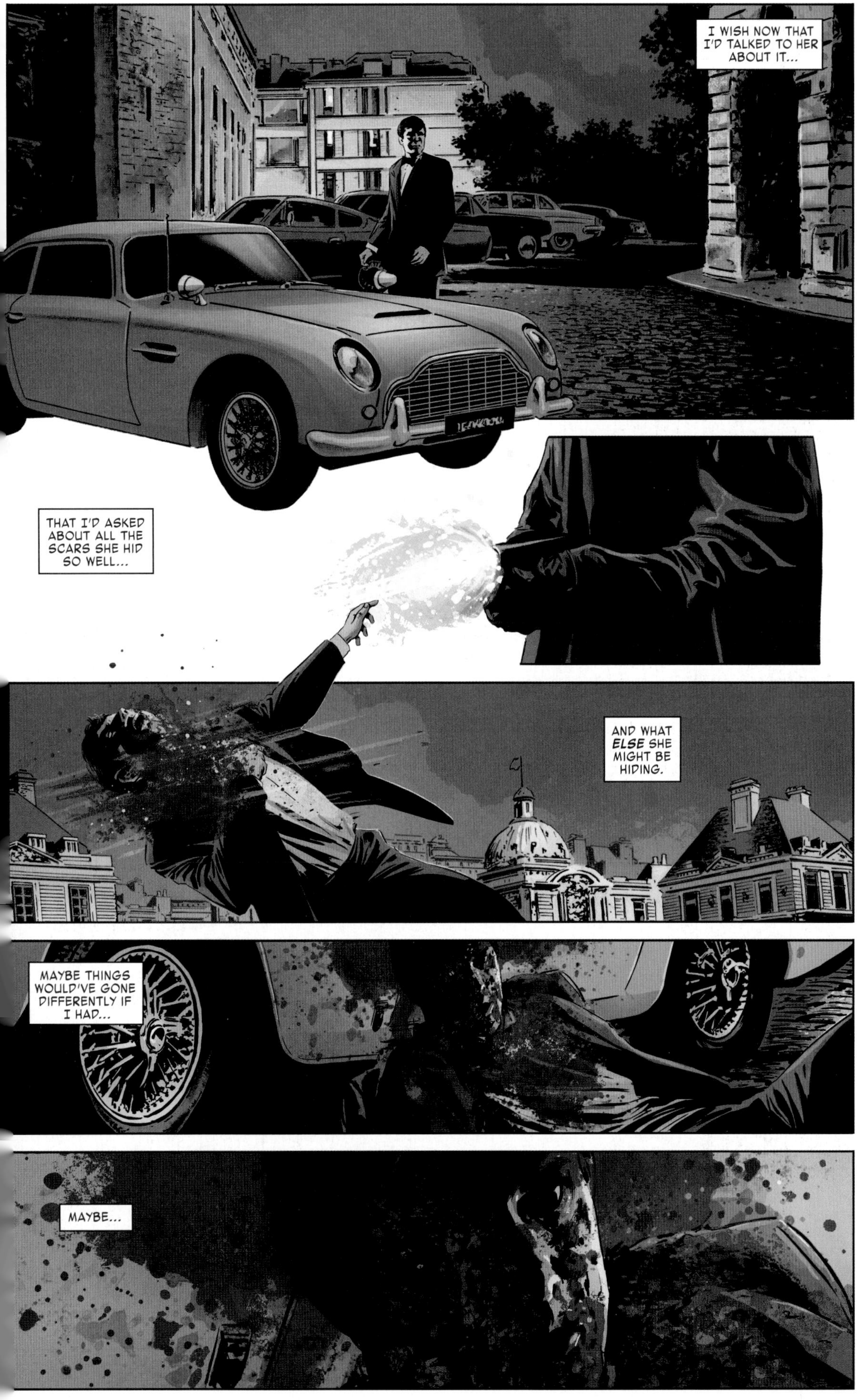
I WISH NOW THAT I'D TALKED TO HER ABOUT IT...
THAT I'D ASKED ABOUT ALL THE SCARS SHE HID SO WELL...
AND WHAT ELSE SHE MIGHT BE HIDING.
MAYBE THINGS WOULD'VE GONE DIFFERENTLY IF I HAD...
MAYBE...

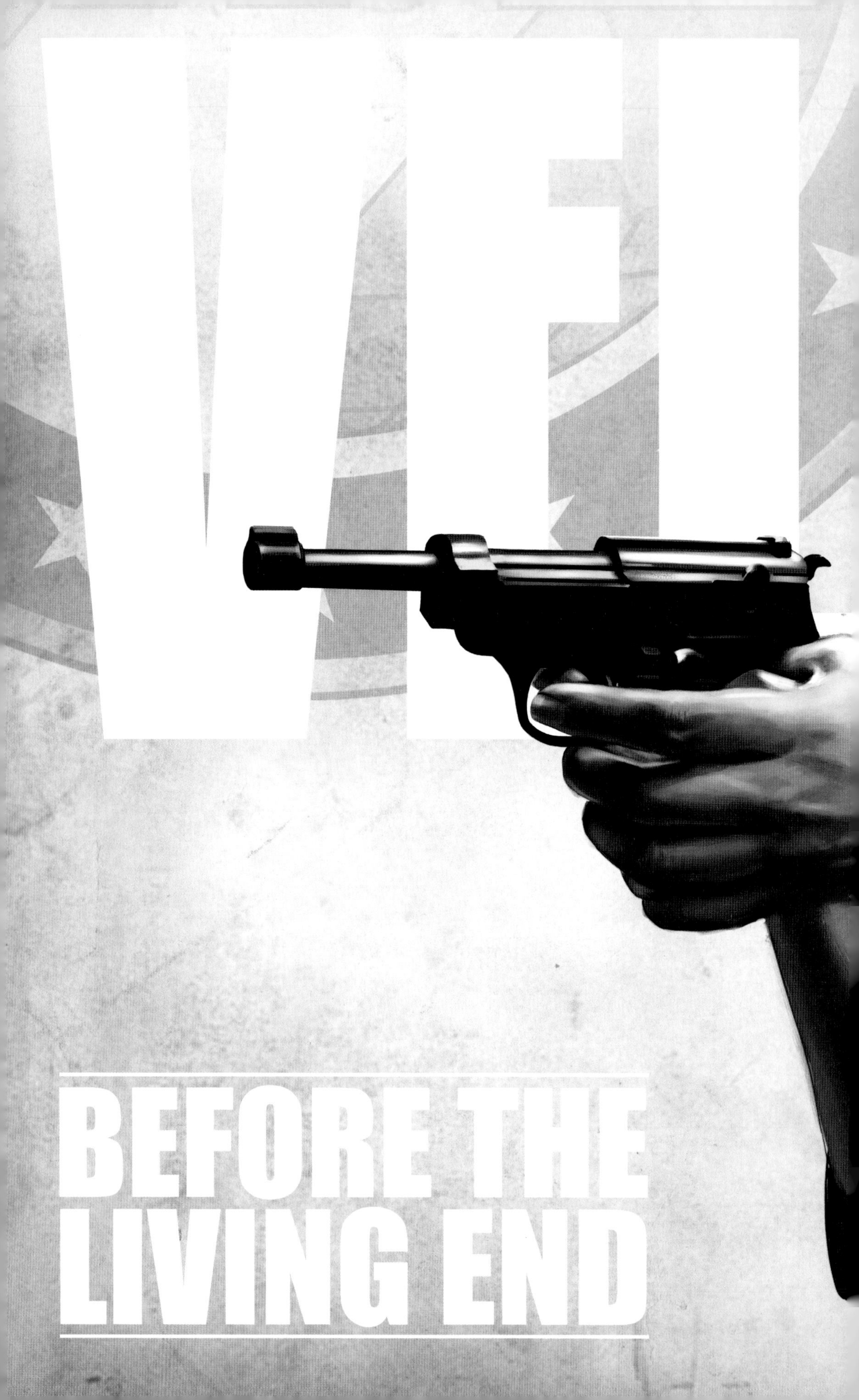
BEFORE THE
LIVING END

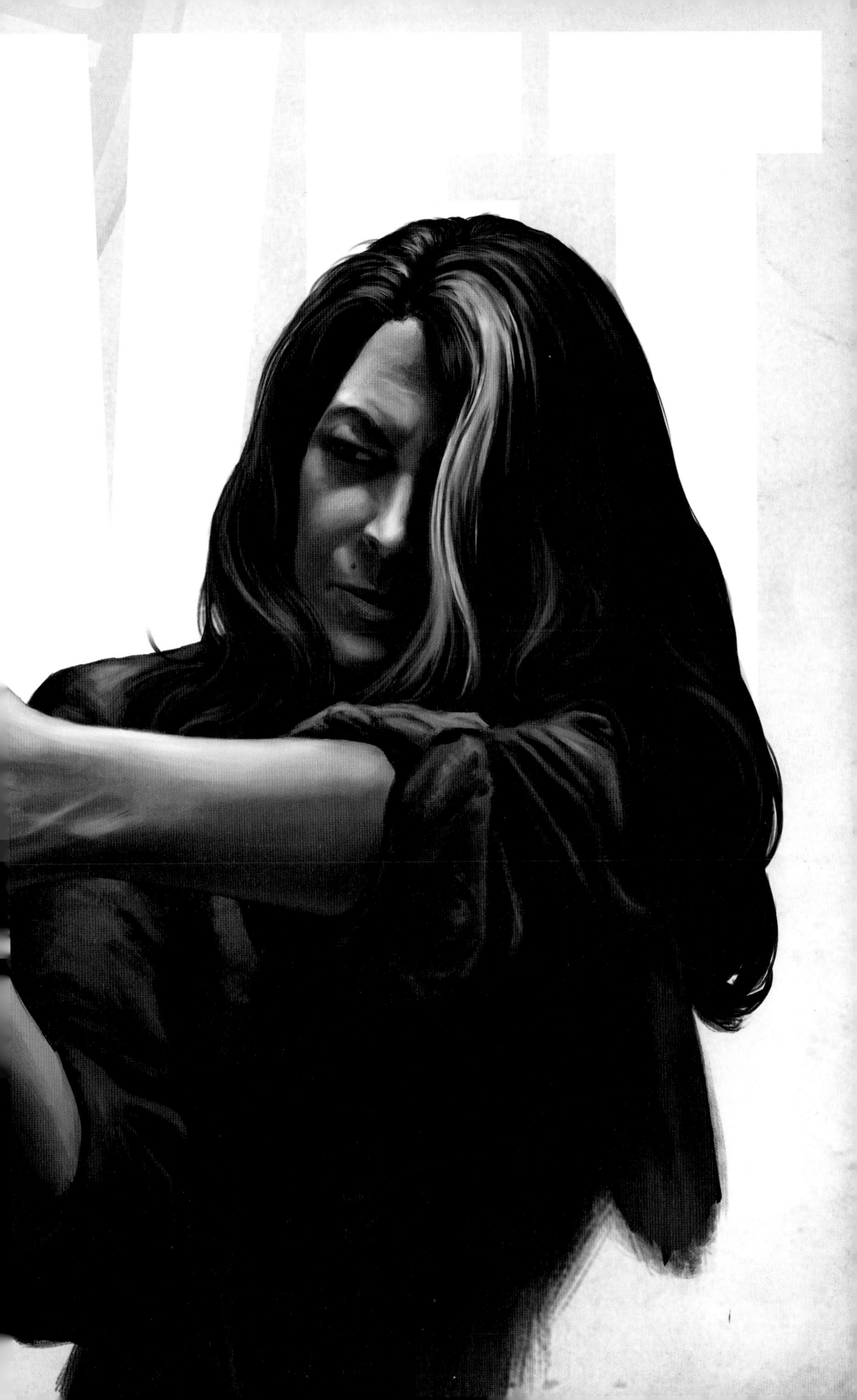

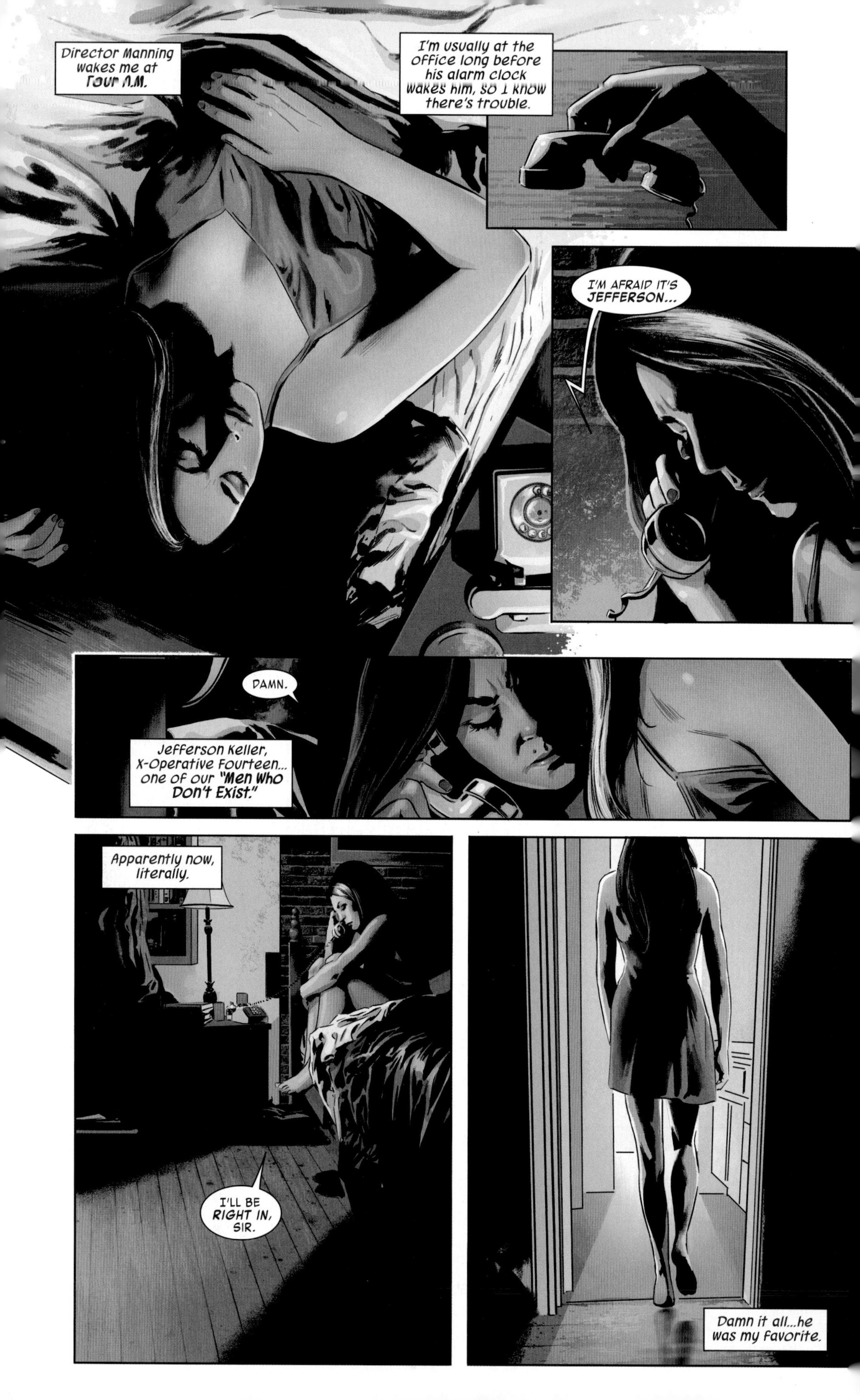
Director Manning wakes me at four A.M.
I'm usually at the office long before his alarm clock wakes him, so I know there's trouble.
I'M AFRAID IT'S JEFFERSON...
DAMN.
Jefferson Keller, X-Operative Fourteen... one of our "Men Who Don't Exist."
Apparently now, literally.
I'LL BE RIGHT IN, SIR.
Damn it all...he was my favorite.

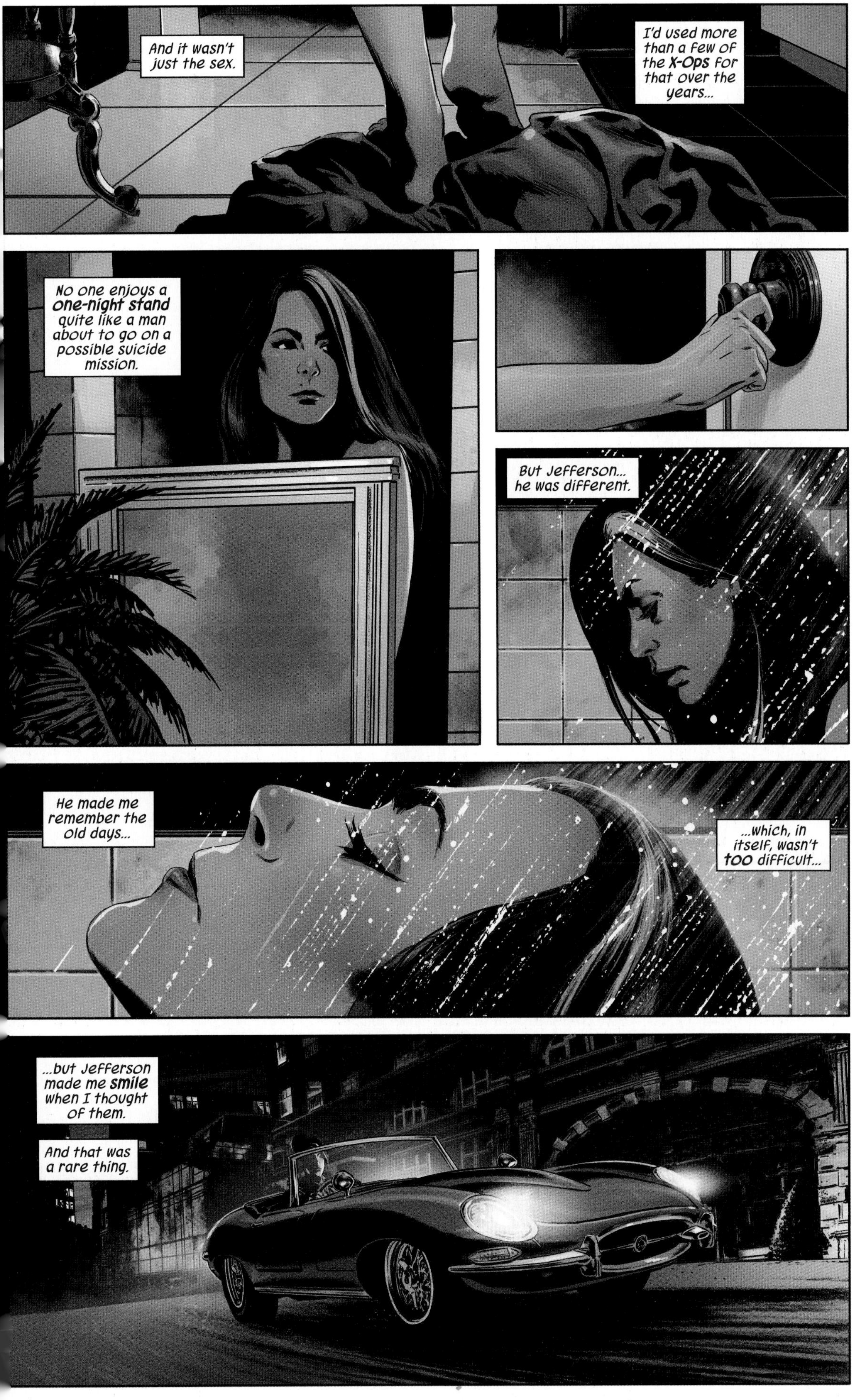
And it wasn't just the sex.
I'd used more than a few of the X-Ops for that over the years...
No one enjoys a one-night stand quite like a man about to go on a possible suicide mission.
But Jefferson... he was different.
He made me remember the old days...
...which, in itself, wasn't too difficult...
...but Jefferson made me smile when I thought of them.
And that was a rare thing.

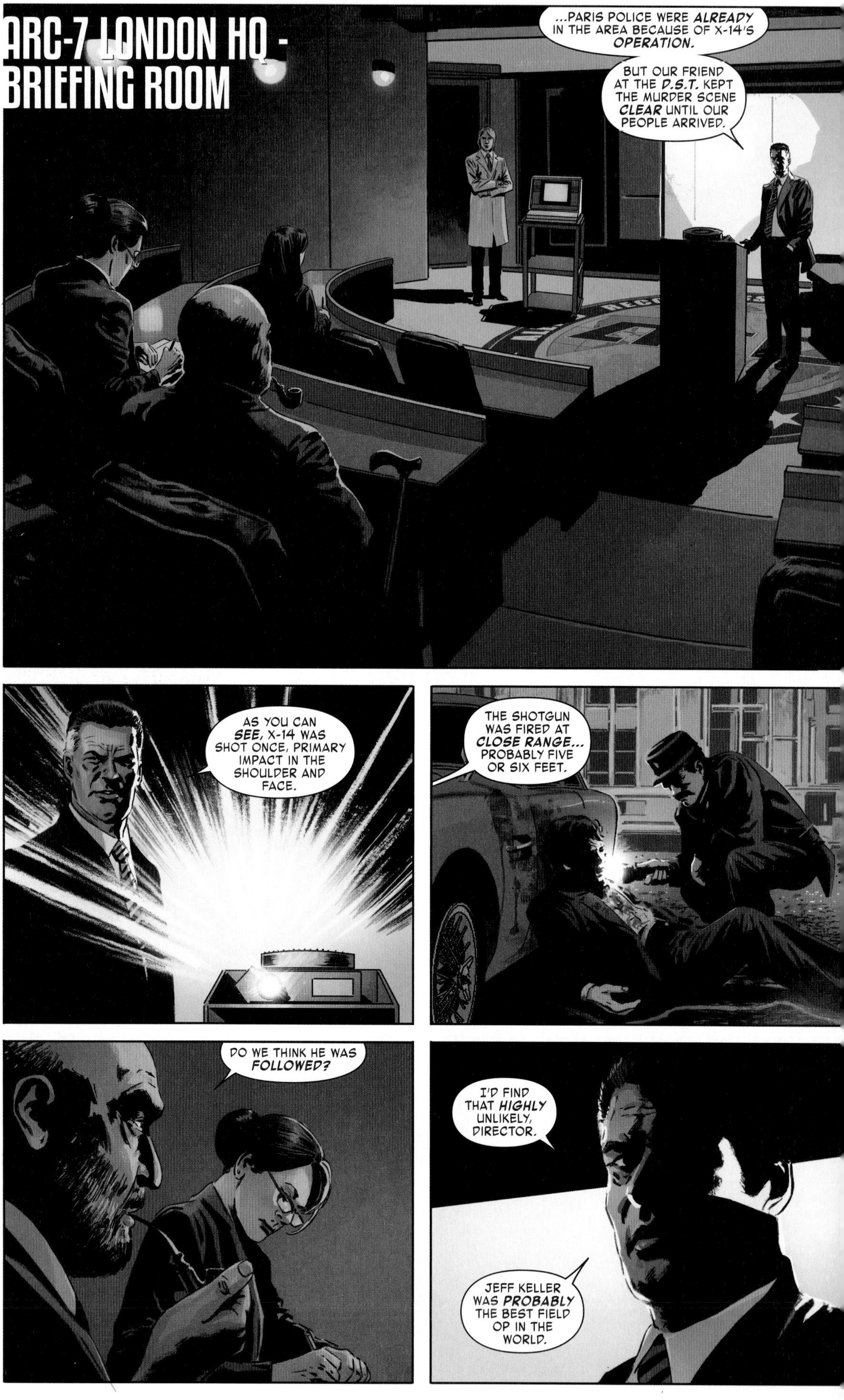
ARC-7 LONDON HQ - BRIEFING ROOM
...PARIS POLICE WERE ALREADY IN THE AREA BECAUSE OF X-14'S OPERATION.
BUT OUR FRIEND AT THE D.S.T. KEPT THE MURDER SCENE CLEAR UNTIL OUR PEOPLE ARRIVED.
AS YOU CAN SEE, X-14 WAS SHOT ONCE, PRIMARY IMPACT IN THE SHOULDER AND FACE.
THE SHOTGUN WAS FIRED AT CLOSE RANGE... PROBABLY FIVE OR SIX FEET.
DO WE THINK HE WAS FOLLOWED?
I'D FIND THAT HIGHLY UNLIKELY, DIRECTOR.
JEFF KELLER WAS PROBABLY THE BEST FIELD OP IN THE WORLD.

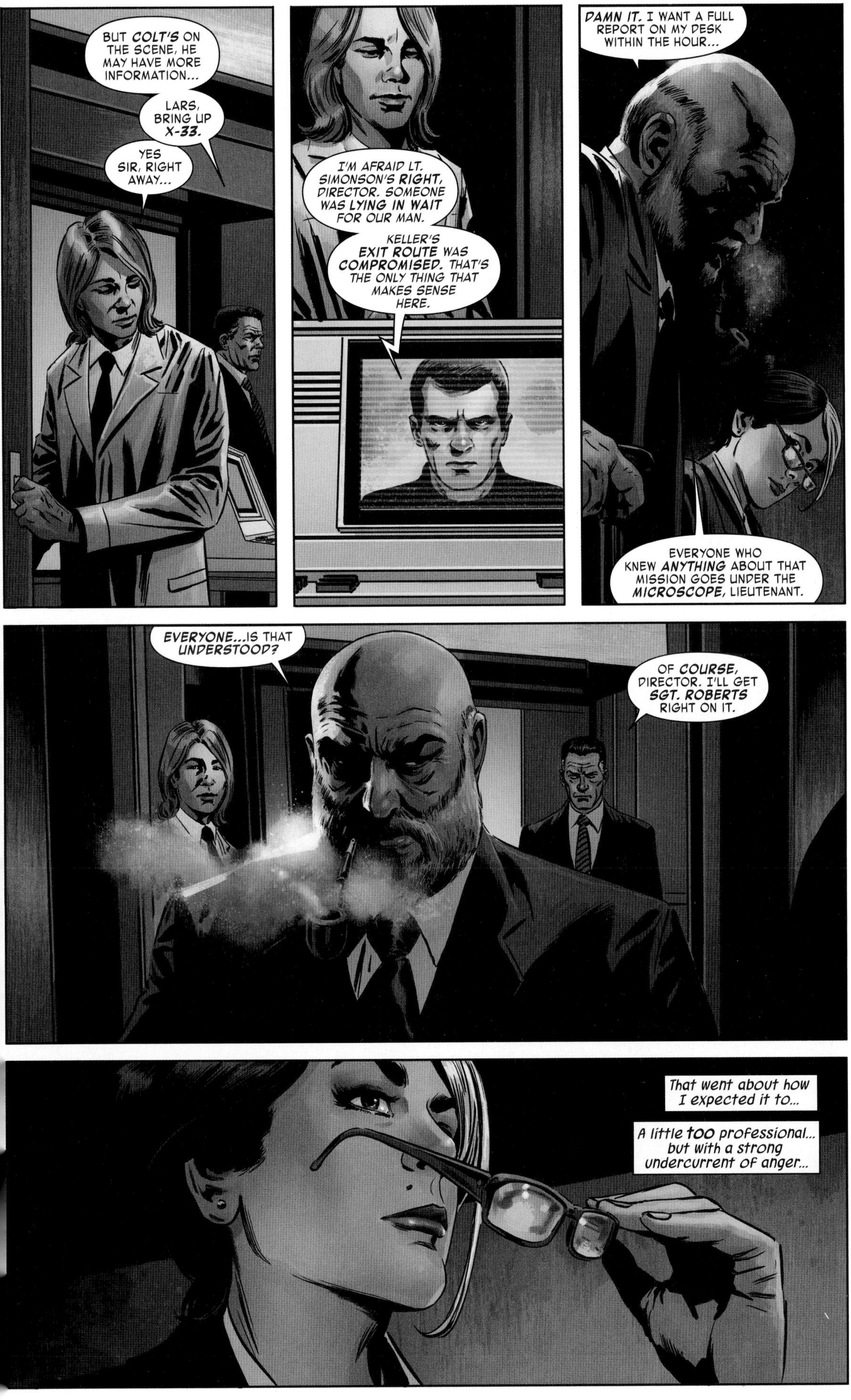

BUT COLT'S ON THE SCENE, HE MAY HAVE MORE INFORMATION...
LARS, BRING UP X-33.
YES SIR, RIGHT AWAY...
I'M AFRAID LT. SIMONSON'S RIGHT, DIRECTOR. SOMEONE WAS LYING IN WAIT FOR OUR MAN.
KELLER'S EXIT ROUTE WAS COMPROMISED. THAT'S THE ONLY THING THAT MAKES SENSE HERE.
DAMN IT. I WANT A FULL REPORT ON MY DESK WITHIN THE HOUR...
EVERYONE WHO KNEW ANYTHING ABOUT THAT MISSION GOES UNDER THE MICROSCOPE, LIEUTENANT.
EVERYONE...IS THAT UNDERSTOOD?
OF COURSE, DIRECTOR. I'LL GET SGT. ROBERTS RIGHT ON IT.
That went about how I expected it to...
A little TOO professional... but with a strong undercurrent of anger...

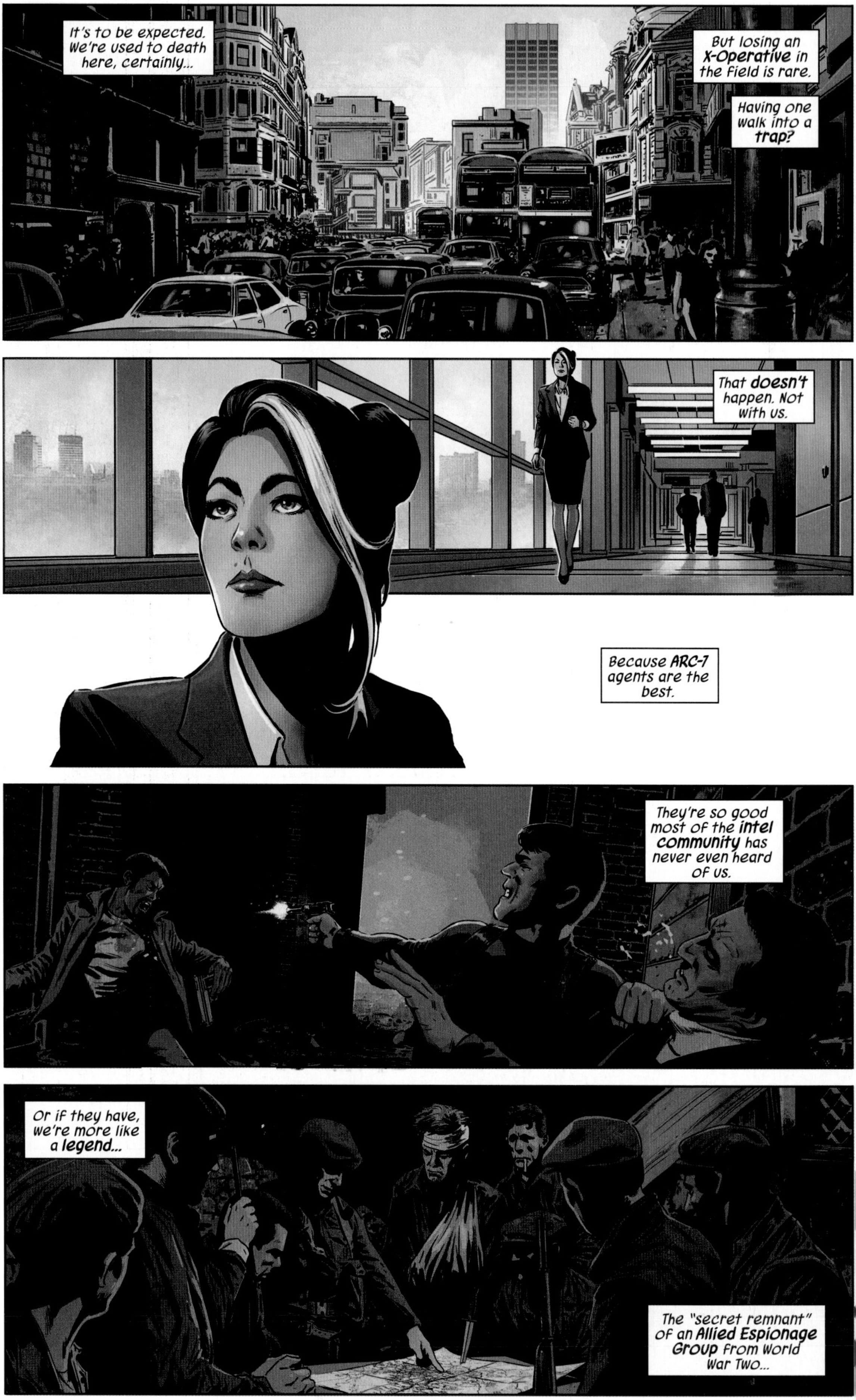

It's to be expected. We're used to death here, certainly...
But losing an X-Operative in the field is rare.
Having one walk into a trap?
That doesn't happen. Not with us.
Because ARC-7 agents are the best.
They're so good most of the intel community has never even heard of us.
Or if they have, we're more like a legend...
The "secret remnant" of an Allied Espionage Group from World War Two...

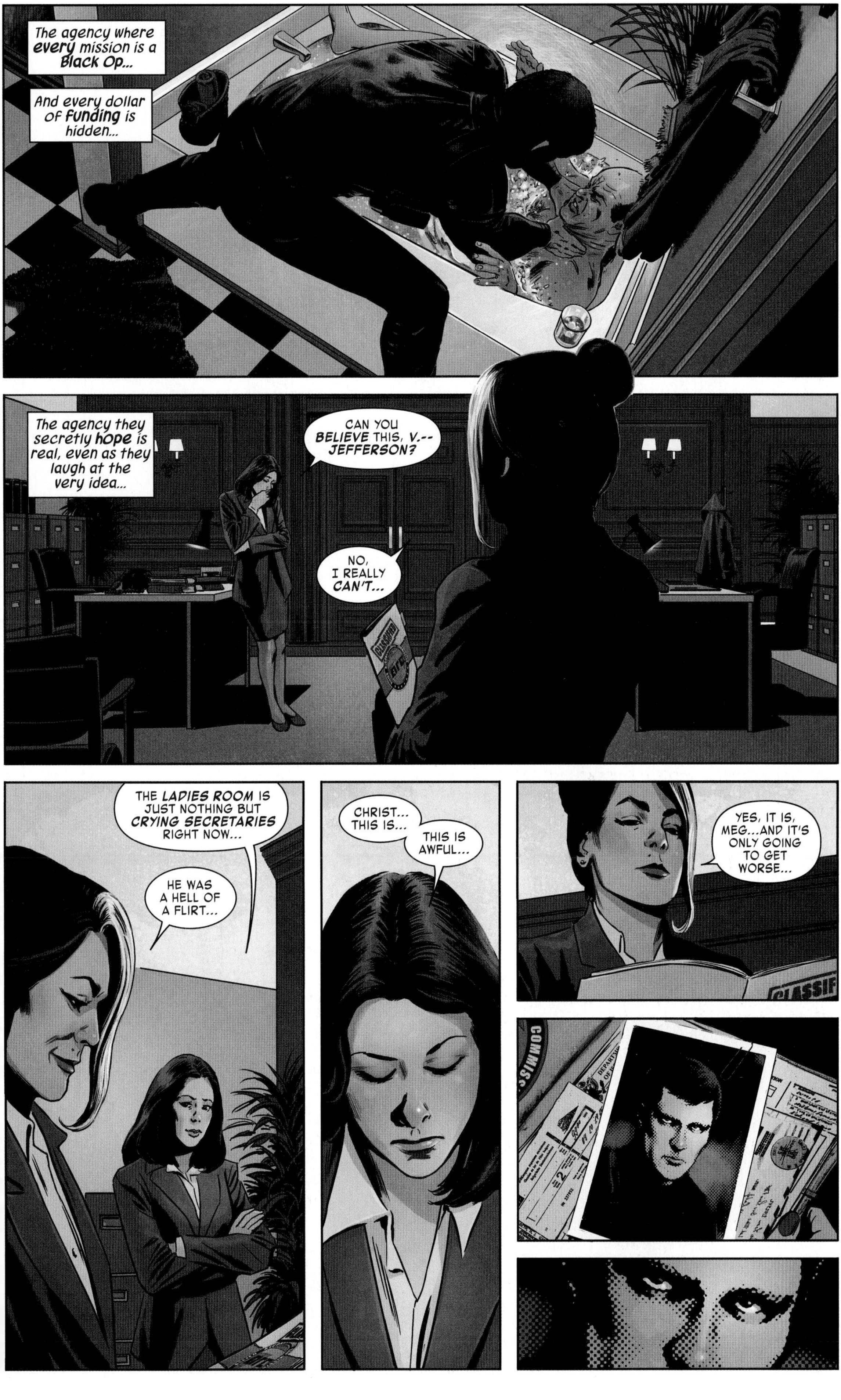
The agency where every mission is a Black Op...
And every dollar of funding is hidden...
The agency they secretly hope is real, even as they laugh at the very idea...
CAN YOU BELIEVE THIS, V.-- JEFFERSON?
NO, I REALLY CAN'T...
THE LADIES ROOM IS JUST NOTHING BUT CRYING SECRETARIES RIGHT NOW...
HE WAS A HELL OF A FLIRT...
CHRIST... THIS IS...
THIS IS AWFUL...
YES, IT IS, MEG...AND IT'S ONLY GOING TO GET WORSE...

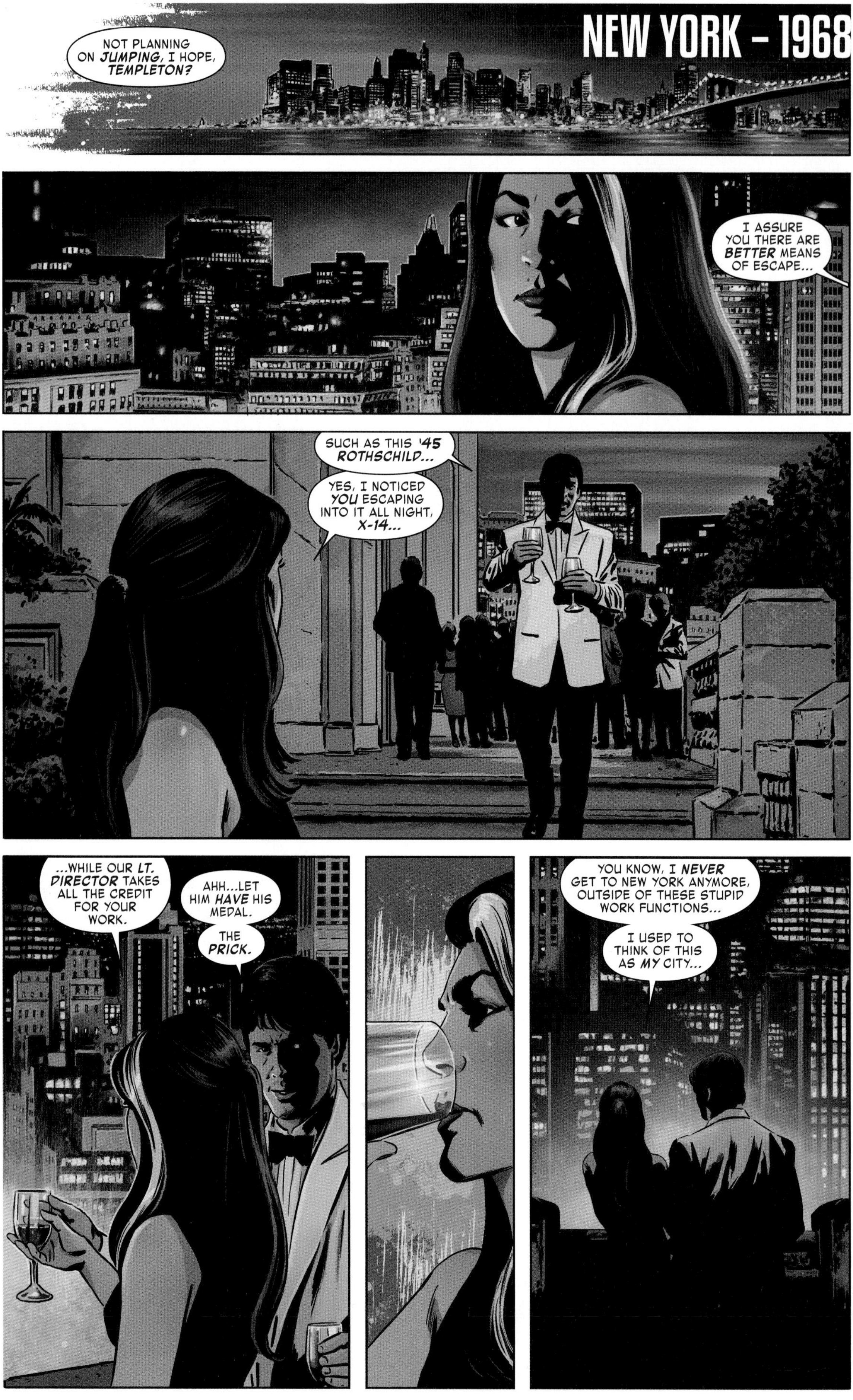
NEW YORK - 1968
NOT PLANNING ON JUMPING, I HOPE, TEMPLETON?
I ASSURE YOU THERE ARE BETTER MEANS OF ESCAPE...
SUCH AS THIS '45 ROTHSCHILD...
YES, I NOTICED YOU ESCAPING INTO IT ALL NIGHT, X-14...
...WHILE OUR LT. DIRECTOR TAKES ALL THE CREDIT FOR YOUR WORK.
AHH...LET HIM HAVE HIS MEDAL.
THE PRICK.
YOU KNOW, I NEVER GET TO NEW YORK ANYMORE, OUTSIDE OF THESE STUPID WORK FUNCTIONS...
I USED TO THINK OF THIS AS MY CITY...

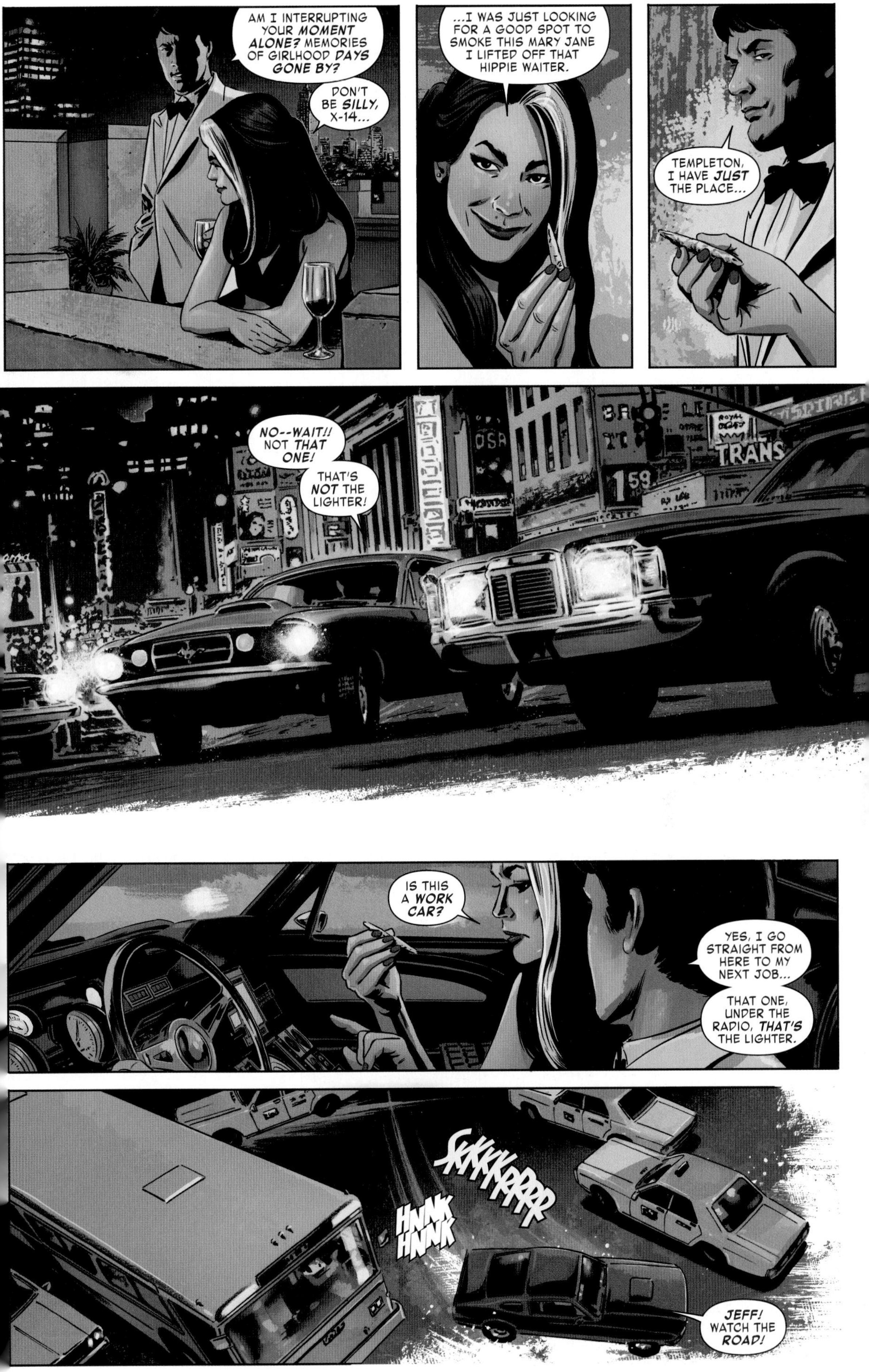
AM I INTERRUPTING YOUR MOMENT ALONE? MEMORIES OF GIRLHOOD DAYS GONE BY?
DON'T BE SILLY, X-14...
...I WAS JUST LOOKING FOR A GOOD SPOT TO SMOKE THIS MARY JANE I LIFTED OFF THAT HIPPIE WAITER.
TEMPLETON, I HAVE JUST THE PLACE...
NO--WAIT!! NOT THAT ONE!
THAT'S NOT THE LIGHTER!
TRANS
IS THIS A WORK CAR?
YES, I GO STRAIGHT FROM HERE TO MY NEXT JOB...
THAT ONE, UNDER THE RADIO, THAT'S THE LIGHTER.
SKKKKRRRR
HNNK HNNK
JEFF! WATCH THE ROAD!

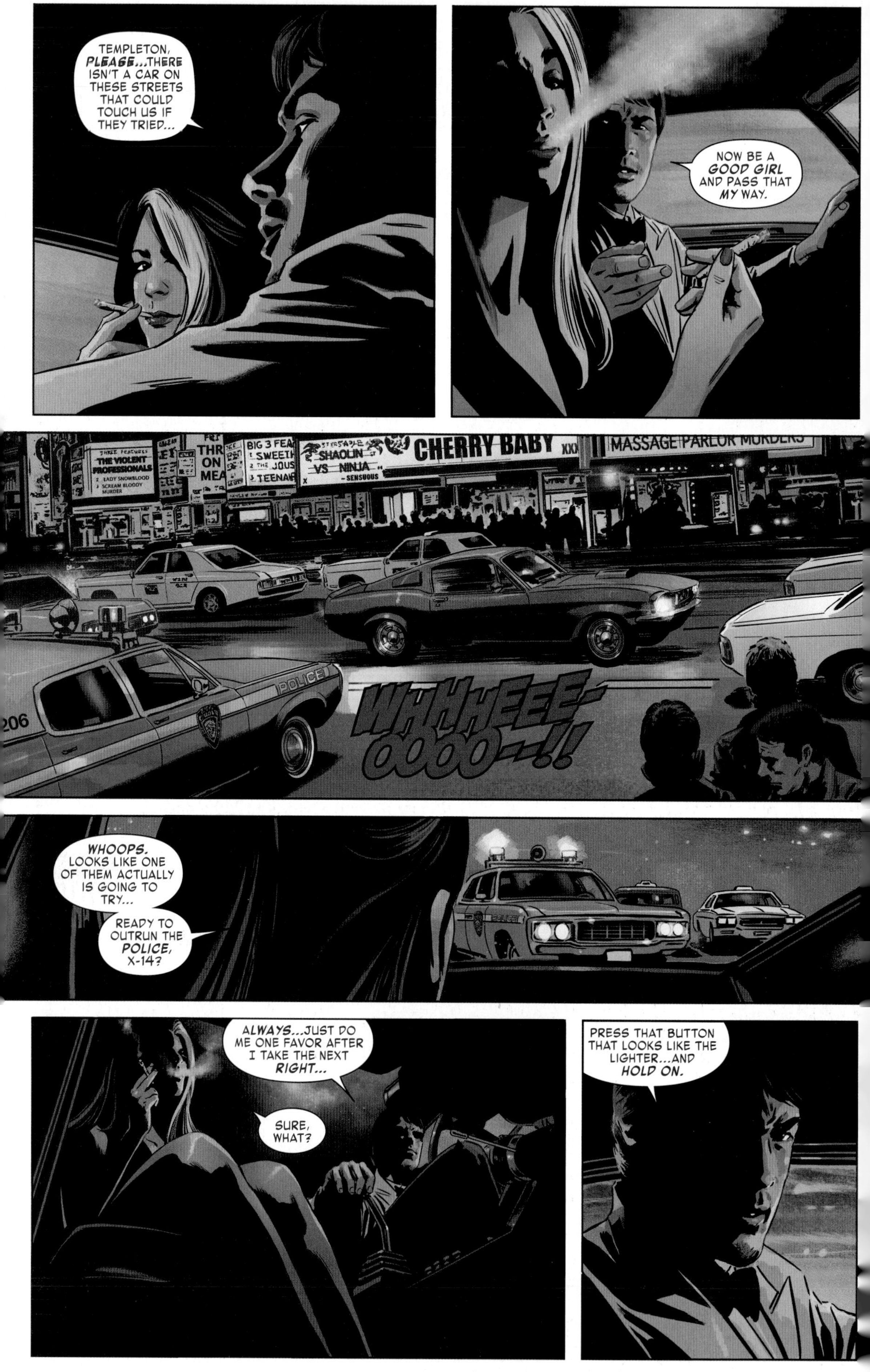
TEMPLETON, PLEASE...THERE ISN'T A CAR ON THESE STREETS THAT COULD TOUCH US IF THEY TRIED...
NOW BE A GOOD GIRL AND PASS THAT MY WAY.
THREE FEATURES THE VIOLENT PROFESSIONALS
LADY SNOWBLOOD
SCREAM BLOODY MURDER
SHAOLIN VS NINJA
CHERRY BABY
MASSAGE PARLOR MURDERS
POLICE
206
WHHHEEE-OOOO--!!
WHOOPS. LOOKS LIKE ONE OF THEM ACTUALLY IS GOING TO TRY...
READY TO OUTRUN THE POLICE, X-14?
ALWAYS...JUST DO ME ONE FAVOR AFTER I TAKE THE NEXT RIGHT...
SURE, WHAT?
PRESS THAT BUTTON THAT LOOKS LIKE THE LIGHTER...AND HOLD ON.

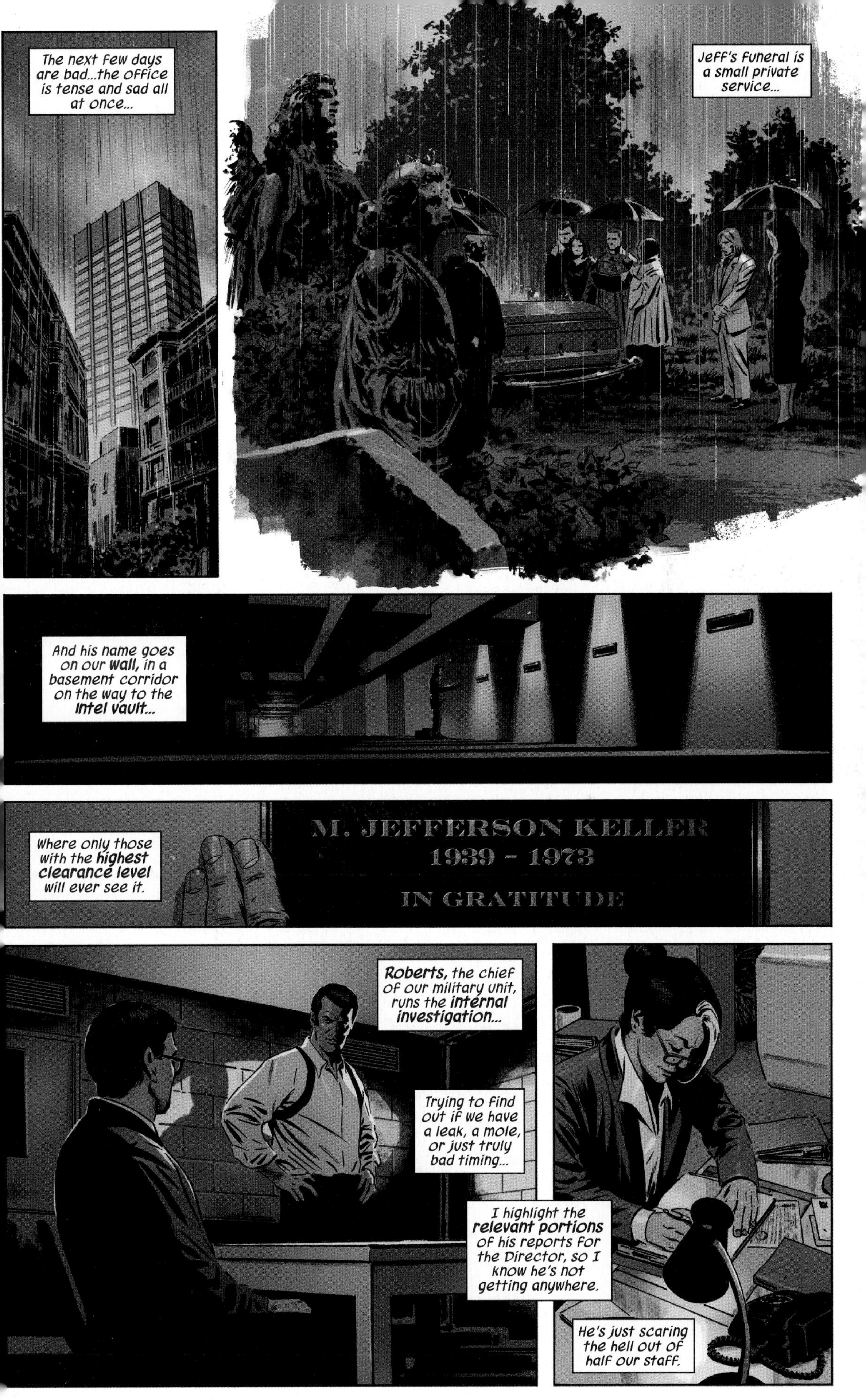
The next few days are bad...the office is tense and sad all at once...
Jeff's funeral is a small private service...
And his name goes on our **wall,** in a basement corridor on the way to the **Intel vault...**
Where only those with the **highest clearance level** will ever see it.
M. JEFFERSON KELLER
1939 - 1973
IN GRATITUDE
Roberts, the chief of our military unit, runs the **internal investigation...**
Trying to find out if we have a leak, a mole, or just truly bad timing...
I highlight the **relevant portions** of his reports for the Director, so I know he's not getting anywhere.
He's just scaring the hell out of half our staff.

Colt's investigation in the **field** isn't bringing much joy, either.

Analyzing surveillance photos, searching customs reports at airports and train stations...

...talking to **sources** who don't know anything.

at 12:00 noon, however, he did not appear until approximately 4:30 m., when approximately 5 individuals attended the first ting consisting of the following individuals:

It's weeks like **this** that I hate my job.

I'm watching this case grow **colder** with every document that crosses my desk...

And all I'm doing is "highlighting the relevant portions."

That's probably the **first** thing that gets me in trouble...that frustration...

THIS **ALL** OF X-14'S REPORTS BACK THROUGH '72, DAISY...?

YES MA'AM, THE UNREDACTED ONES...

THAT **IS** WHAT THE DIRECTOR **WANTED**, ISN'T IT?

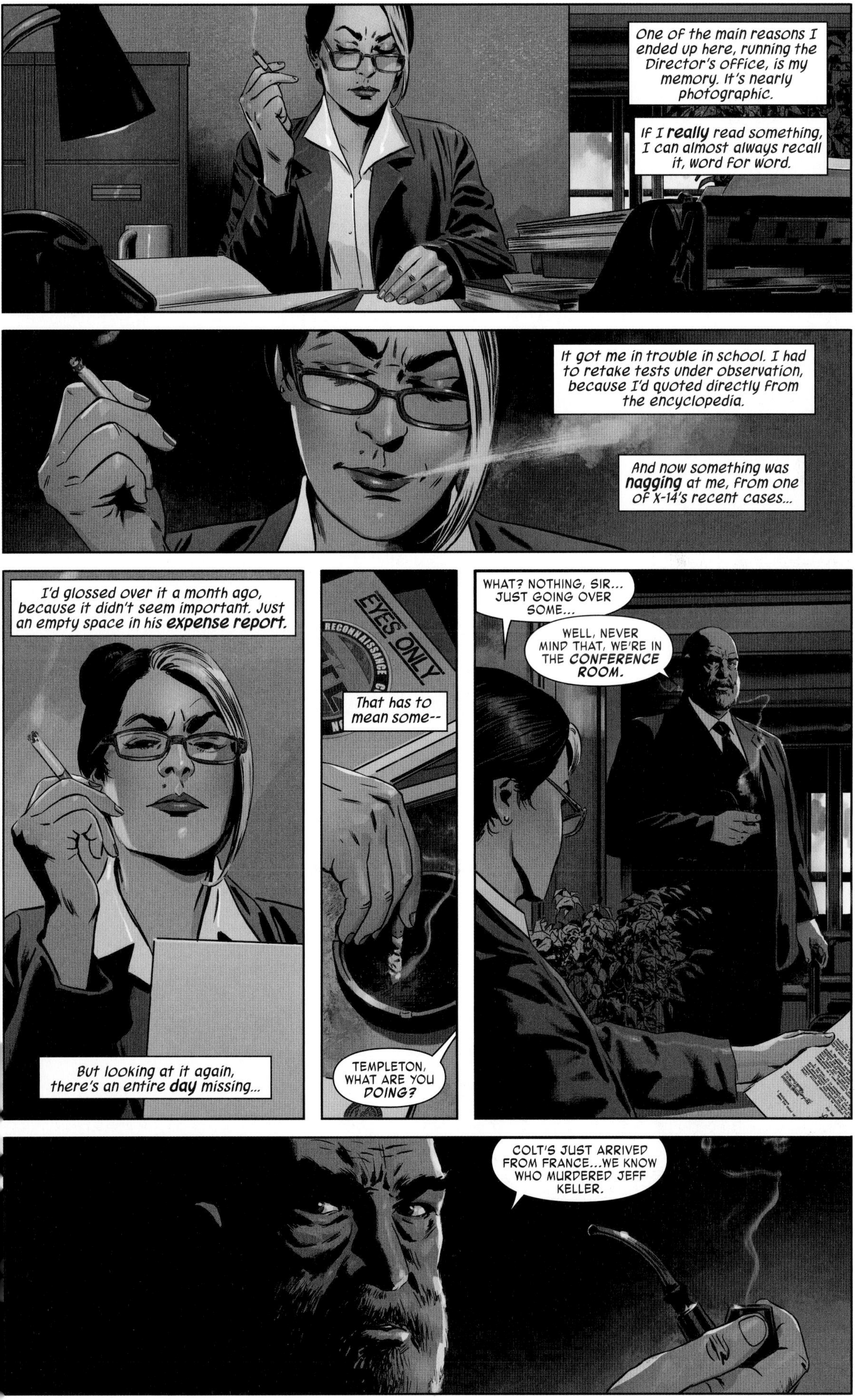
One of the main reasons I ended up here, running the Director's office, is my memory. It's nearly photographic.
If I really read something, I can almost always recall it, word for word.
It got me in trouble in school. I had to retake tests under observation, because I'd quoted directly from the encyclopedia.
And now something was nagging at me, from one of X-14's recent cases...
I'd glossed over it a month ago, because it didn't seem important. Just an empty space in his expense report.
But looking at it again, there's an entire day missing...
EYES ONLY
RECONNAISSANCE
That has to mean some--
TEMPLETON, WHAT ARE YOU DOING?
WHAT? NOTHING, SIR... JUST GOING OVER SOME...
WELL, NEVER MIND THAT, WE'RE IN THE CONFERENCE ROOM.
COLT'S JUST ARRIVED FROM FRANCE...WE KNOW WHO MURDERED JEFF KELLER.

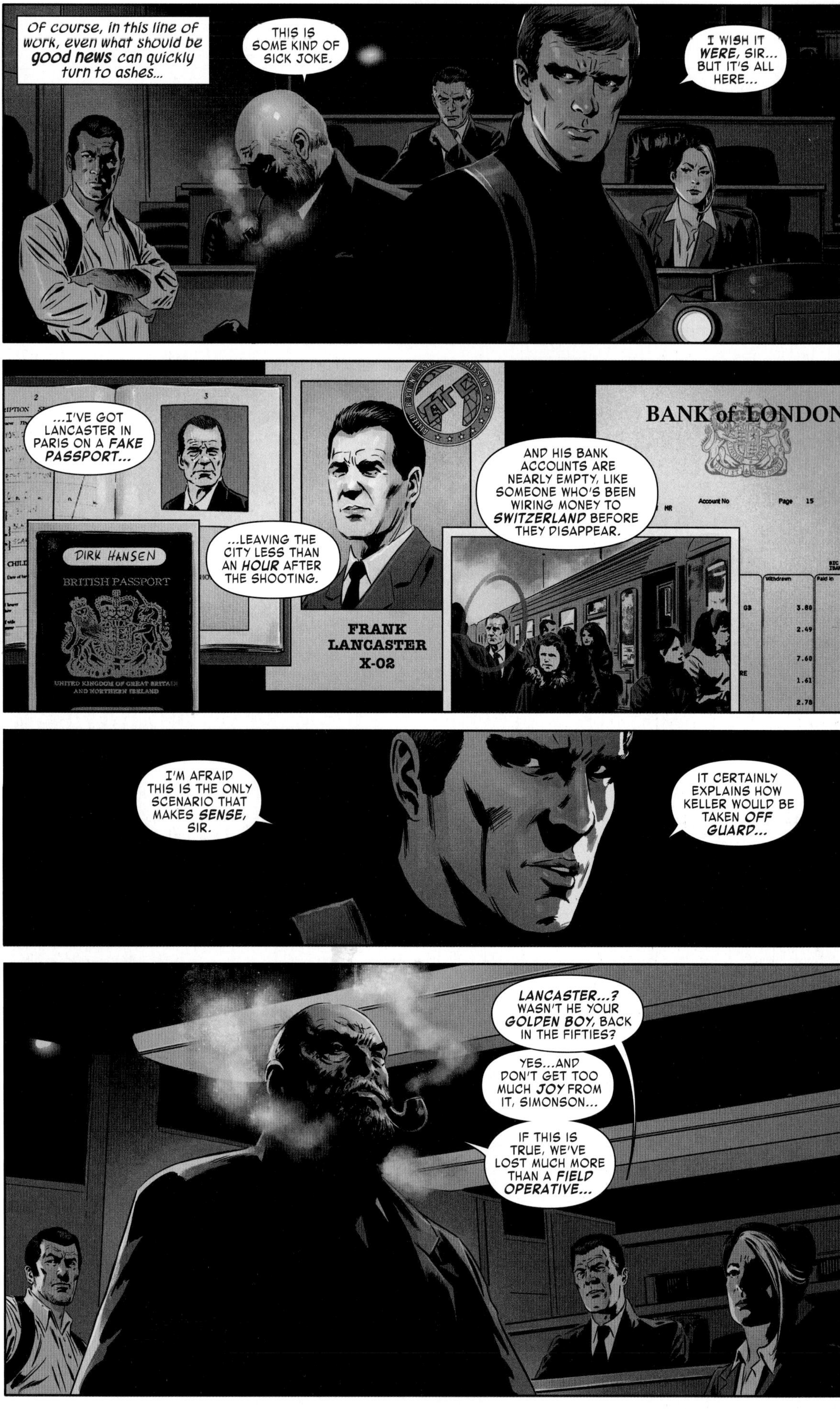
Of course, in this line of work, even what should be good news can quickly turn to ashes...
THIS IS SOME KIND OF SICK JOKE.
I WISH IT WERE, SIR... BUT IT'S ALL HERE...
...I'VE GOT LANCASTER IN PARIS ON A FAKE PASSPORT...
DIRK HANSEN
BRITISH PASSPORT
UNITED KINGDOM OF GREAT BRITAIN AND NORTHERN IRELAND
...LEAVING THE CITY LESS THAN AN HOUR AFTER THE SHOOTING.
FRANK LANCASTER X-02
BANK of LONDON
AND HIS BANK ACCOUNTS ARE NEARLY EMPTY, LIKE SOMEONE WHO'S BEEN WIRING MONEY TO SWITZERLAND BEFORE THEY DISAPPEAR.
Account No
Page 15
Withdrawn
Paid in
3.80
2.49
7.60
1.61
2.78
I'M AFRAID THIS IS THE ONLY SCENARIO THAT MAKES SENSE, SIR.
IT CERTAINLY EXPLAINS HOW KELLER WOULD BE TAKEN OFF GUARD...
LANCASTER...? WASN'T HE YOUR GOLDEN BOY, BACK IN THE FIFTIES?
YES...AND DON'T GET TOO MUCH JOY FROM IT, SIMONSON...
IF THIS IS TRUE, WE'VE LOST MUCH MORE THAN A FIELD OPERATIVE...

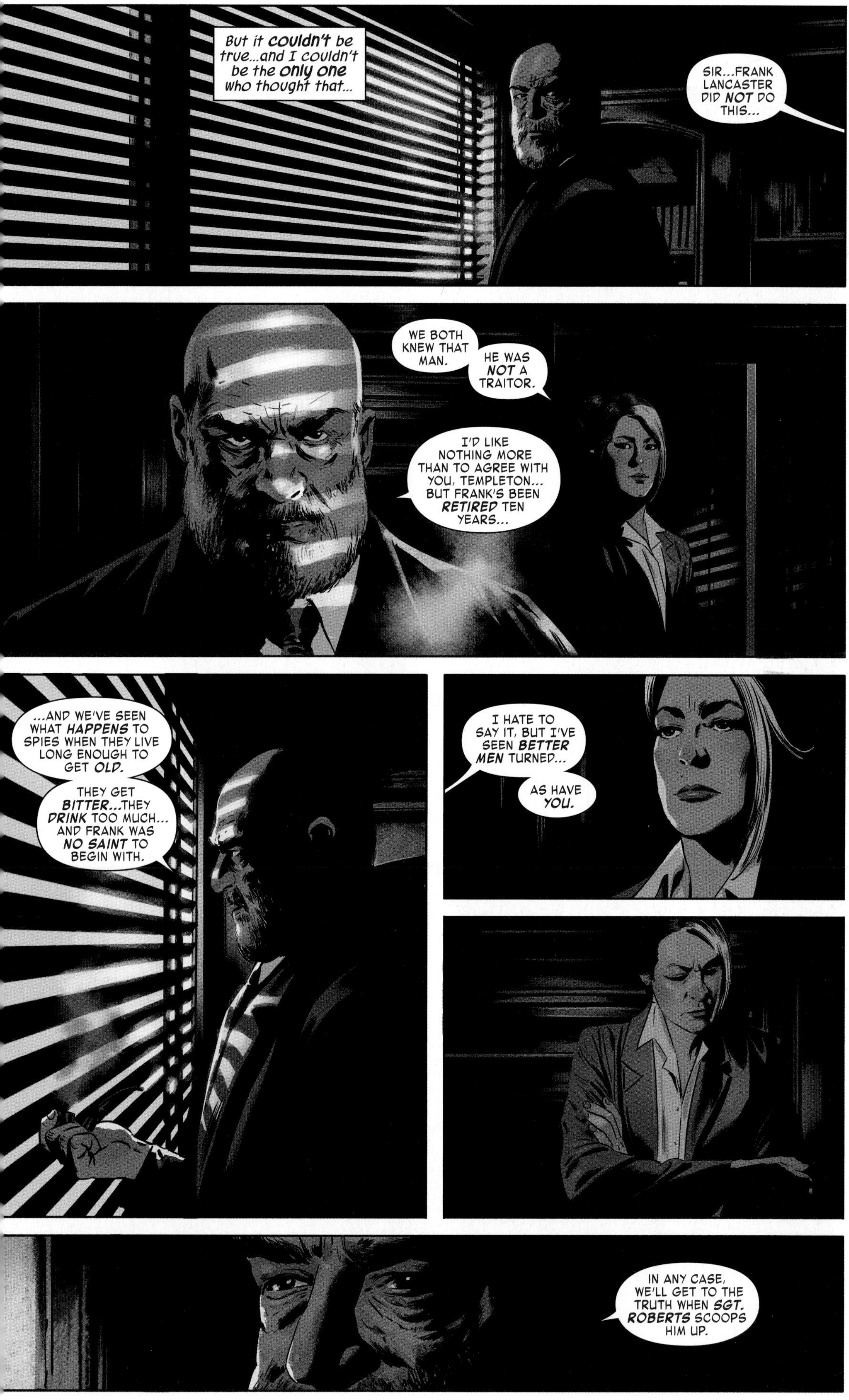
But it **couldn't** be true...and I couldn't be the **only one** who thought that...
SIR...FRANK LANCASTER DID **NOT** DO THIS...
WE BOTH KNEW THAT MAN.
HE WAS **NOT** A TRAITOR.
I'D LIKE NOTHING MORE THAN TO AGREE WITH YOU, TEMPLETON... BUT FRANK'S BEEN **RETIRED** TEN YEARS...
...AND WE'VE SEEN WHAT **HAPPENS** TO SPIES WHEN THEY LIVE LONG ENOUGH TO GET **OLD.**
THEY GET **BITTER...**THEY **DRINK** TOO MUCH... AND FRANK WAS **NO SAINT** TO BEGIN WITH.
I HATE TO SAY IT, BUT I'VE SEEN **BETTER MEN** TURNED...
AS HAVE **YOU.**
IN ANY CASE, WE'LL GET TO THE TRUTH WHEN **SGT. ROBERTS** SCOOPS HIM UP.

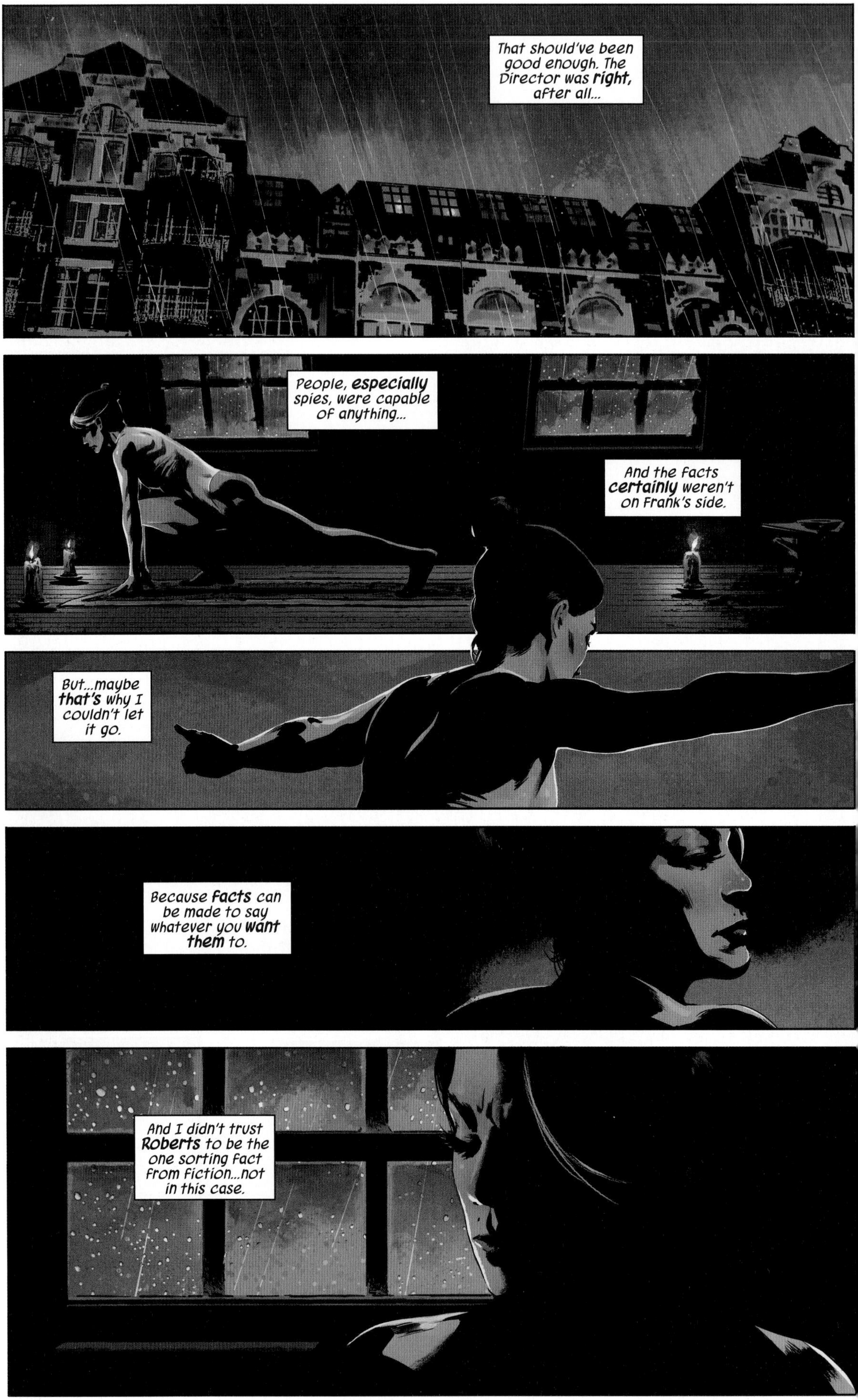
That should've been good enough. The Director was right, after all...
People, especially spies, were capable of anything...
And the facts certainly weren't on Frank's side.
But...maybe that's why I couldn't let it go.
Because facts can be made to say whatever you want them to.
And I didn't trust Roberts to be the one sorting fact from fiction...not in this case.

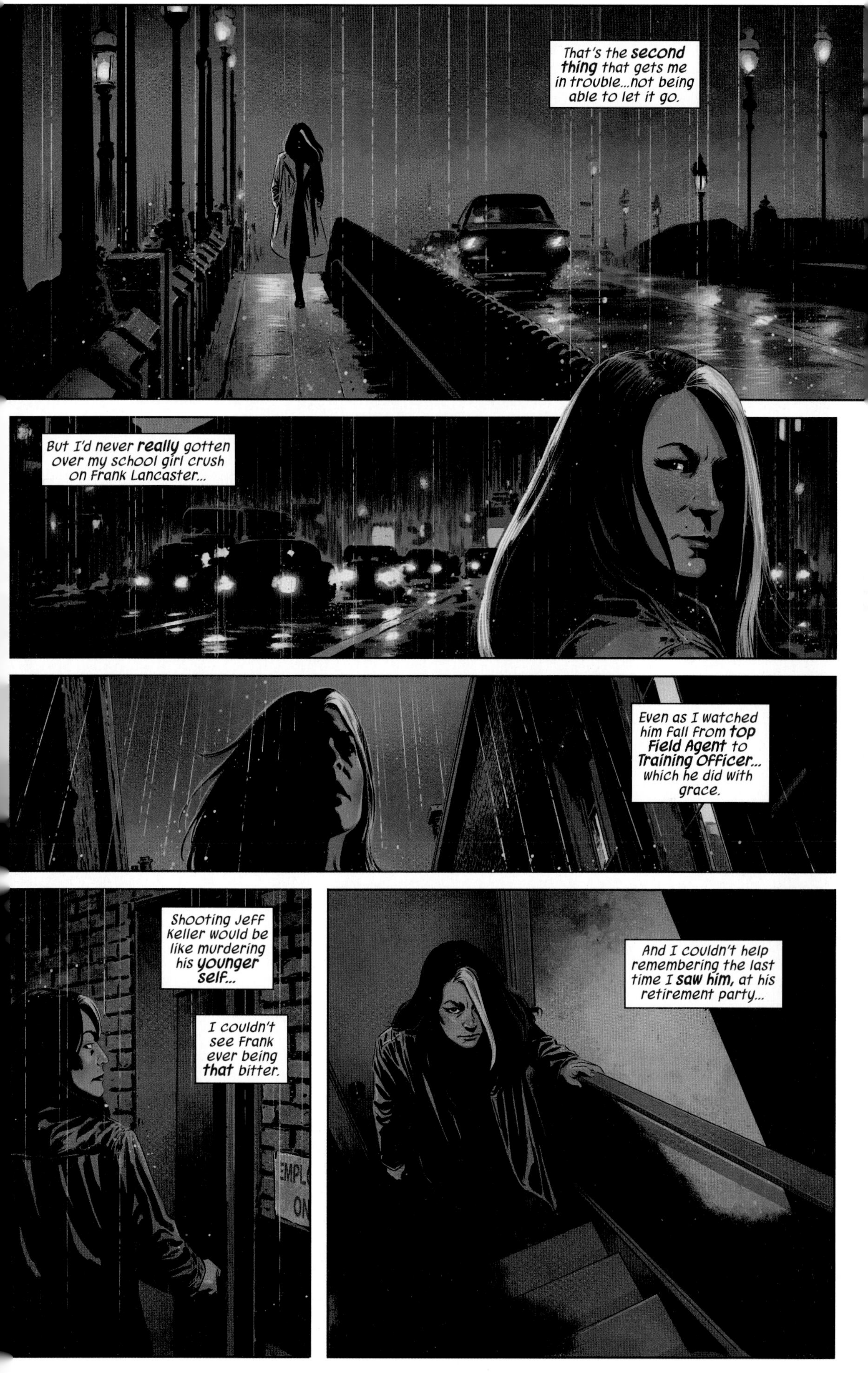
That's the second thing that gets me in trouble...not being able to let it go.
But I'd never really gotten over my school girl crush on Frank Lancaster...
Even as I watched him fall from top Field Agent to Training Officer... which he did with grace.
Shooting Jeff Keller would be like murdering his younger self...
I couldn't see Frank ever being that bitter.
And I couldn't help remembering the last time I saw him, at his retirement party...

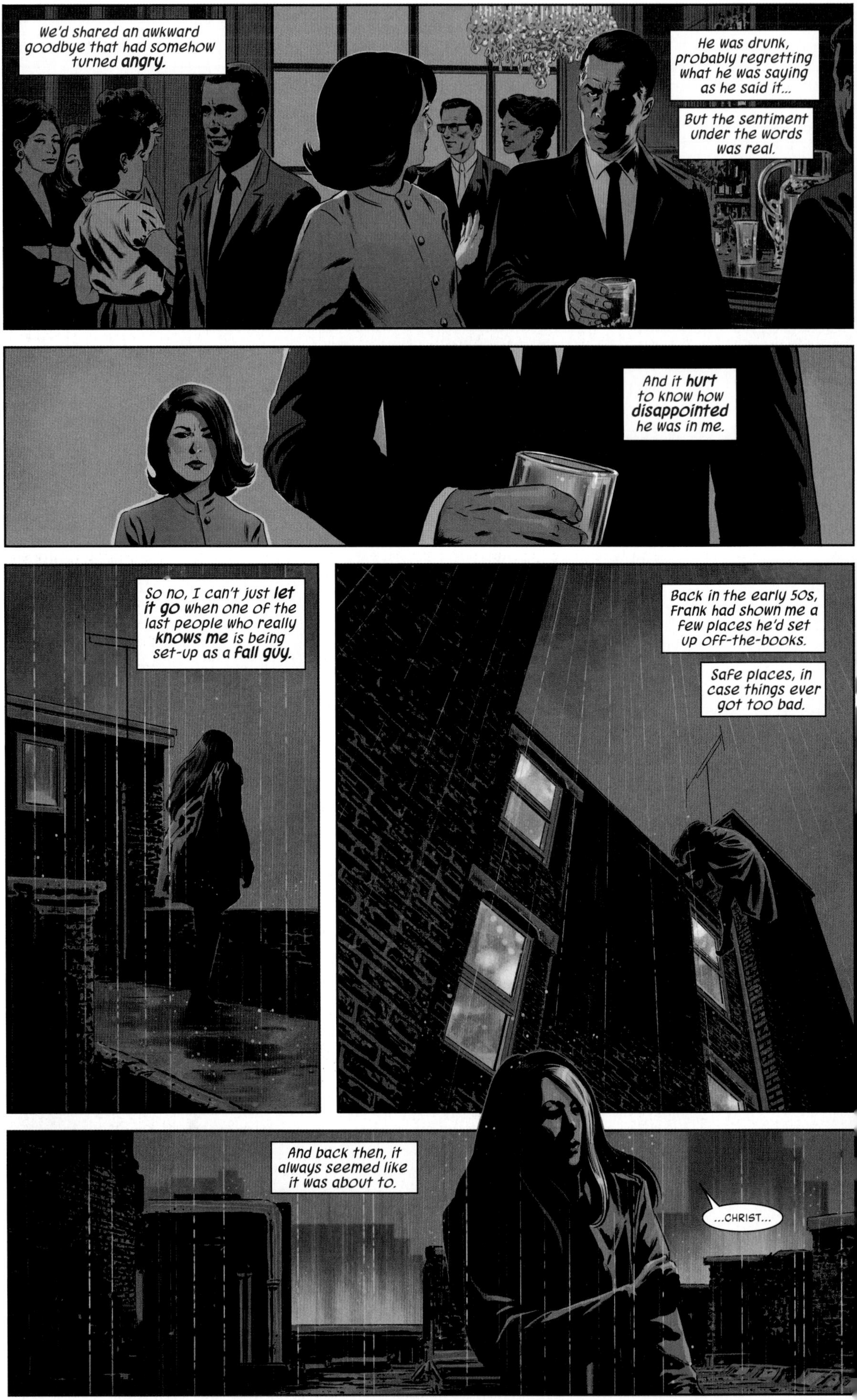
We'd shared an awkward goodbye that had somehow turned angry.
He was drunk, probably regretting what he was saying as he said it...
But the sentiment under the words was real.
And it hurt to know how disappointed he was in me.
So no, I can't just let it go when one of the last people who really knows me is being set-up as a fall guy.
Back in the early 50s, Frank had shown me a few places he'd set up off-the-books.
Safe places, in case things ever got too bad.
And back then, it always seemed like it was about to.
...CHRIST...

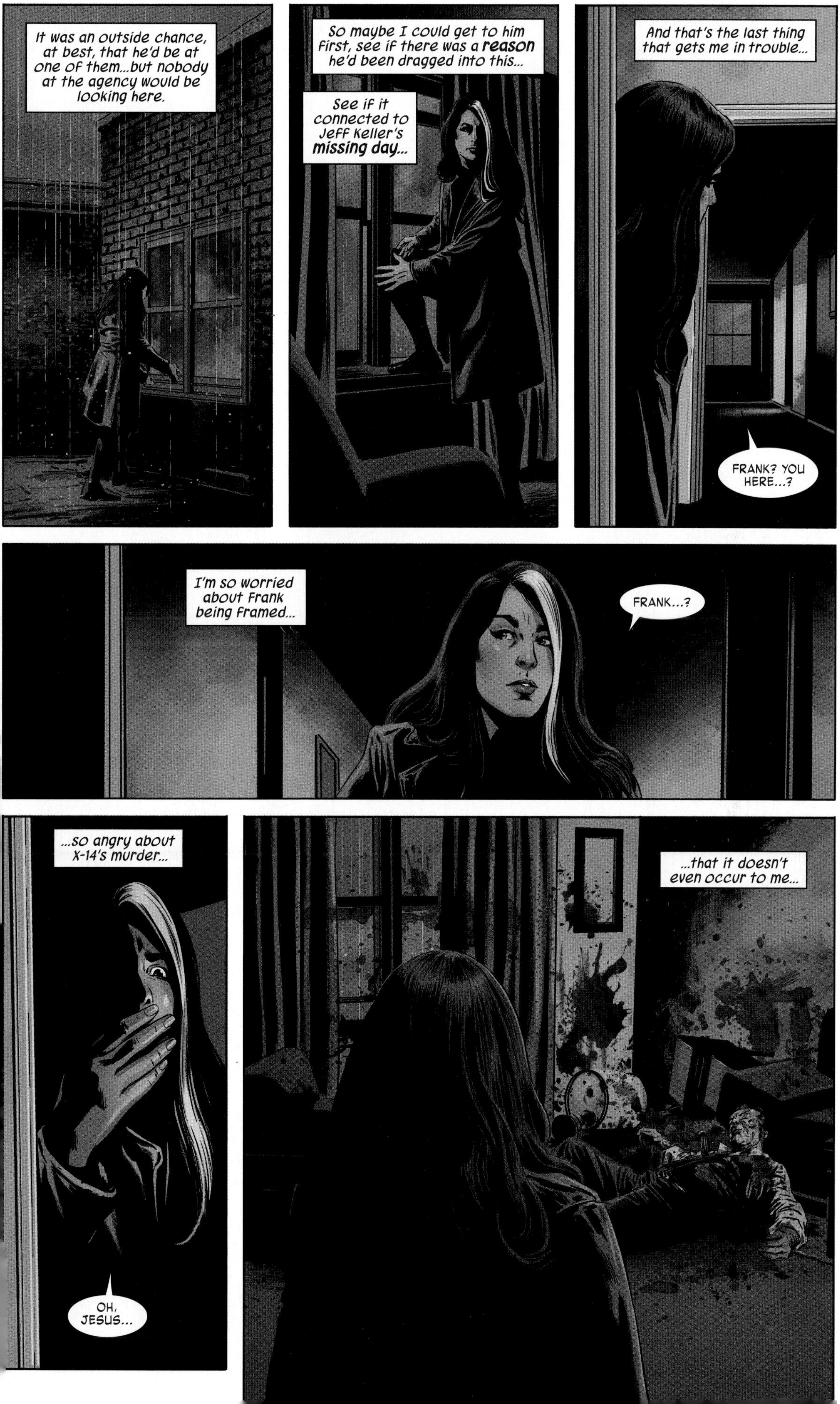
It was an outside chance, at best, that he'd be at one of them...but nobody at the agency would be looking here.
So maybe I could get to him first, see if there was a reason he'd been dragged into this...
See if it connected to Jeff Keller's missing day...
And that's the last thing that gets me in trouble...
FRANK? YOU HERE...?
I'm so worried about Frank being framed...
FRANK...?
...so angry about X-14's murder...
OH, JESUS...
...that it doesn't even occur to me...

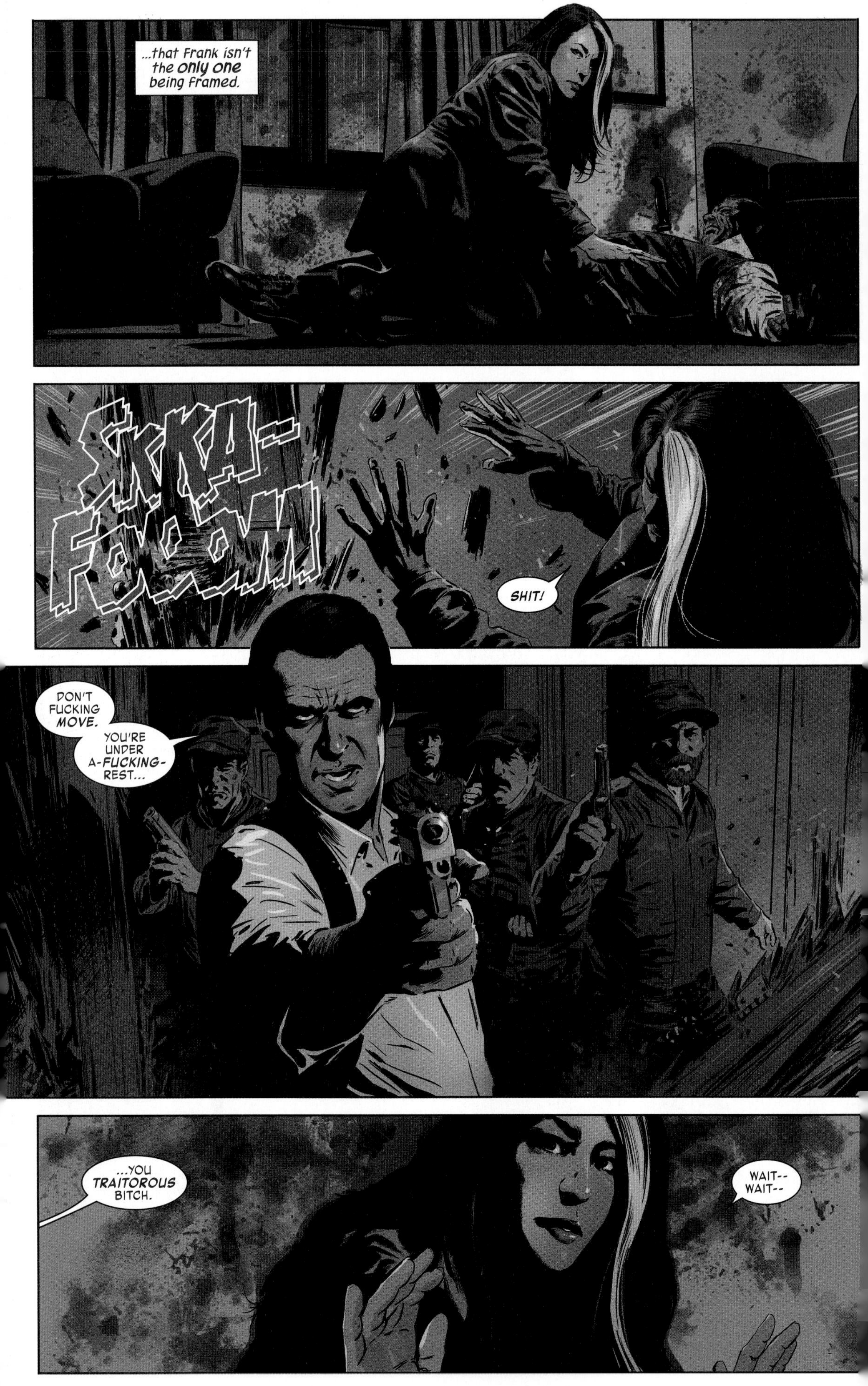
...that Frank isn't the only one being framed.
SHIT!
DON'T FUCKING MOVE.
YOU'RE UNDER A-FUCKING-REST...
...YOU TRAITOROUS BITCH.
WAIT-- WAIT--

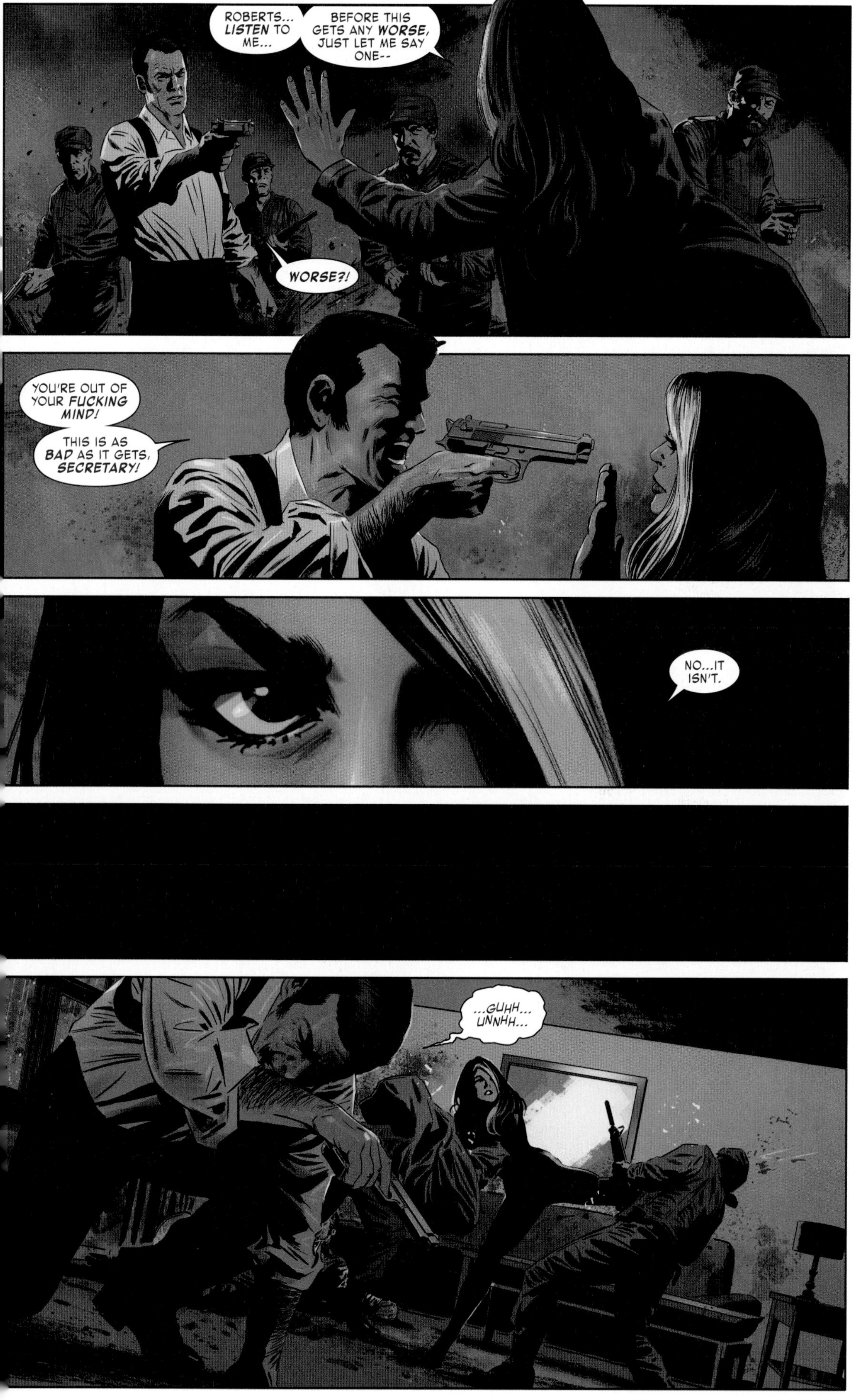
ROBERTS... LISTEN TO ME...
BEFORE THIS GETS ANY WORSE, JUST LET ME SAY ONE--
WORSE?!
YOU'RE OUT OF YOUR FUCKING MIND!
THIS IS AS BAD AS IT GETS, SECRETARY!
NO...IT ISN'T.
...GUHH... UNNHH...

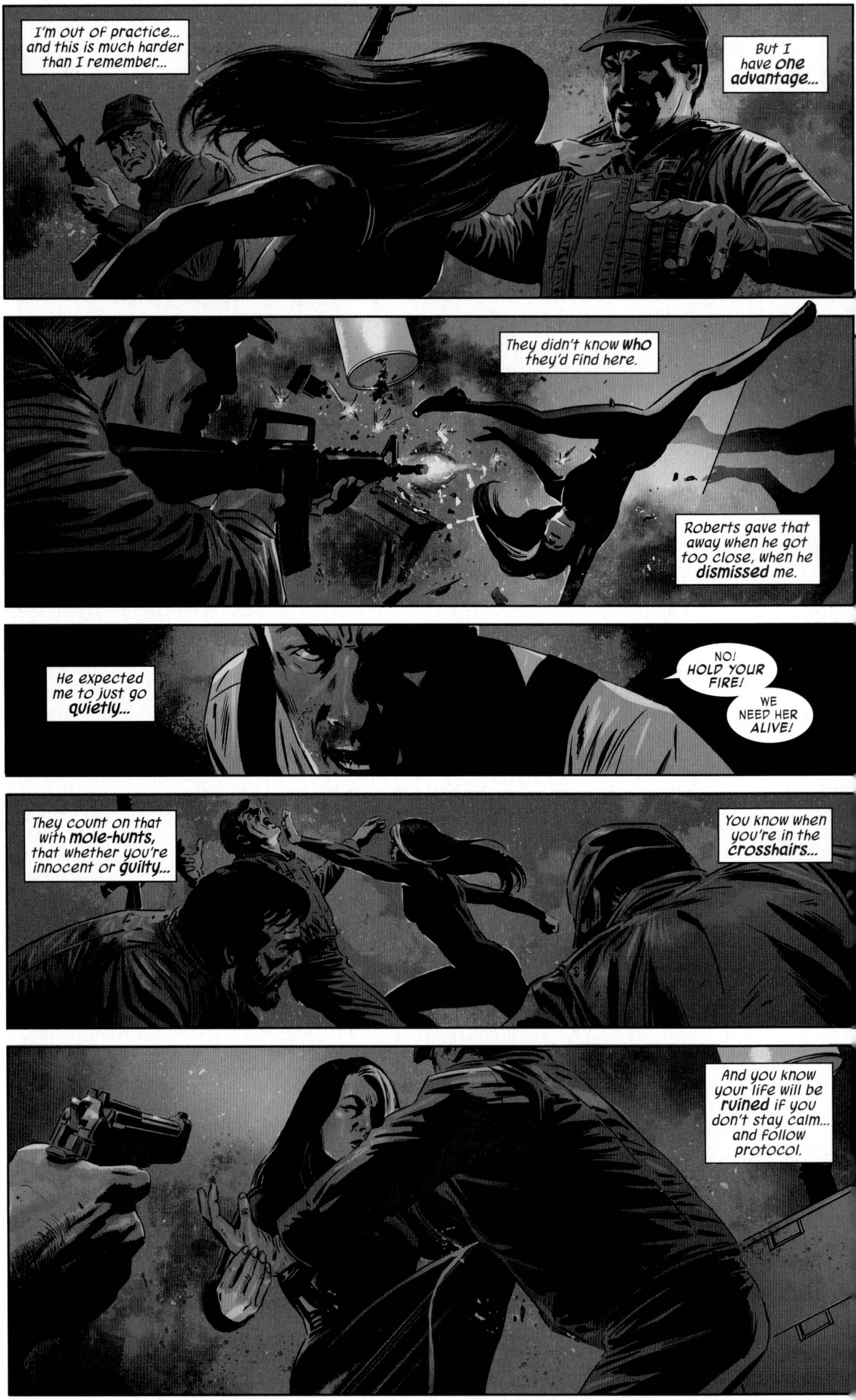

I'm out of practice... and this is much harder than I remember...
But I have one advantage...
They didn't know who they'd find here.
Roberts gave that away when he got too close, when he dismissed me.
He expected me to just go quietly...
NO! HOLD YOUR FIRE!
WE NEED HER ALIVE!
They count on that with mole-hunts, that whether you're innocent or guilty...
You know when you're in the crosshairs...
And you know your life will be ruined if you don't stay calm... and follow protocol.

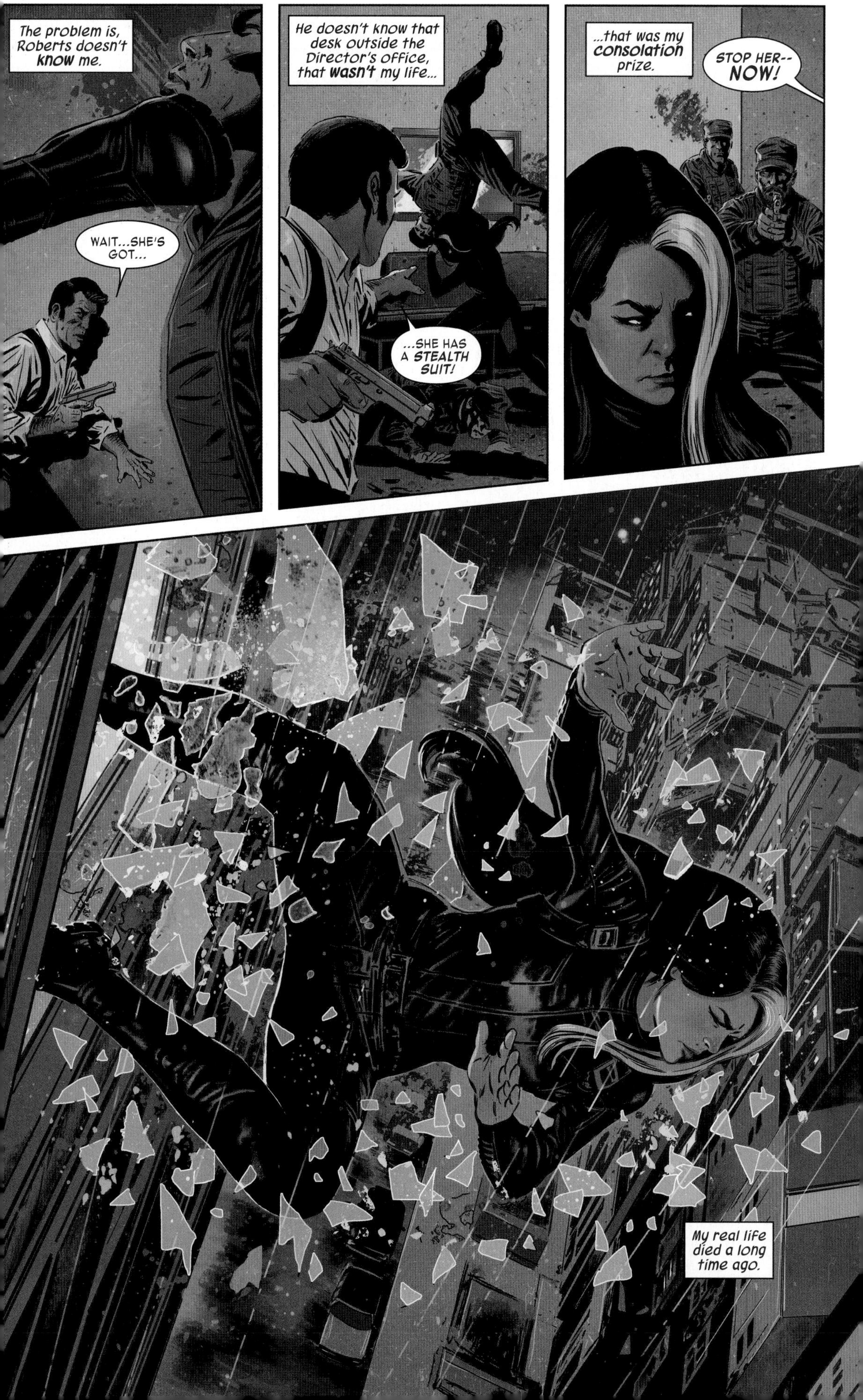
The problem is, Roberts doesn't **know** me.
WAIT...SHE'S GOT...
He doesn't know that desk outside the Director's office, that **wasn't** my life...
...SHE HAS A **STEALTH SUIT!**
...that was my **consolation** prize.
STOP HER-- **NOW!**
My real life died a long time ago.

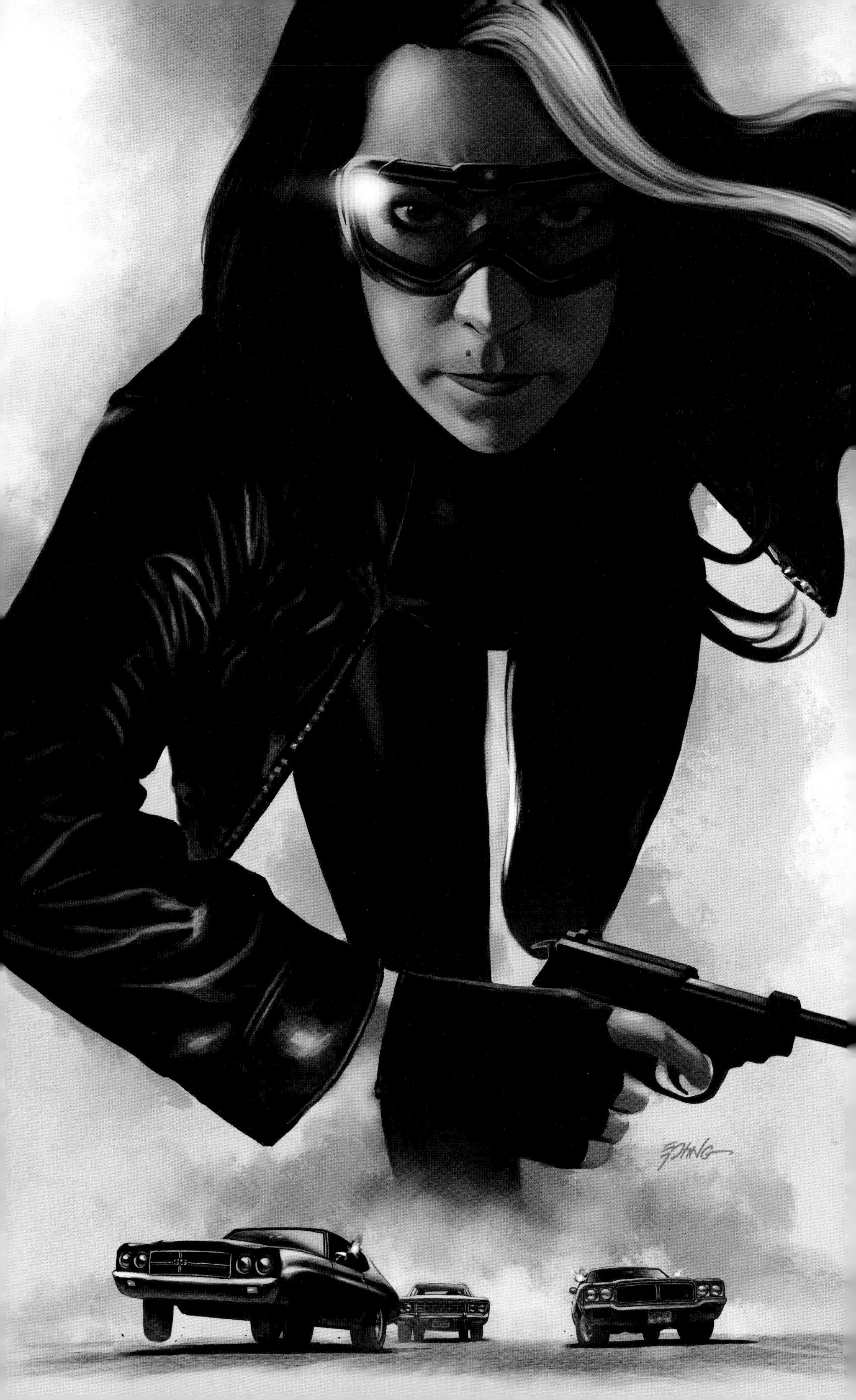

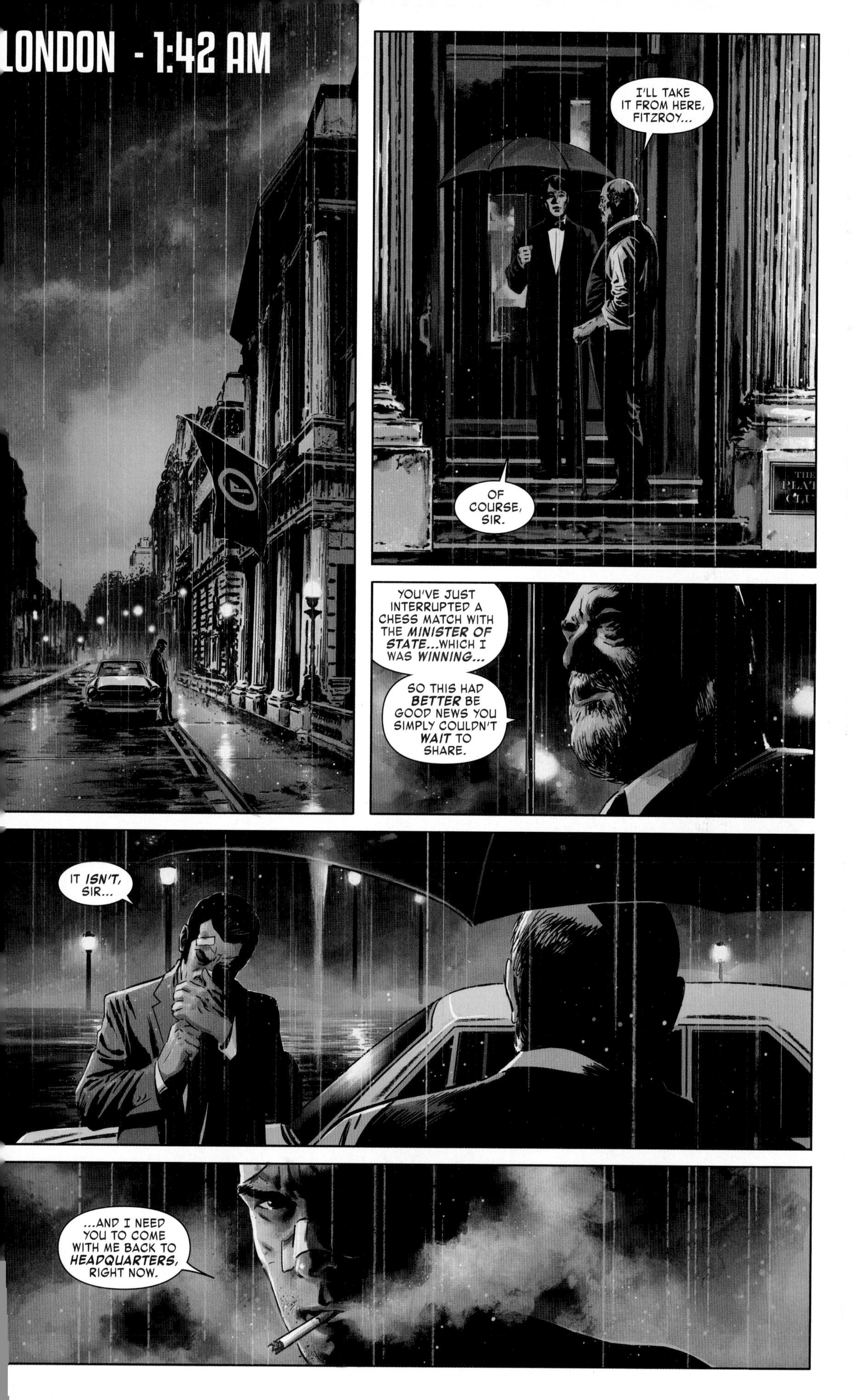
LONDON - 1:42 AM
I'LL TAKE IT FROM HERE, FITZROY...
OF COURSE, SIR.
YOU'VE JUST INTERRUPTED A CHESS MATCH WITH THE MINISTER OF STATE...WHICH I WAS WINNING...
SO THIS HAD BETTER BE GOOD NEWS YOU SIMPLY COULDN'T WAIT TO SHARE.
IT ISN'T, SIR...
...AND I NEED YOU TO COME WITH ME BACK TO HEADQUARTERS, RIGHT NOW.

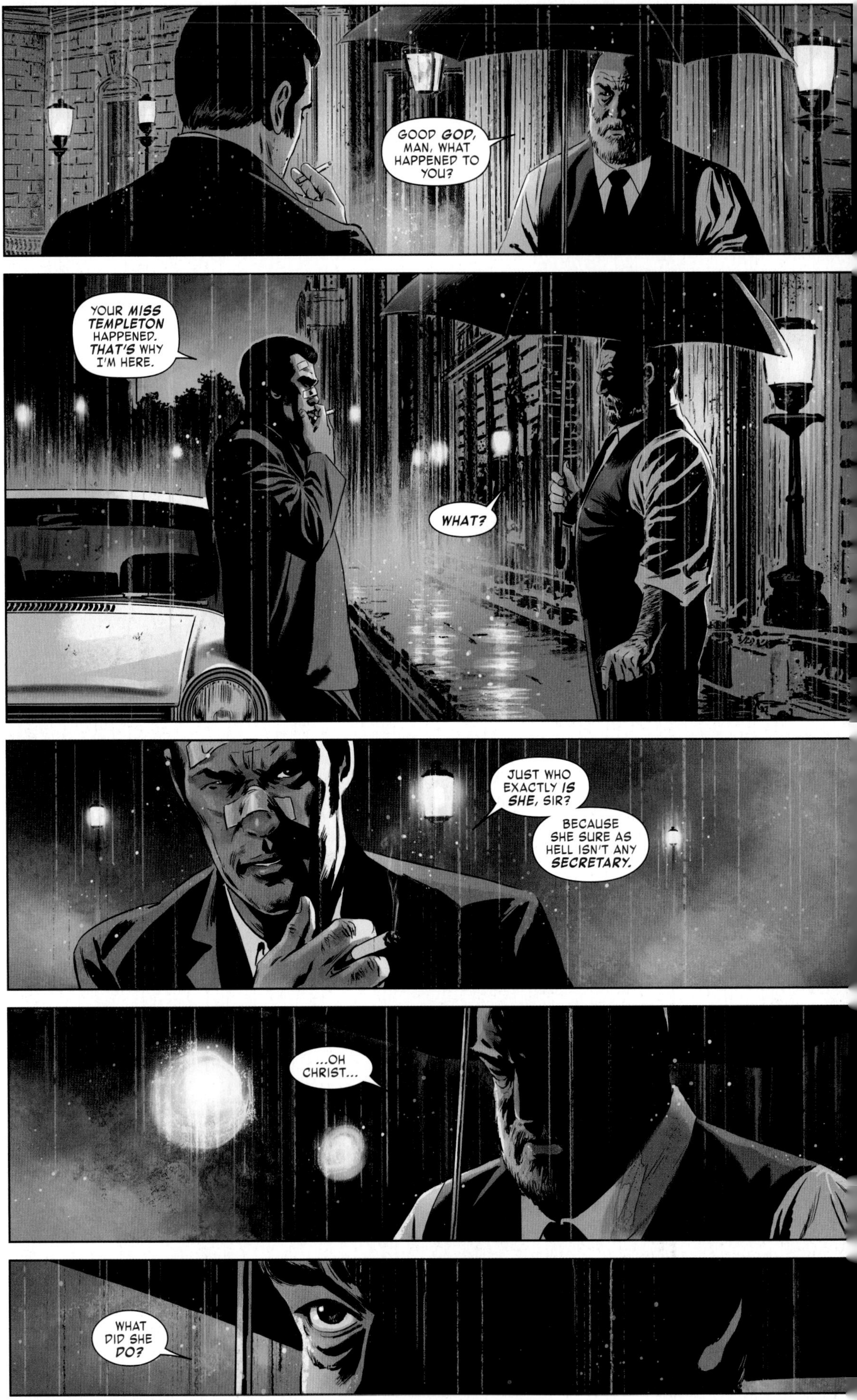
GOOD GOD, MAN, WHAT HAPPENED TO YOU?
YOUR MISS TEMPLETON HAPPENED. THAT'S WHY I'M HERE.
WHAT?
JUST WHO EXACTLY IS SHE, SIR?
BECAUSE SHE SURE AS HELL ISN'T ANY SECRETARY.
...OH CHRIST...
WHAT DID SHE DO?

PART TWO

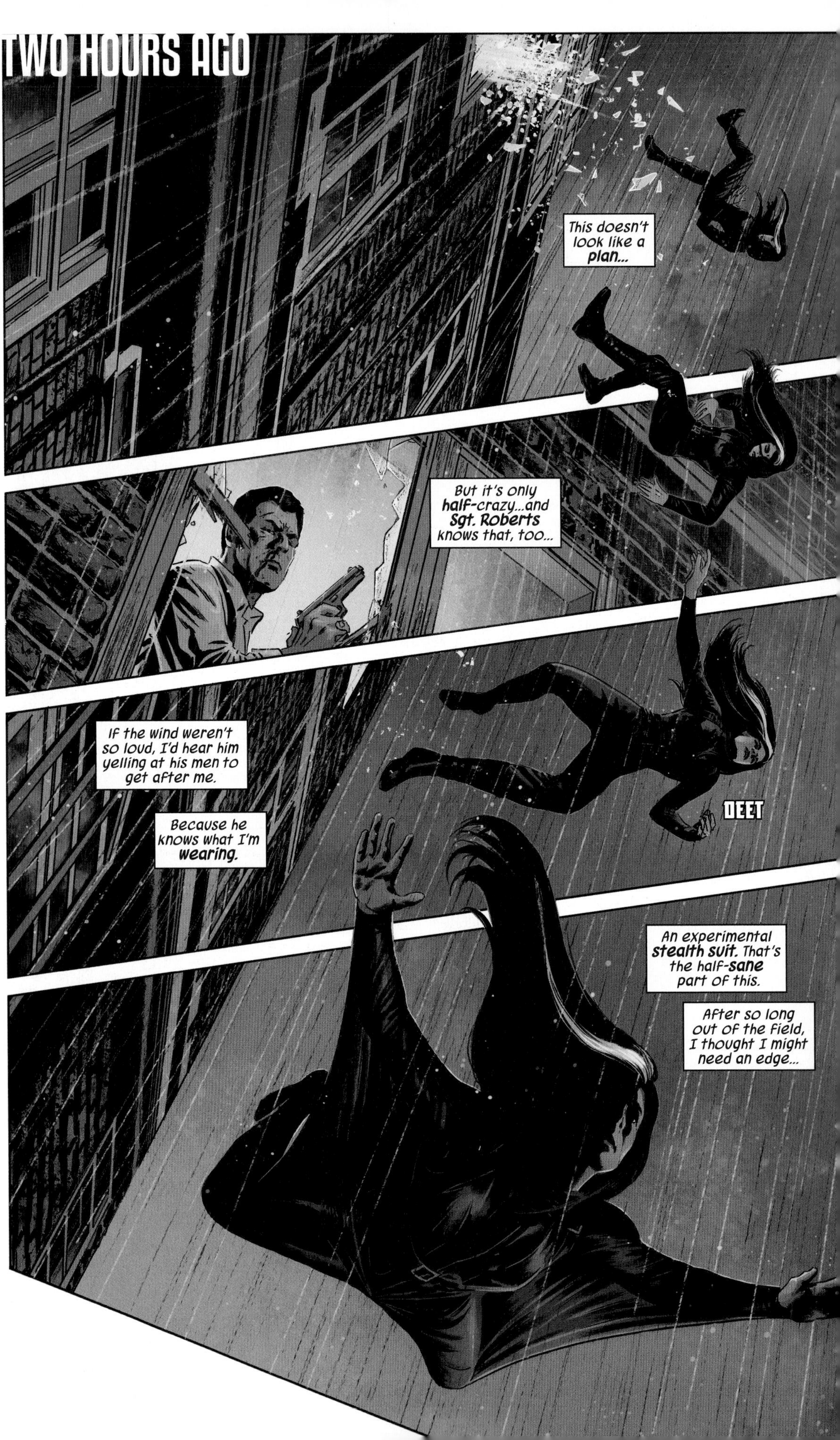
TWO HOURS AGO
This doesn't look like a plan...
But it's only half-crazy...and Sgt. Roberts knows that, too...
If the wind weren't so loud, I'd hear him yelling at his men to get after me.
Because he knows what I'm wearing.
DEET
An experimental stealth suit. That's the half-sane part of this.
After so long out of the field, I thought I might need an edge...

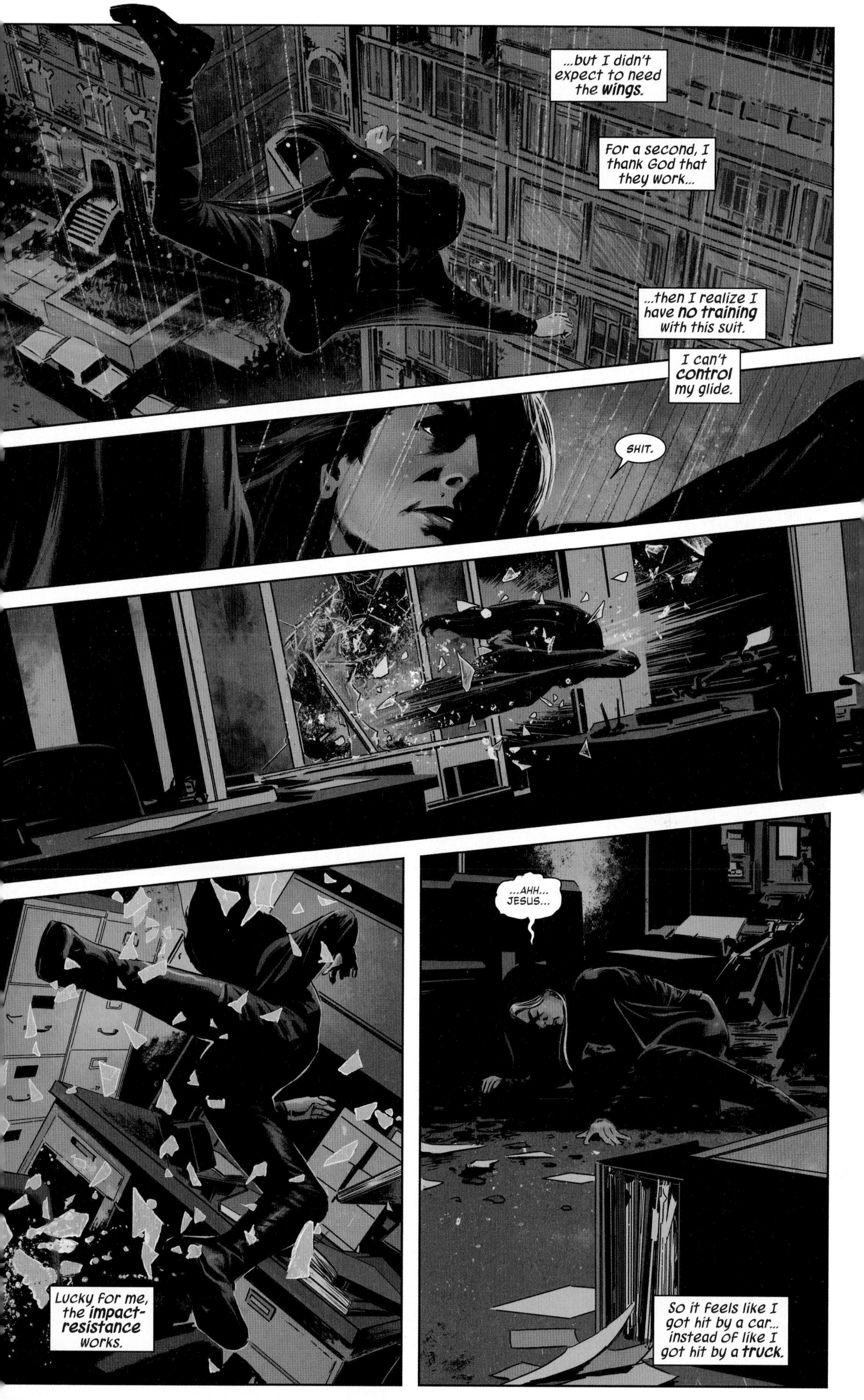
...but I didn't expect to need the **wings**.
For a second, I thank God that they work...
...then I realize I have **no training** with this suit.
I can't **control** my glide.
SHIT.
Lucky for me, the **impact-resistance** works.
...AHH... JESUS...
So it feels like I got hit by a car... instead of like I got hit by a **truck**.

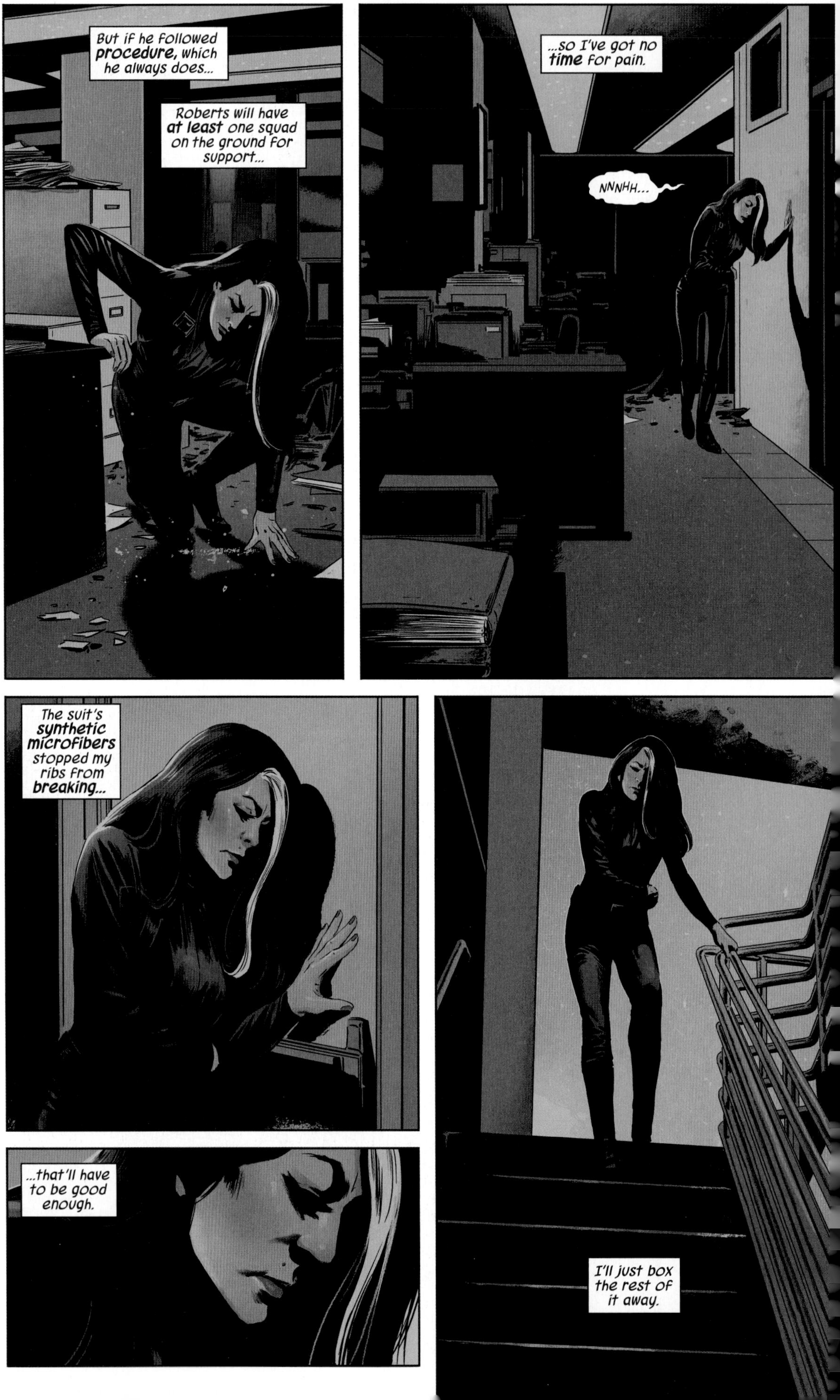
But if he followed procedure, which he always does...
Roberts will have at least one squad on the ground for support...
...so I've got no time for pain.
NNNHH...
The suit's synthetic microfibers stopped my ribs from breaking...
...that'll have to be good enough.
I'll just box the rest of it away.

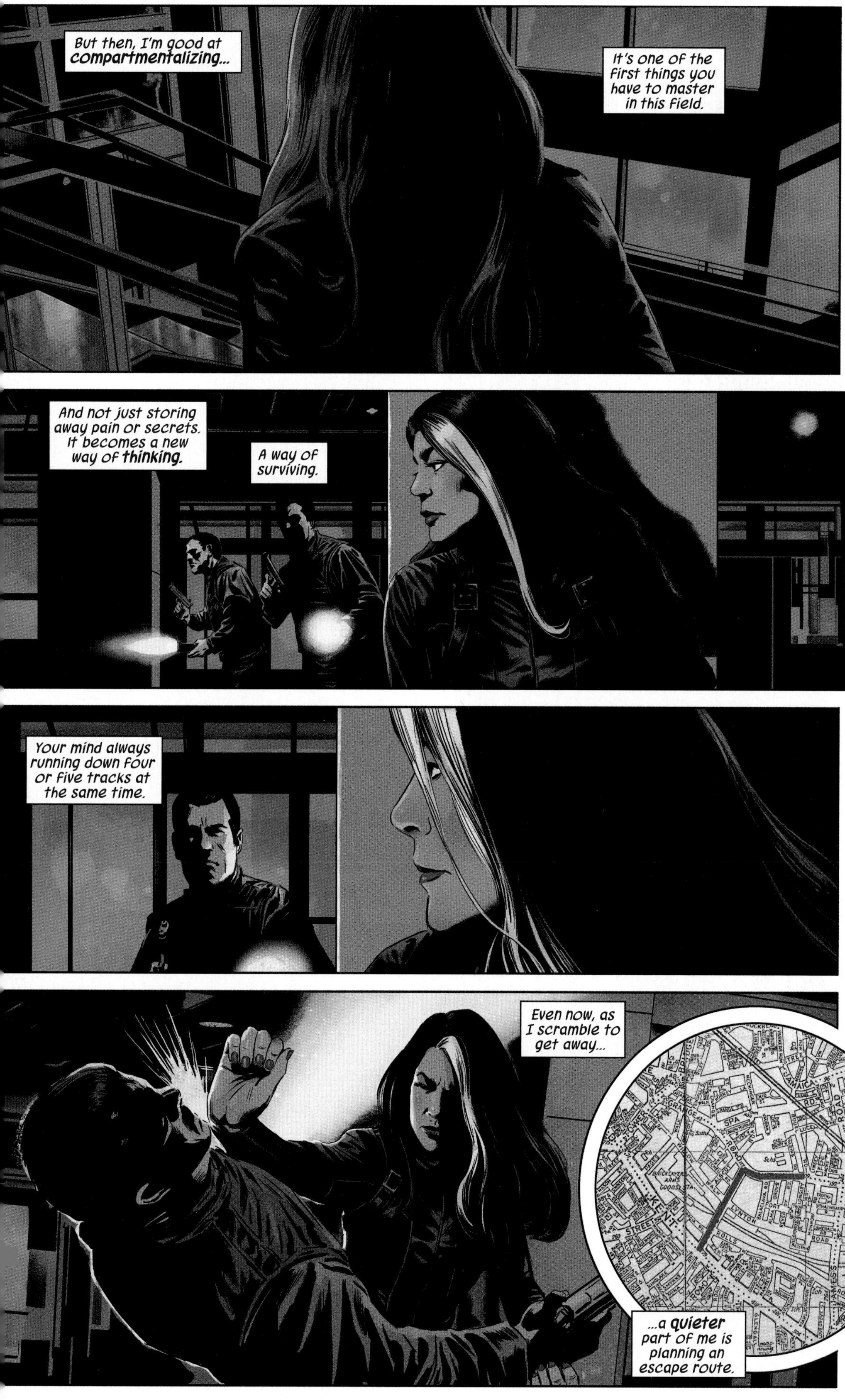
But then, I'm good at compartmentalizing...
It's one of the first things you have to master in this field.
And not just storing away pain or secrets. It becomes a new way of thinking.
A way of surviving.
Your mind always running down four or five tracks at the same time.
Even now, as I scramble to get away...
...a quieter part of me is planning an escape route.

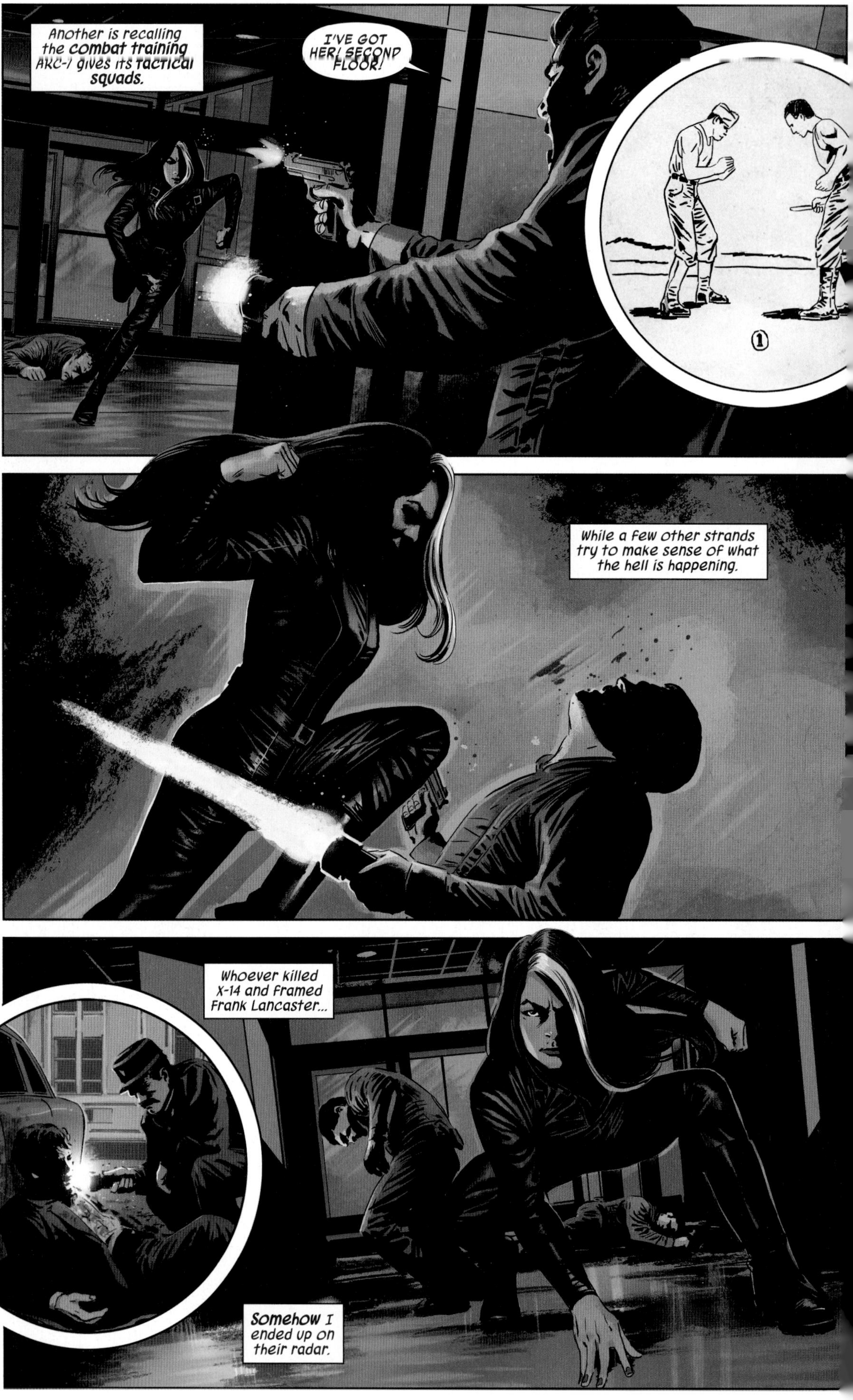
Another is recalling the combat training ARC-7 gives its tactical squads.
I'VE GOT HER! SECOND FLOOR!
1
While a few other strands try to make sense of what the hell is happening.
Whoever killed X-14 and framed Frank Lancaster...
Somehow I ended up on their radar.

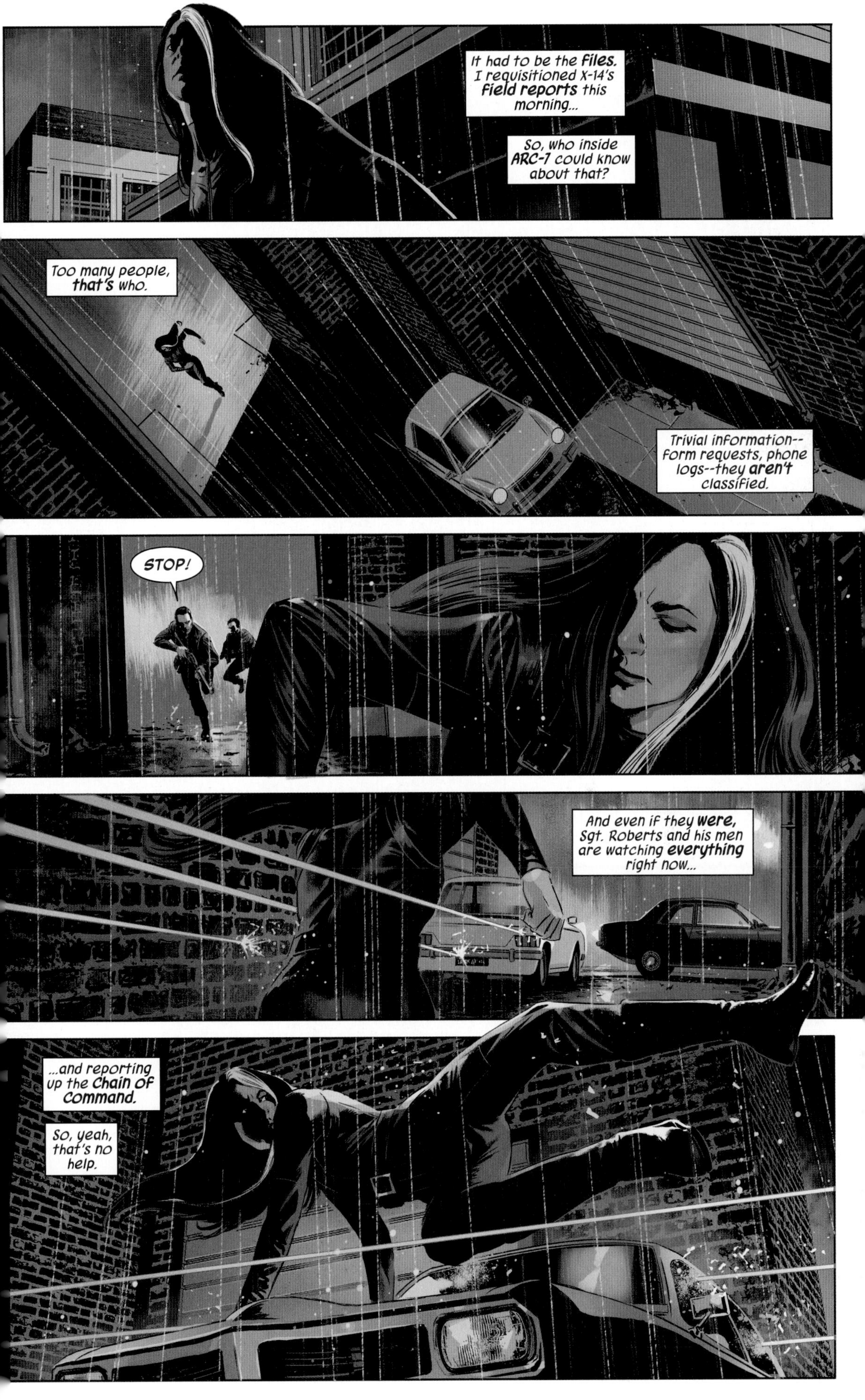

It had to be the files. I requisitioned X-14's field reports this morning...
So, who inside ARC-7 could know about that?
Too many people, that's who.
Trivial information--form requests, phone logs--they aren't classified.
STOP!
And even if they were, Sgt. Roberts and his men are watching everything right now...
...and reporting up the chain of command.
So, yeah, that's no help.

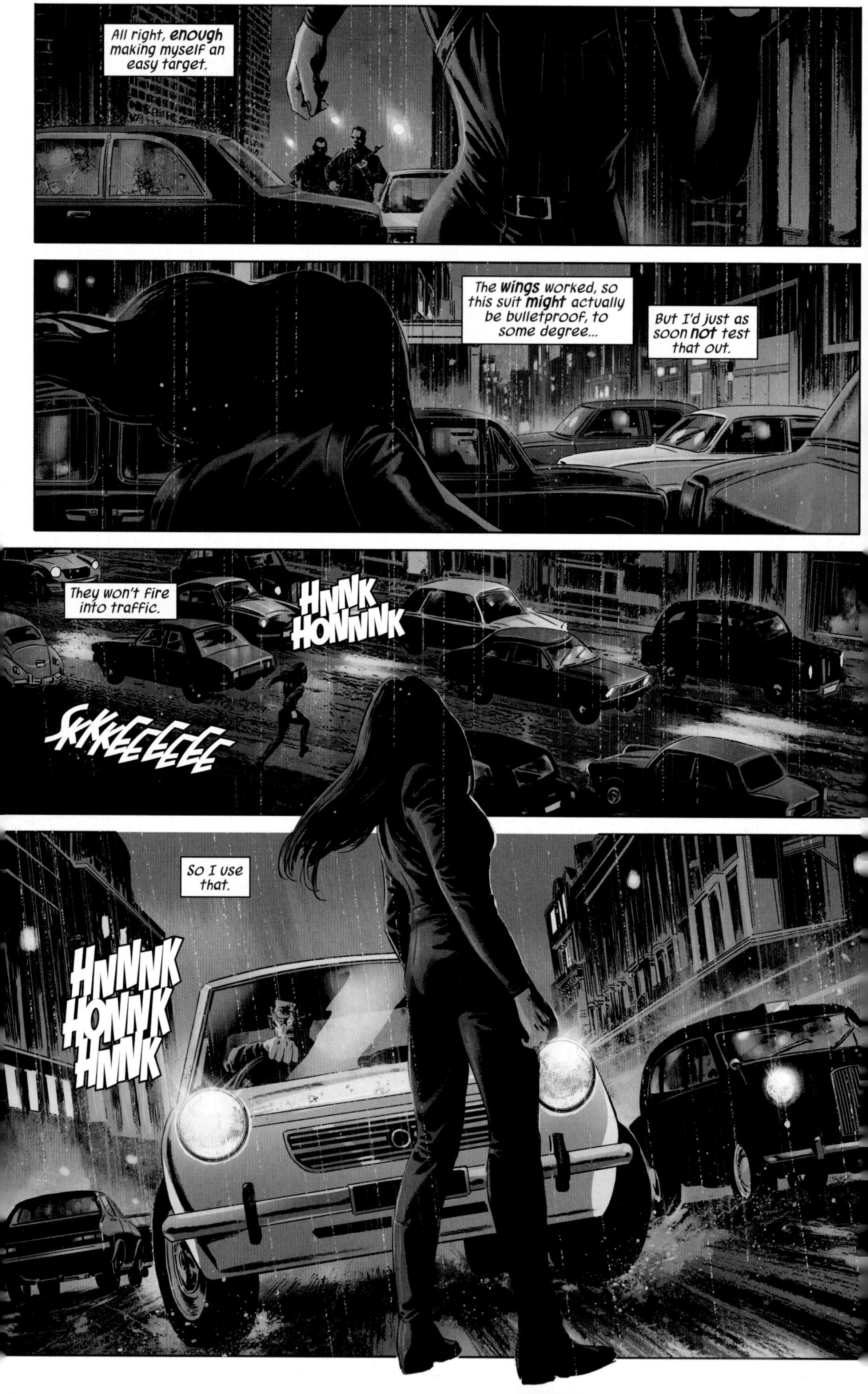
All right, enough making myself an easy target.
The wings worked, so this suit might actually be bulletproof, to some degree...
But I'd just as soon not test that out.
They won't fire into traffic.
HNNK HONNNK
SKKKEEEEEEE
So I use that.
HNNNK HONNK HNNK

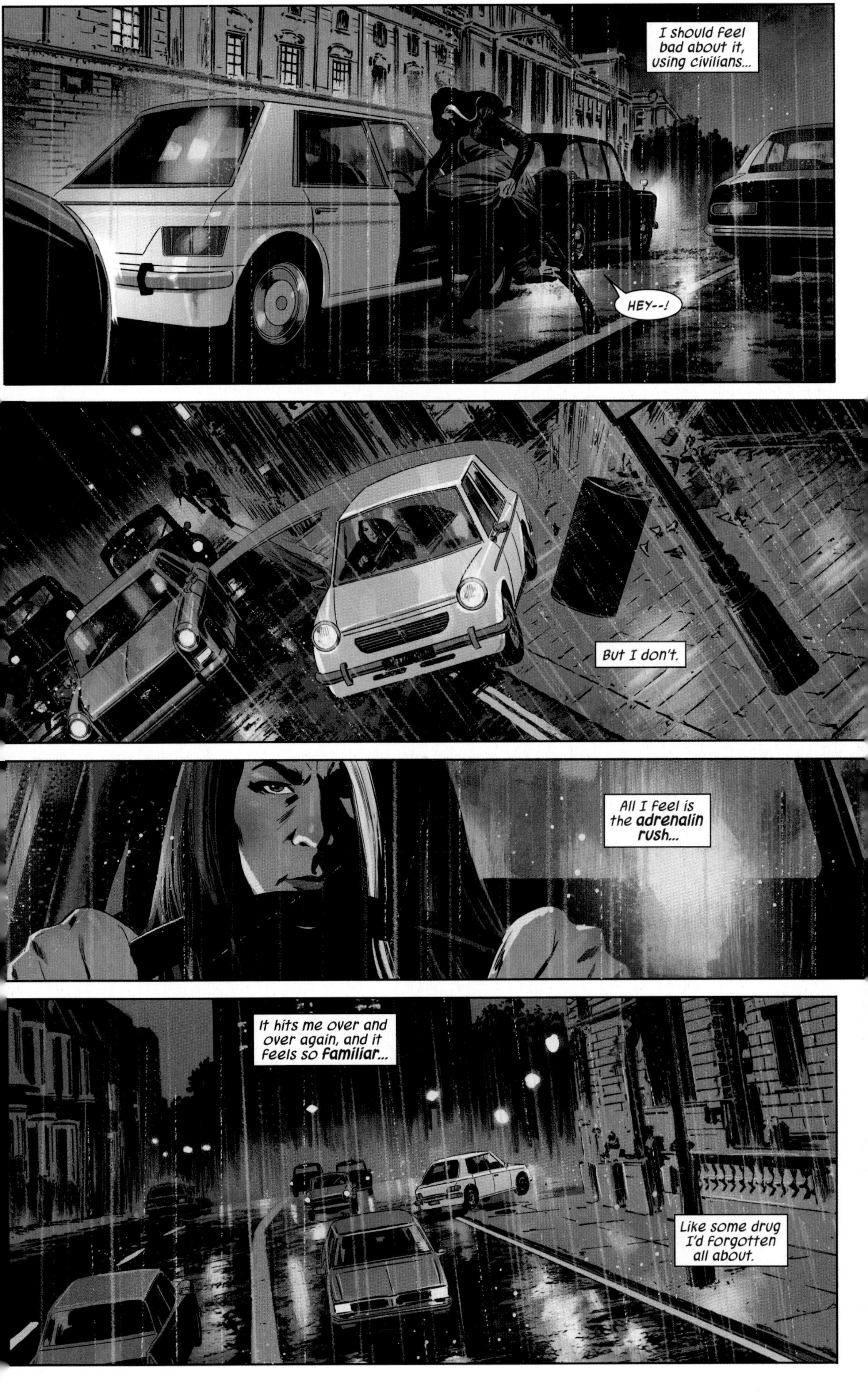
I should feel bad about it, using civilians...
HEY--!
But I don't.
All I feel is the adrenalin rush...
It hits me over and over again, and it feels so familiar...
Like some drug I'd forgotten all about.

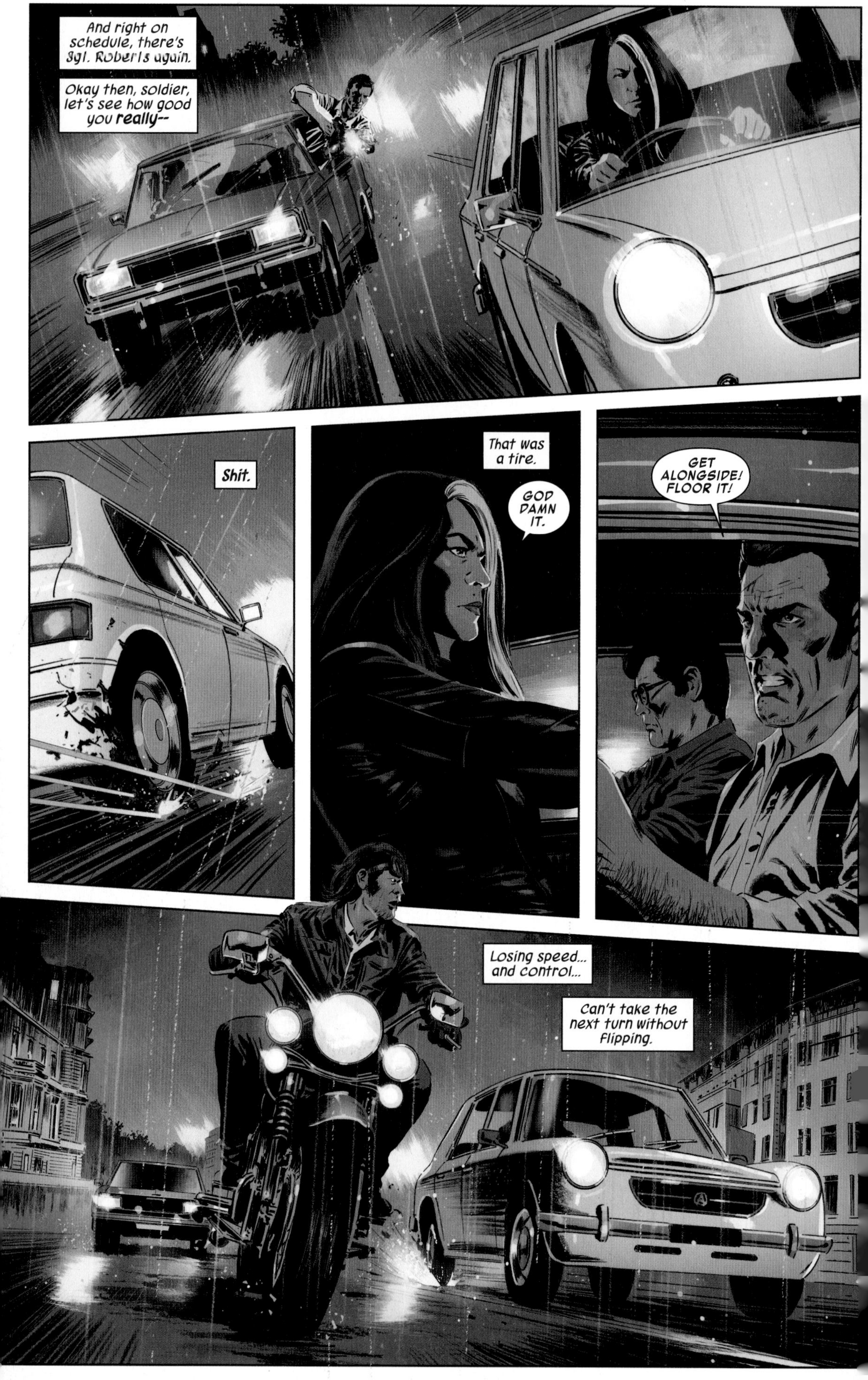
And right on schedule, there's Sgt. Roberts again.
Okay then, soldier, let's see how good you **really**--
Shit.
That was a tire.
GOD DAMN IT.
GET ALONGSIDE! FLOOR IT!
Losing speed... and control...
Can't take the next turn without flipping.

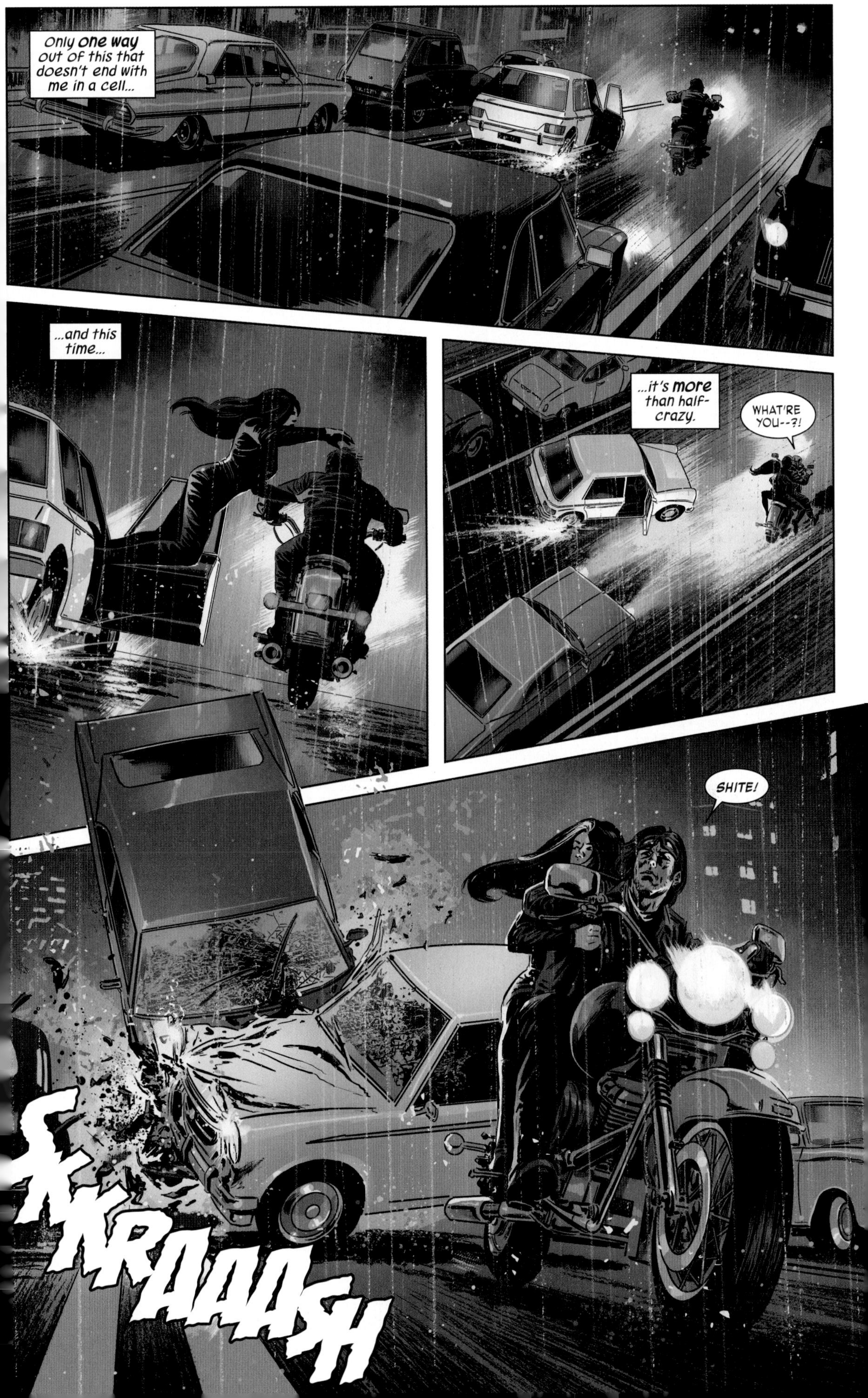
Only one way out of this that doesn't end with me in a cell...
...and this time...
...it's more than half-crazy.
WHAT'RE YOU--?!
SHITE!
SKRAAASH

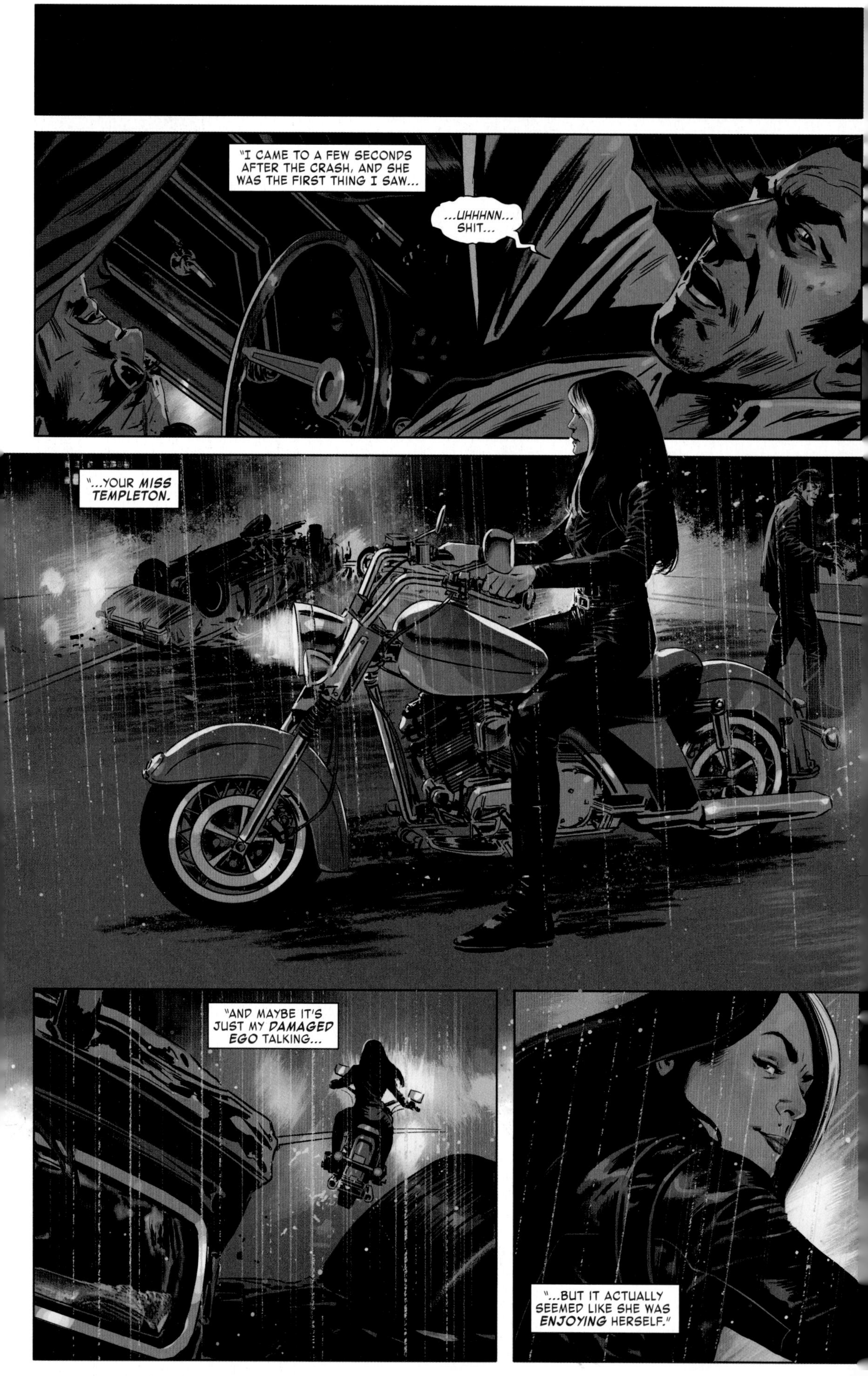
"I CAME TO A FEW SECONDS AFTER THE CRASH, AND SHE WAS THE FIRST THING I SAW...
...UHHHNN... SHIT...
"...YOUR MISS TEMPLETON.
"AND MAYBE IT'S JUST MY DAMAGED EGO TALKING...
"...BUT IT ACTUALLY SEEMED LIKE SHE WAS ENJOYING HERSELF."

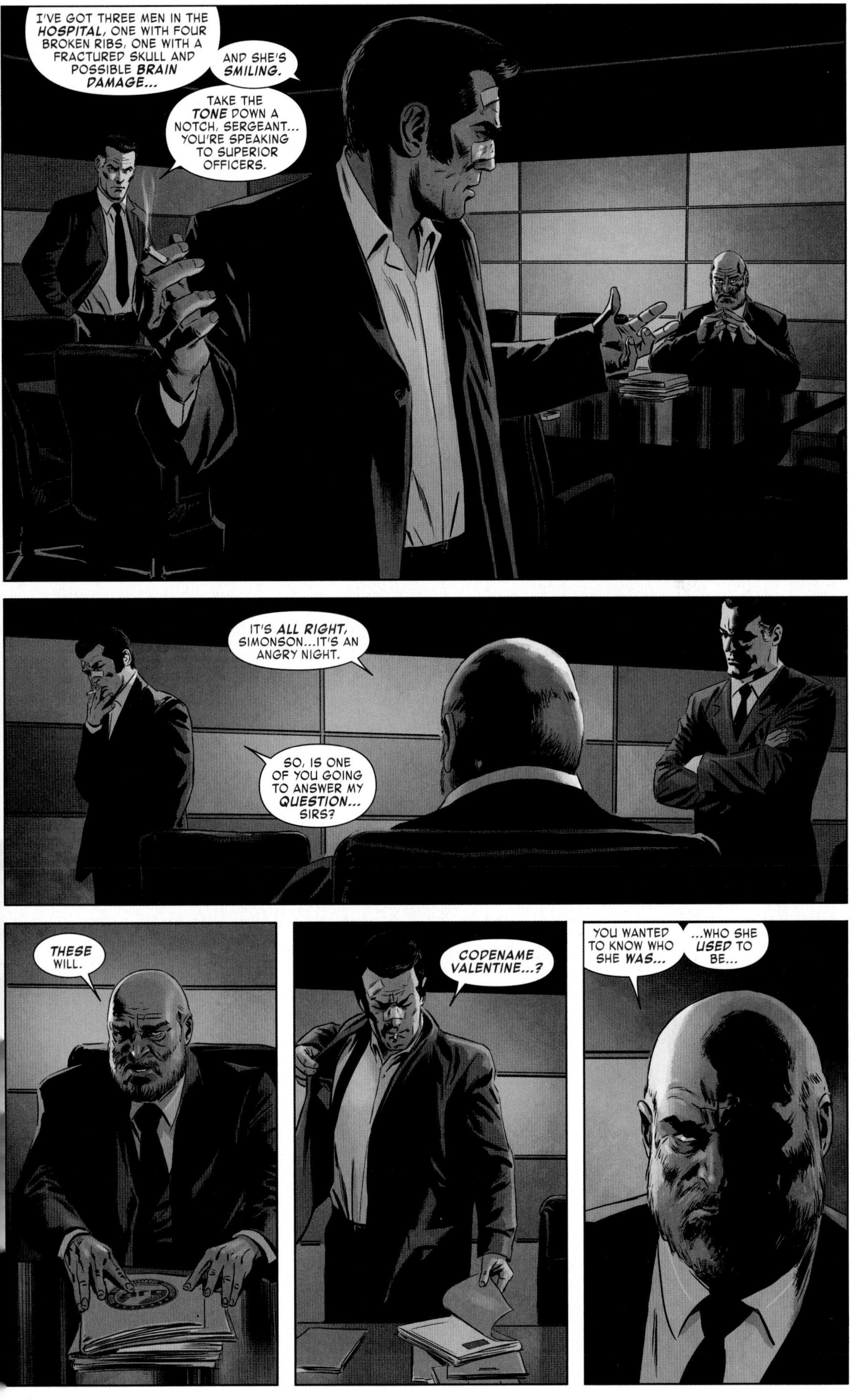
I'VE GOT THREE MEN IN THE HOSPITAL, ONE WITH FOUR BROKEN RIBS, ONE WITH A FRACTURED SKULL AND POSSIBLE BRAIN DAMAGE...
AND SHE'S SMILING.
TAKE THE TONE DOWN A NOTCH, SERGEANT... YOU'RE SPEAKING TO SUPERIOR OFFICERS.
IT'S ALL RIGHT, SIMONSON...IT'S AN ANGRY NIGHT.
SO, IS ONE OF YOU GOING TO ANSWER MY QUESTION... SIRS?
THESE WILL.
CODENAME VALENTINE...?
YOU WANTED TO KNOW WHO SHE WAS...
...WHO SHE USED TO BE...

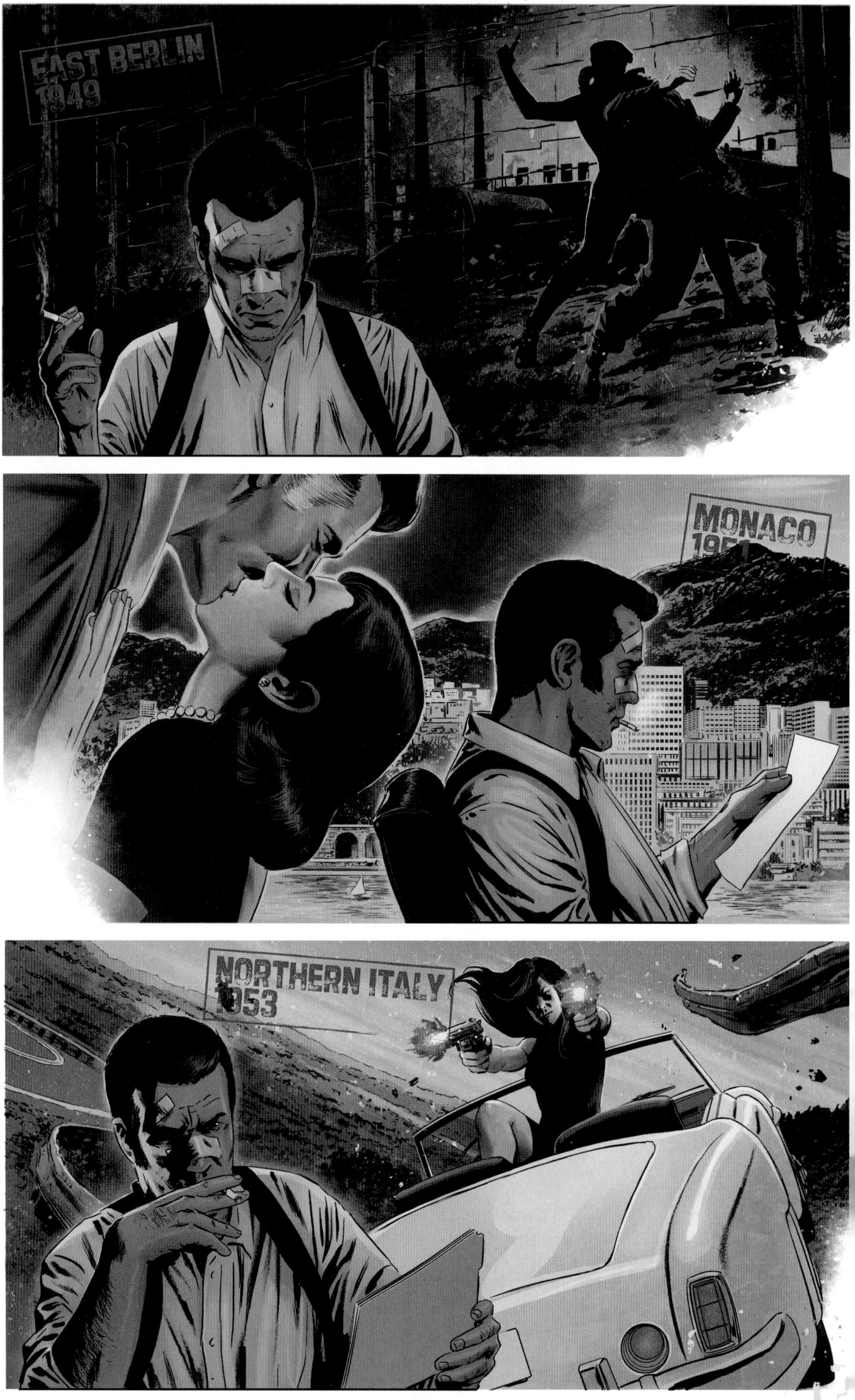
EAST BERLIN
1949
MONACO
NORTHERN ITALY
1953

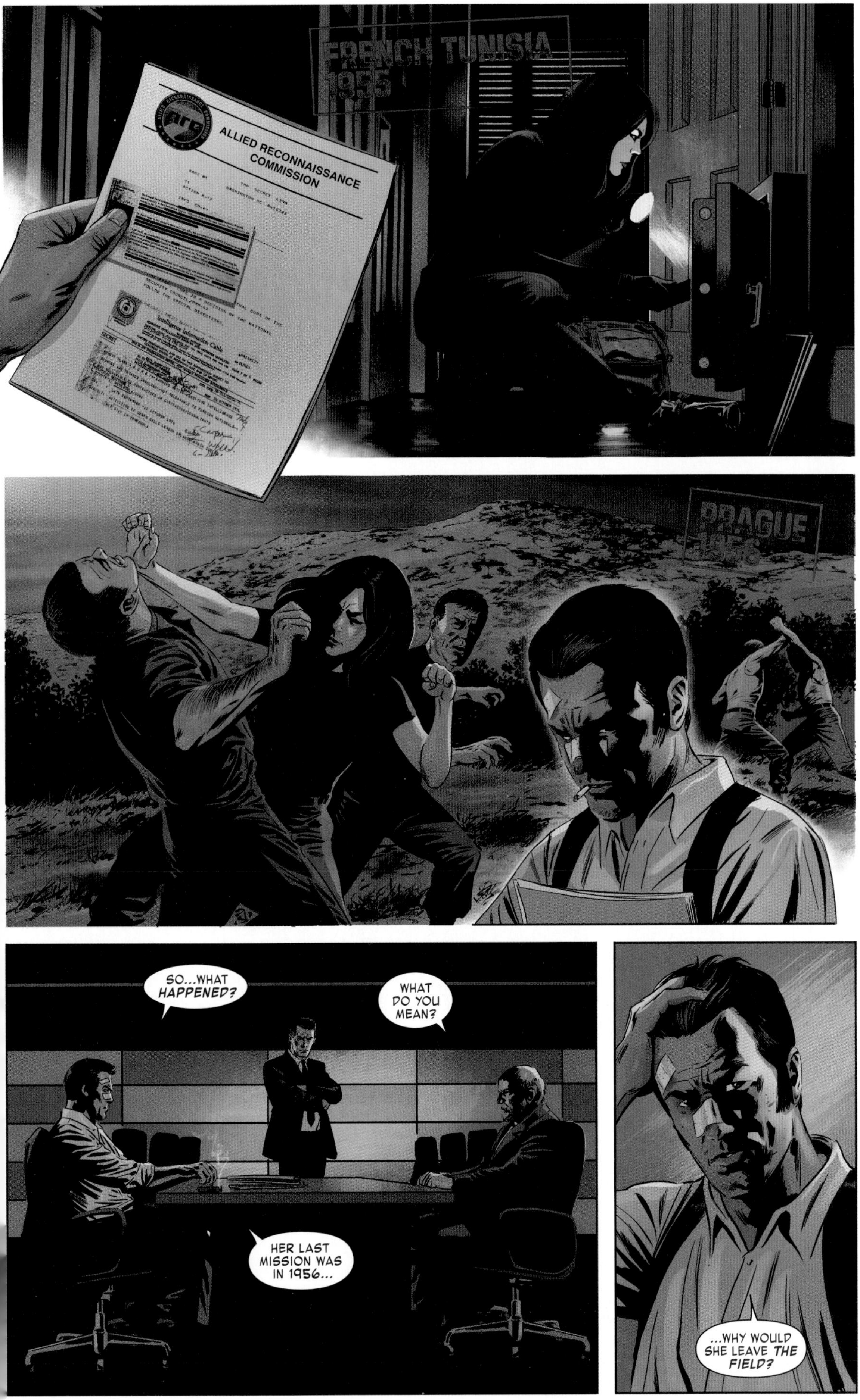
FRENCH TUNISIA 1955
ALLIED RECONNAISSANCE COMMISSION
PRAGUE
SO...WHAT HAPPENED?
WHAT DO YOU MEAN?
HER LAST MISSION WAS IN 1956...
...WHY WOULD SHE LEAVE THE FIELD?

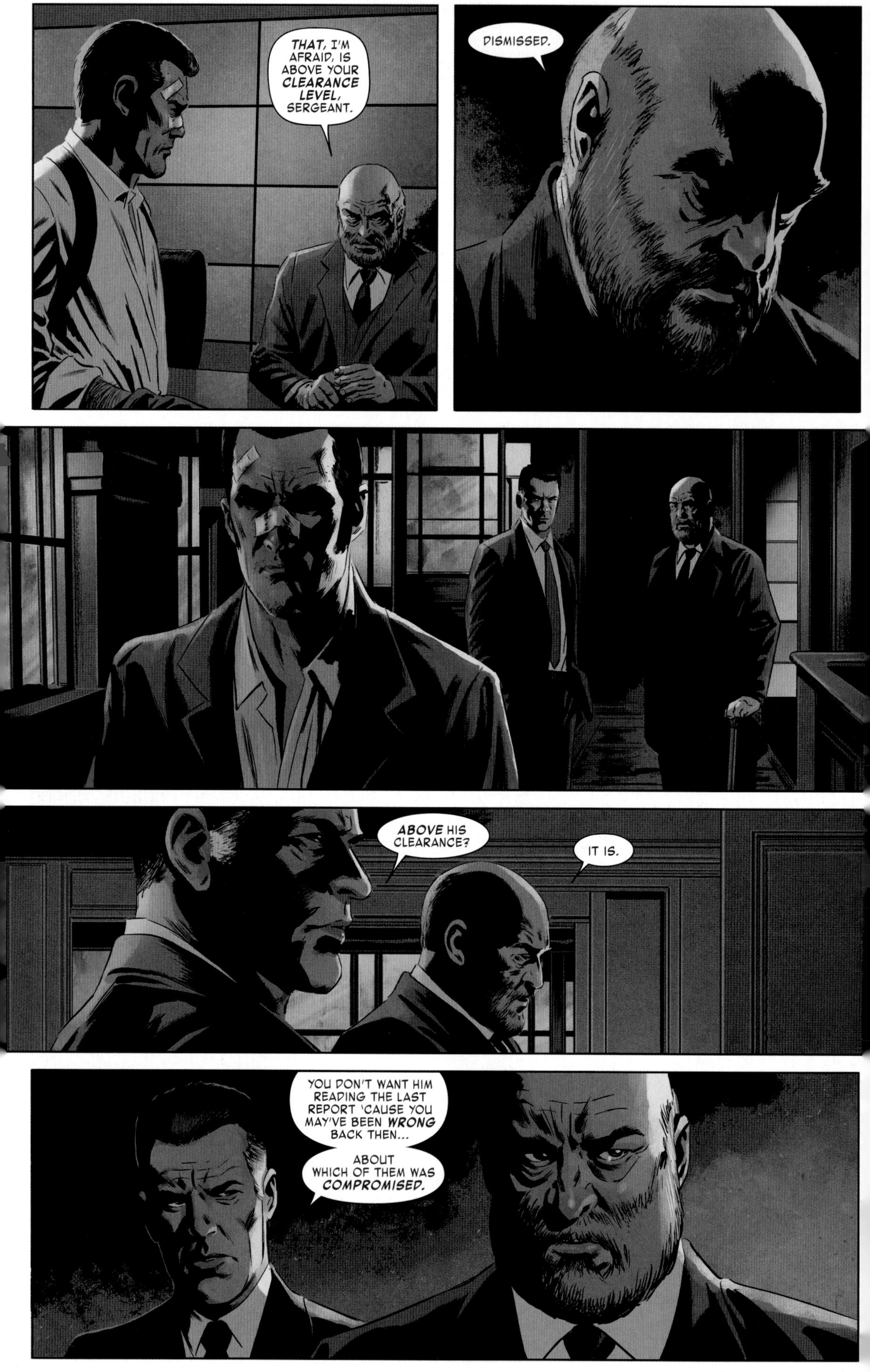
THAT, I'M AFRAID, IS ABOVE YOUR CLEARANCE LEVEL, SERGEANT.
DISMISSED.
ABOVE HIS CLEARANCE?
IT IS.
YOU DON'T WANT HIM READING THE LAST REPORT 'CAUSE YOU MAY'VE BEEN WRONG BACK THEN...
ABOUT WHICH OF THEM WAS COMPROMISED.

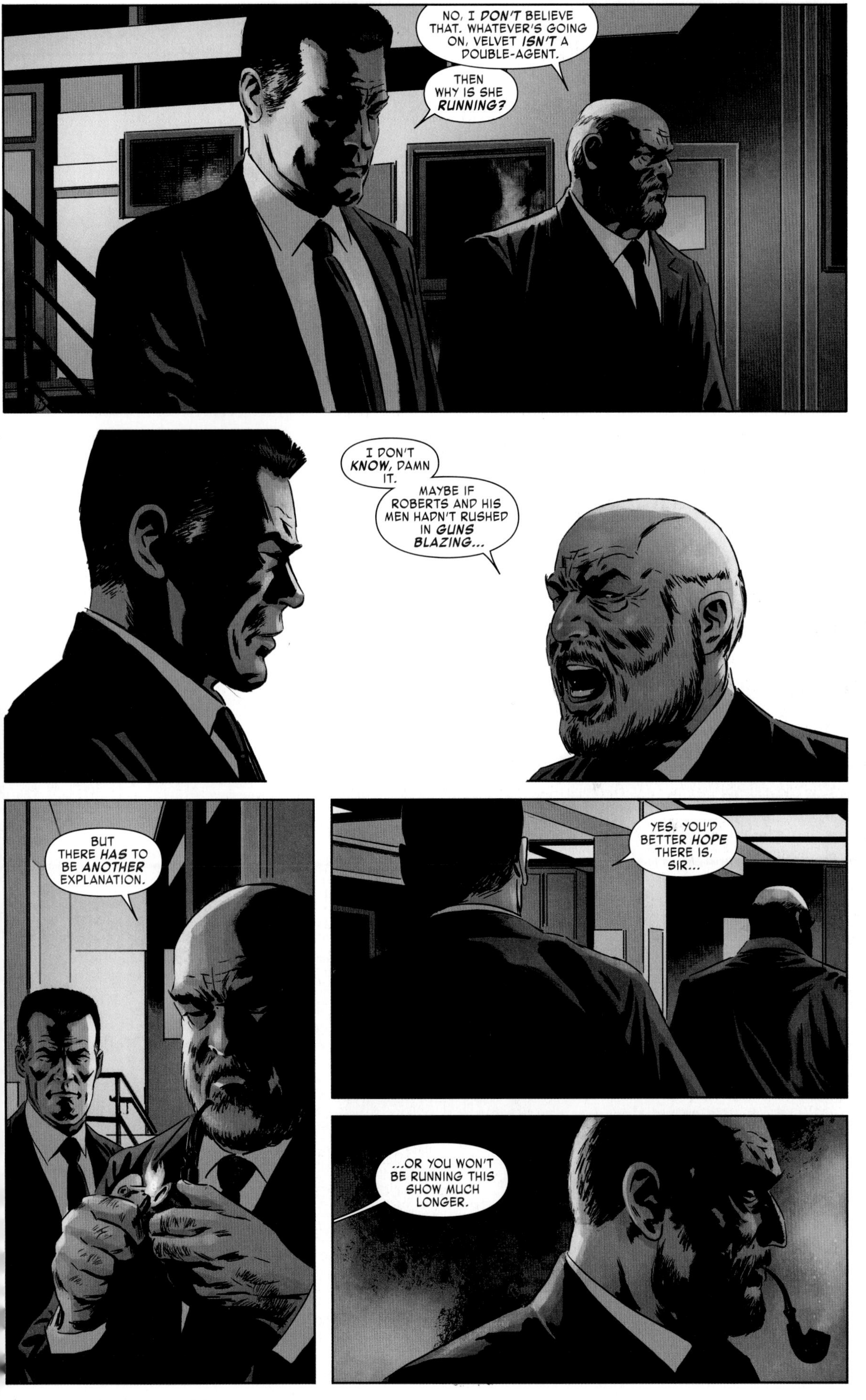
NO, I DON'T BELIEVE THAT. WHATEVER'S GOING ON, VELVET ISN'T A DOUBLE-AGENT.
THEN WHY IS SHE RUNNING?
I DON'T KNOW, DAMN IT.
MAYBE IF ROBERTS AND HIS MEN HADN'T RUSHED IN GUNS BLAZING...
BUT THERE HAS TO BE ANOTHER EXPLANATION.
YES. YOU'D BETTER HOPE THERE IS, SIR...
...OR YOU WON'T BE RUNNING THIS SHOW MUCH LONGER.

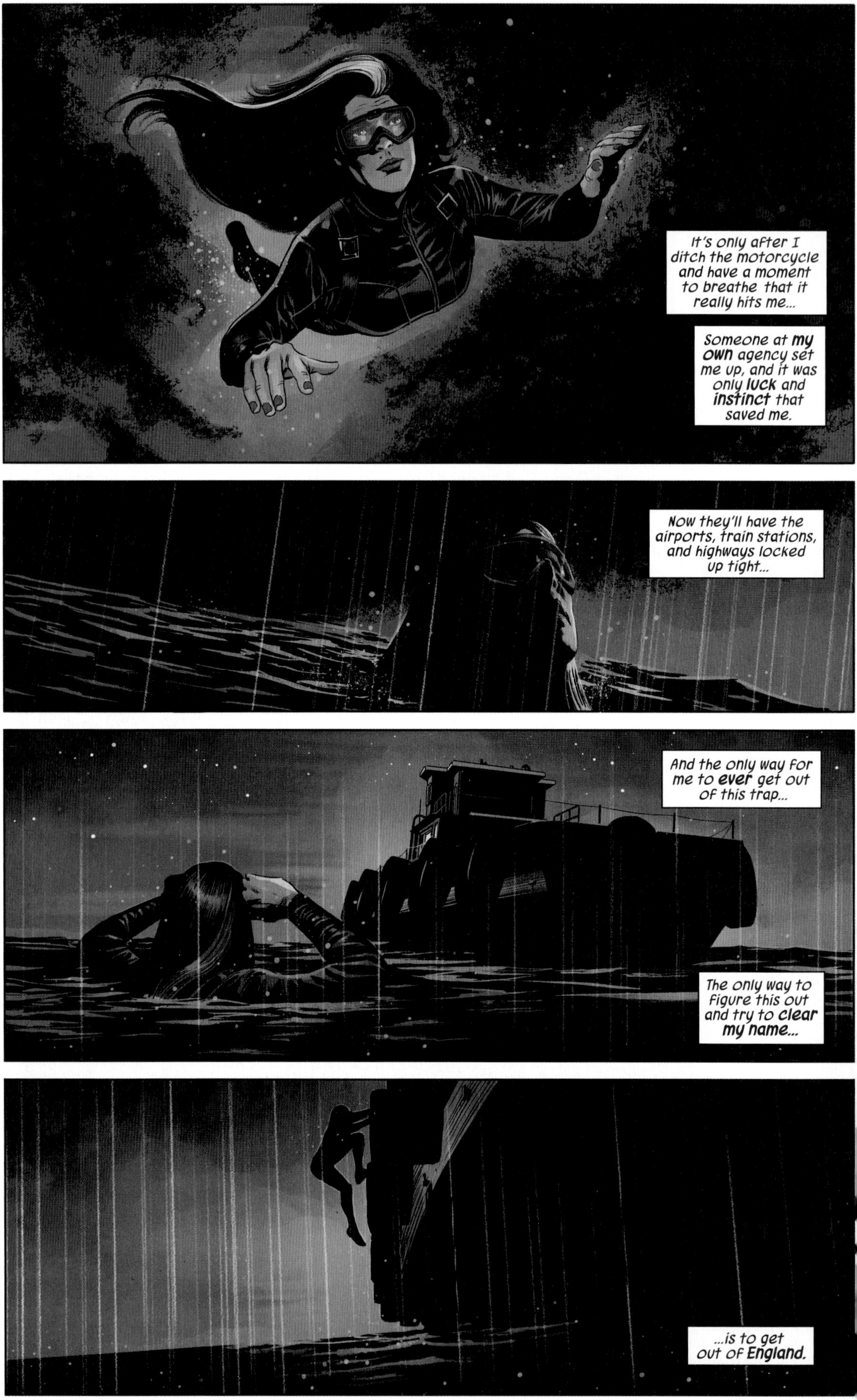
It's only after I ditch the motorcycle and have a moment to breathe that it really hits me...
Someone at my own agency set me up, and it was only luck and instinct that saved me.
Now they'll have the airports, train stations, and highways locked up tight...
And the only way for me to ever get out of this trap...
The only way to figure this out and try to clear my name...
...is to get out of England.

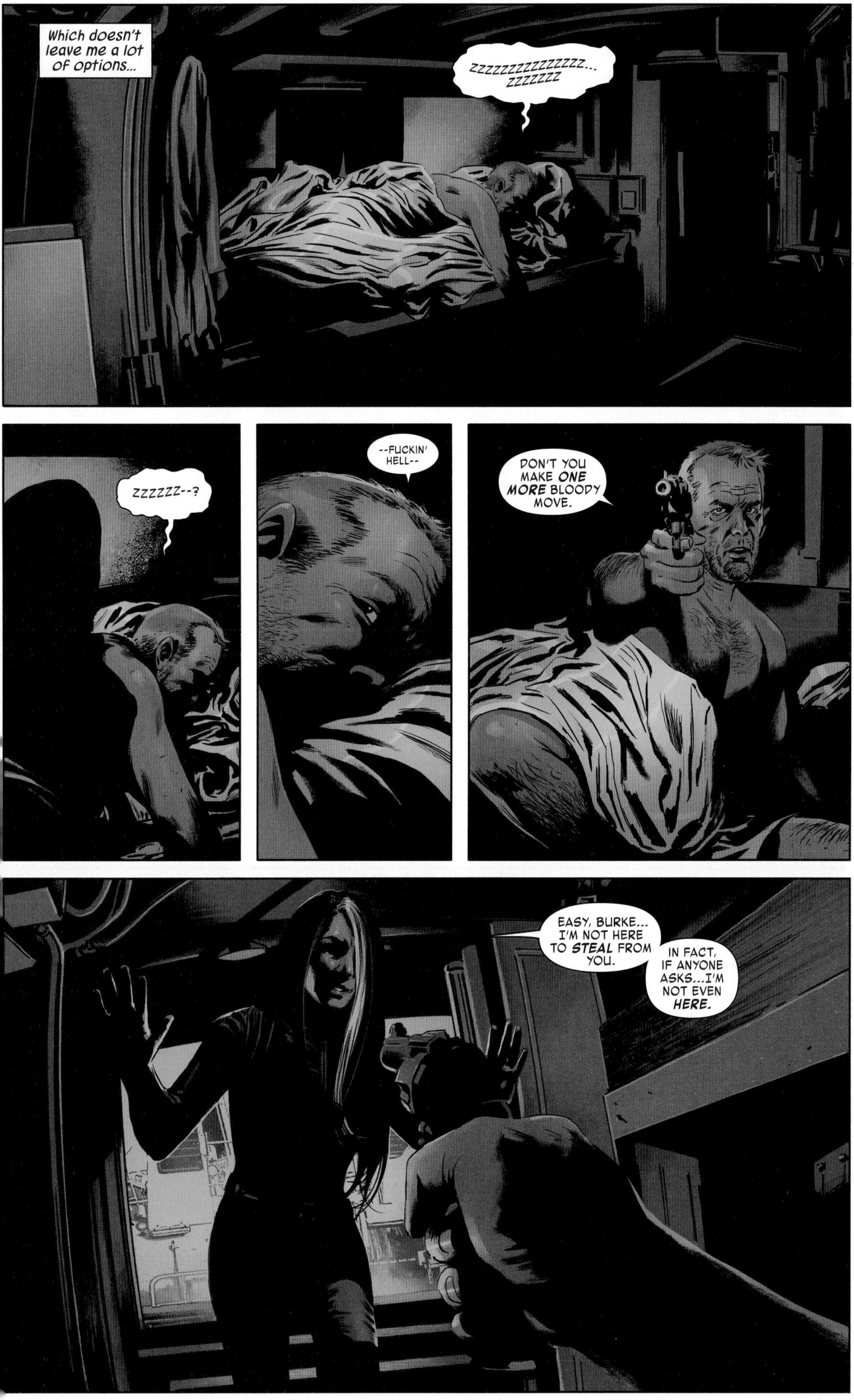
Which doesn't leave me a lot of options...
ZZZZZZZZZZZZZZZ... ZZZZZZZ
ZZZZZZ--?
--FUCKIN' HELL--
DON'T YOU MAKE ONE MORE BLOODY MOVE.
EASY, BURKE... I'M NOT HERE TO STEAL FROM YOU.
IN FACT, IF ANYONE ASKS...I'M NOT EVEN HERE.

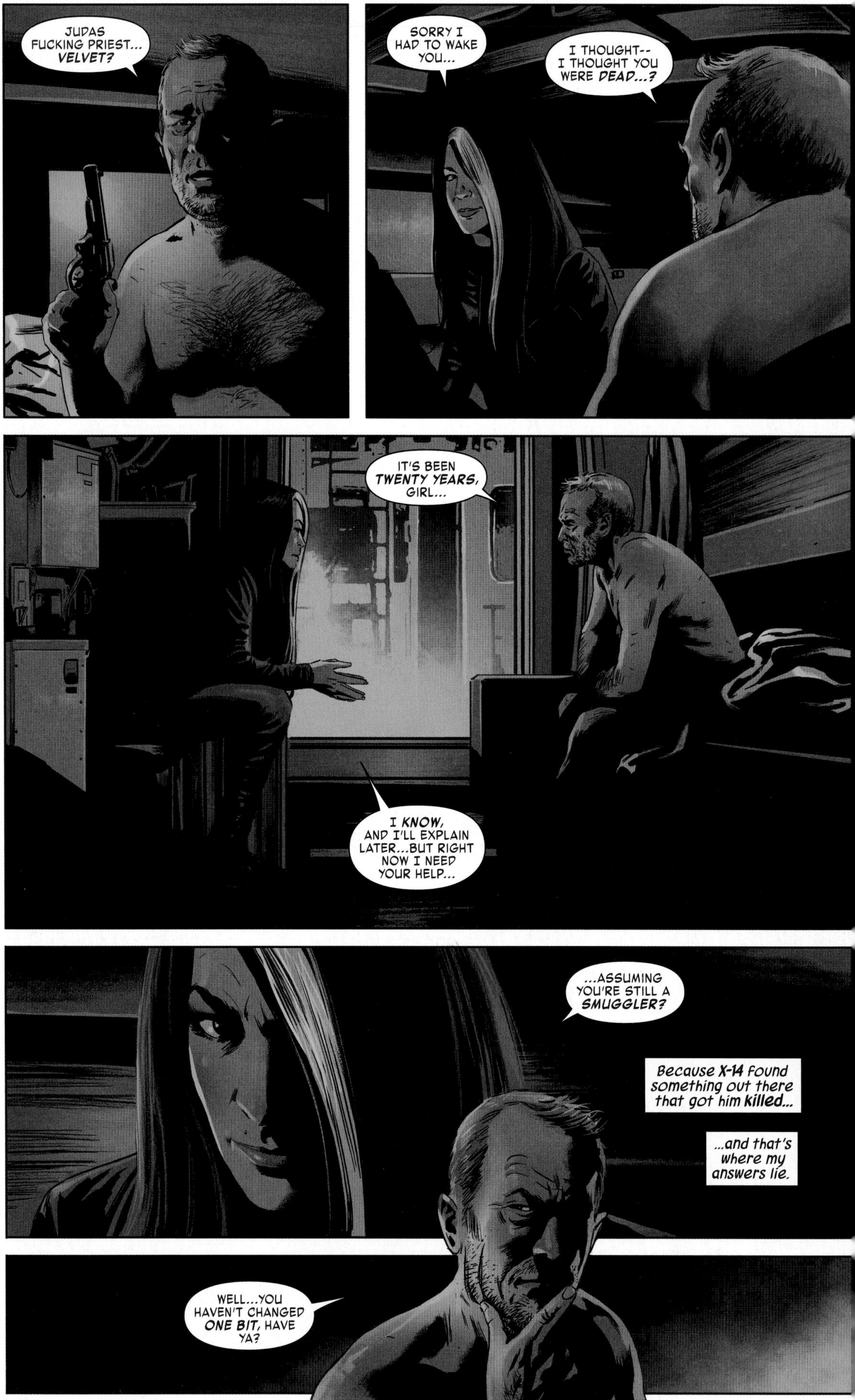
JUDAS FUCKING PRIEST... VELVET?
SORRY I HAD TO WAKE YOU...
I THOUGHT-- I THOUGHT YOU WERE DEAD...?
IT'S BEEN TWENTY YEARS, GIRL...
I KNOW, AND I'LL EXPLAIN LATER...BUT RIGHT NOW I NEED YOUR HELP...
...ASSUMING YOU'RE STILL A SMUGGLER?
Because X-14 found something out there that got him killed...
...and that's where my answers lie.
WELL...YOU HAVEN'T CHANGED ONE BIT, HAVE YA?

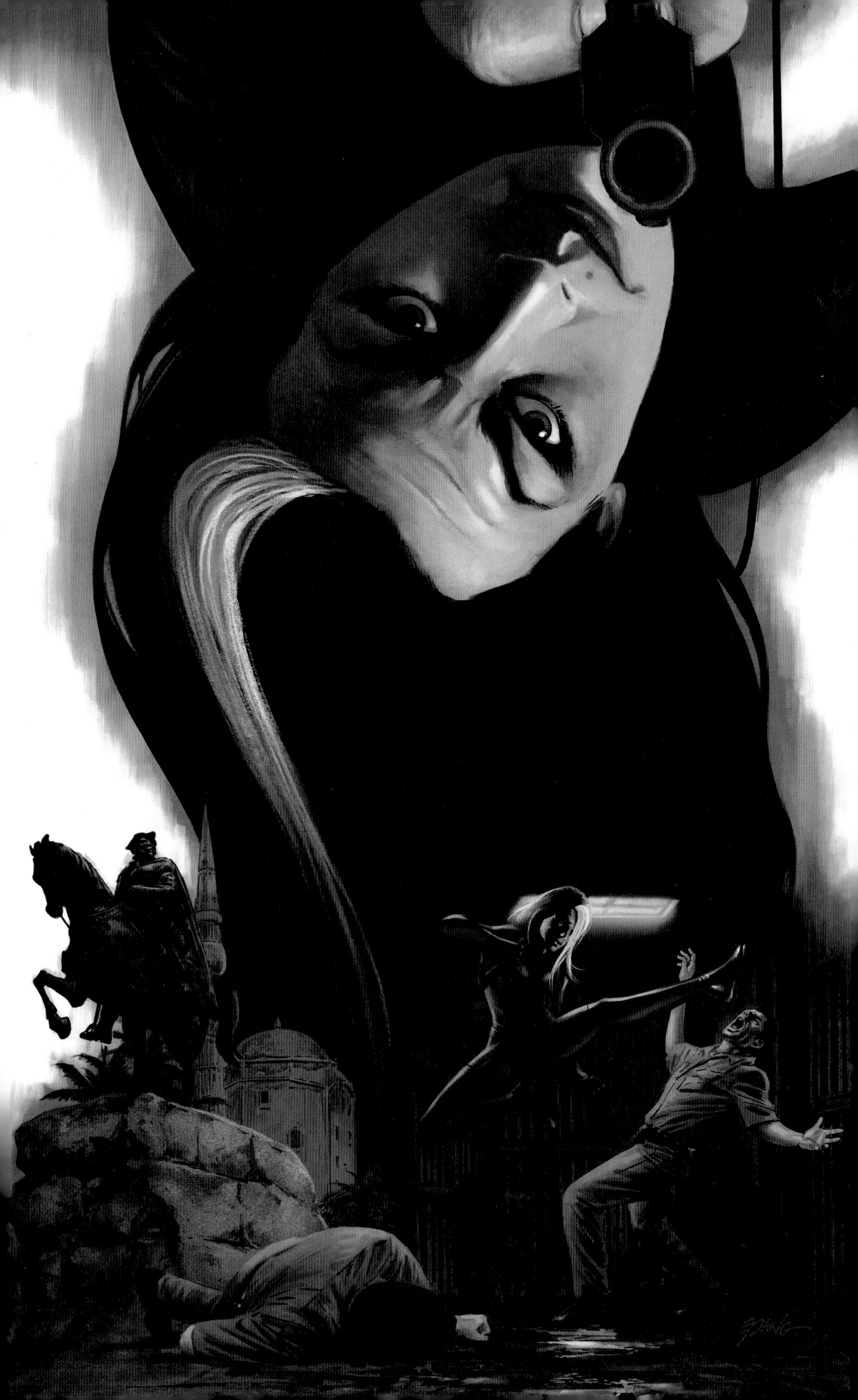

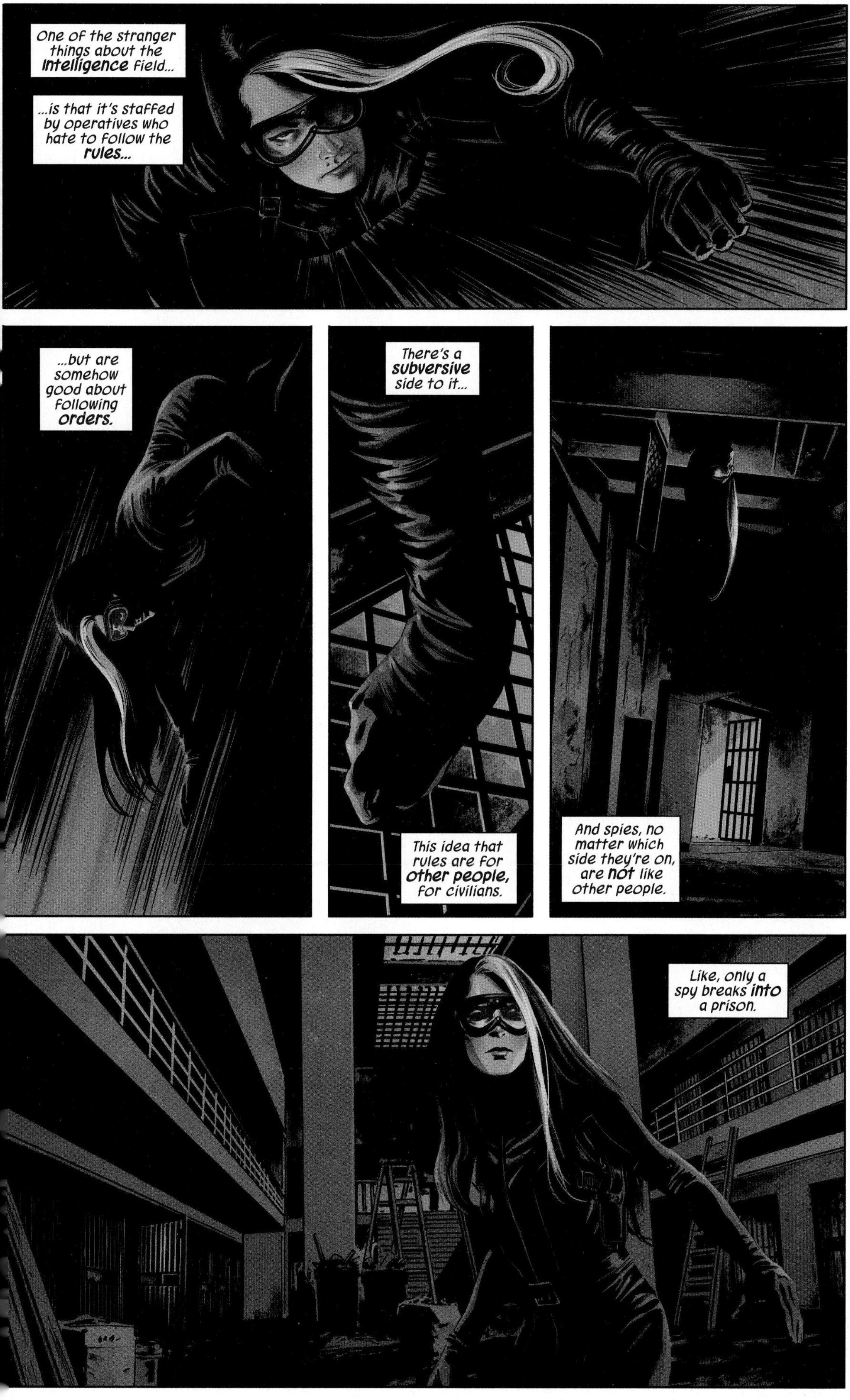
One of the stranger things about the intelligence field...
...is that it's staffed by operatives who hate to follow the rules...
...but are somehow good about following orders.
There's a subversive side to it...
This idea that rules are for other people, for civilians.
And spies, no matter which side they're on, are not like other people.
Like, only a spy breaks into a prison.

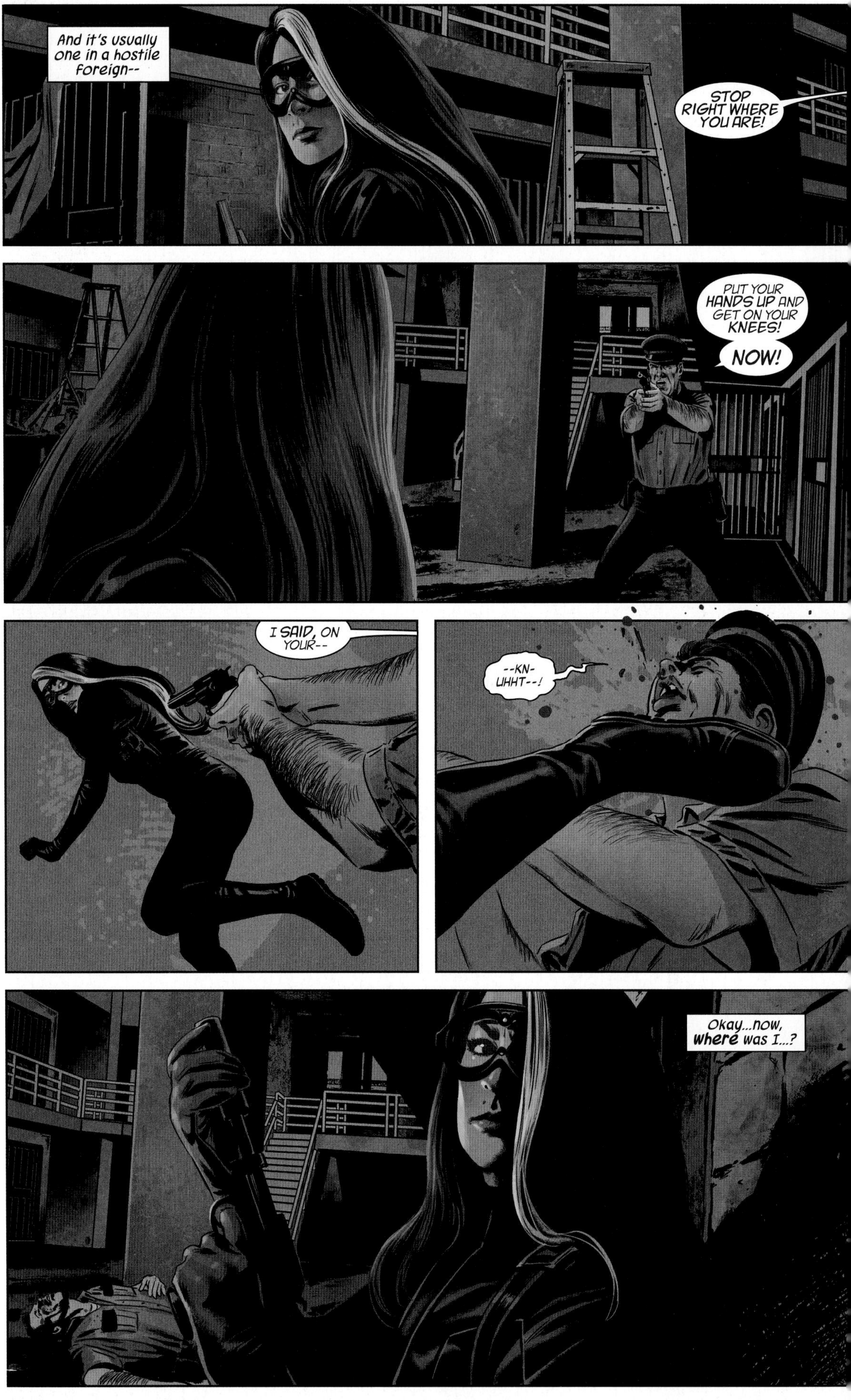
And it's usually one in a hostile foreign--
STOP RIGHT WHERE YOU ARE!
PUT YOUR HANDS UP AND GET ON YOUR KNEES!
NOW!
I SAID, ON YOUR--
--KN- UHHT--!
Okay...now, where was I...?

PART THREE

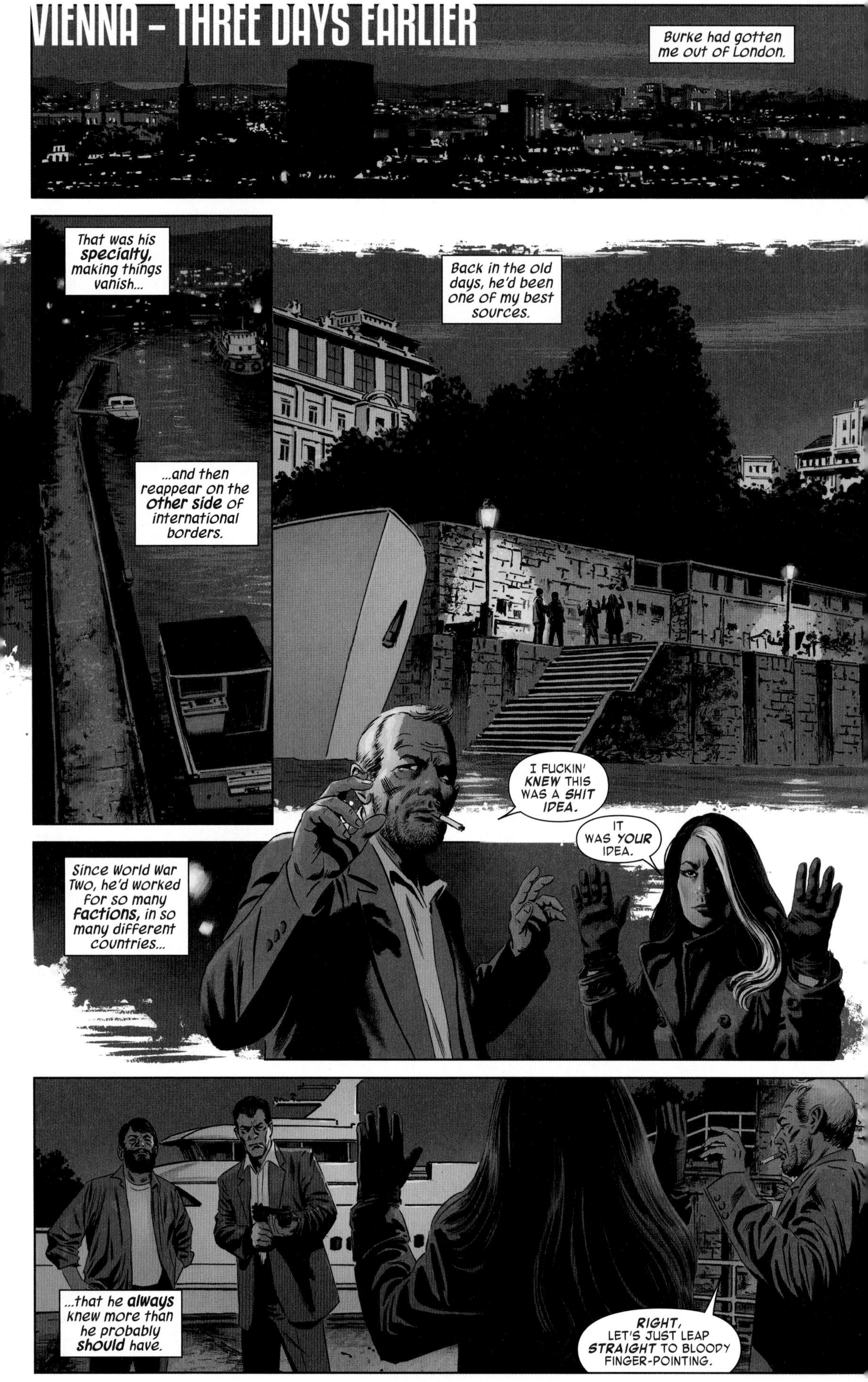
VIENNA - THREE DAYS EARLIER
Burke had gotten me out of London.
That was his specialty, making things vanish...
Back in the old days, he'd been one of my best sources.
...and then reappear on the other side of international borders.
I FUCKIN' KNEW THIS WAS A SHIT IDEA.
IT WAS YOUR IDEA.
Since World War Two, he'd worked for so many factions, in so many different countries...
...that he always knew more than he probably should have.
RIGHT, LET'S JUST LEAP STRAIGHT TO BLOODY FINGER-POINTING.

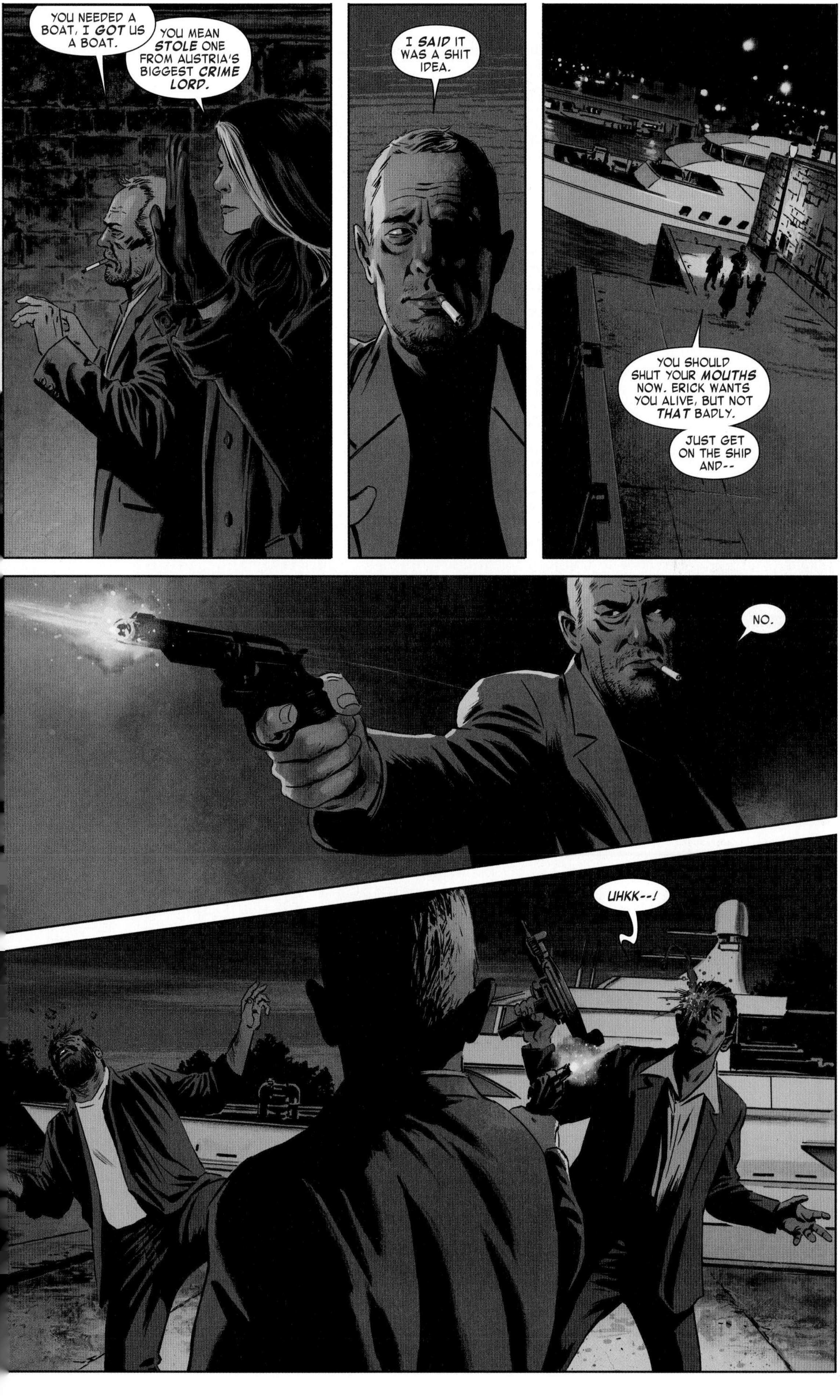
YOU NEEDED A BOAT, I GOT US A BOAT.
YOU MEAN STOLE ONE FROM AUSTRIA'S BIGGEST CRIME LORD.
I SAID IT WAS A SHIT IDEA.
YOU SHOULD SHUT YOUR MOUTHS NOW. ERICK WANTS YOU ALIVE, BUT NOT THAT BADLY.
JUST GET ON THE SHIP AND--
NO.
UHKK--!

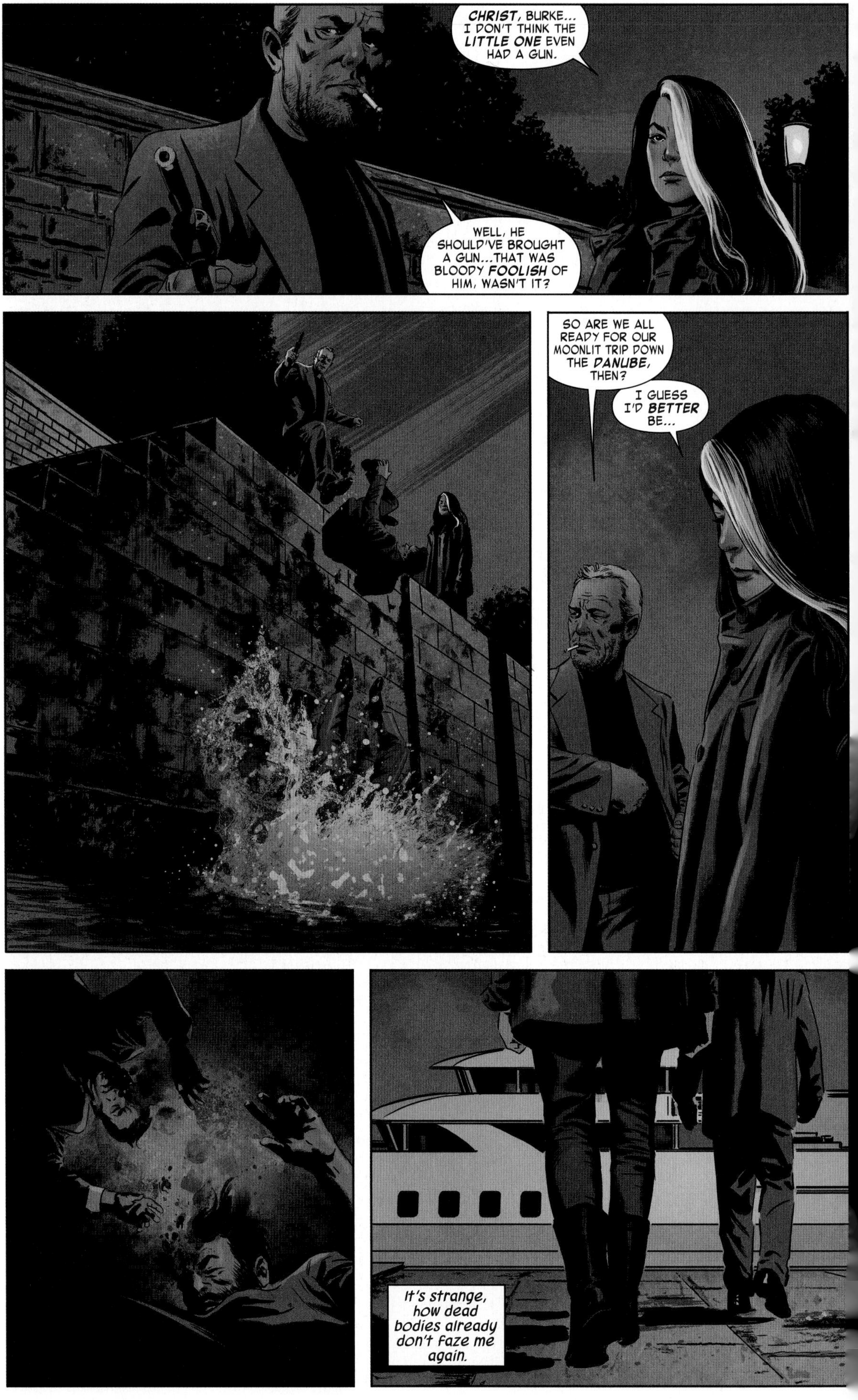
CHRIST, BURKE... I DON'T THINK THE LITTLE ONE EVEN HAD A GUN.
WELL, HE SHOULD'VE BROUGHT A GUN...THAT WAS BLOODY FOOLISH OF HIM, WASN'T IT?
SO ARE WE ALL READY FOR OUR MOONLIT TRIP DOWN THE DANUBE, THEN?
I GUESS I'D BETTER BE...
It's strange, how dead bodies already don't faze me again.

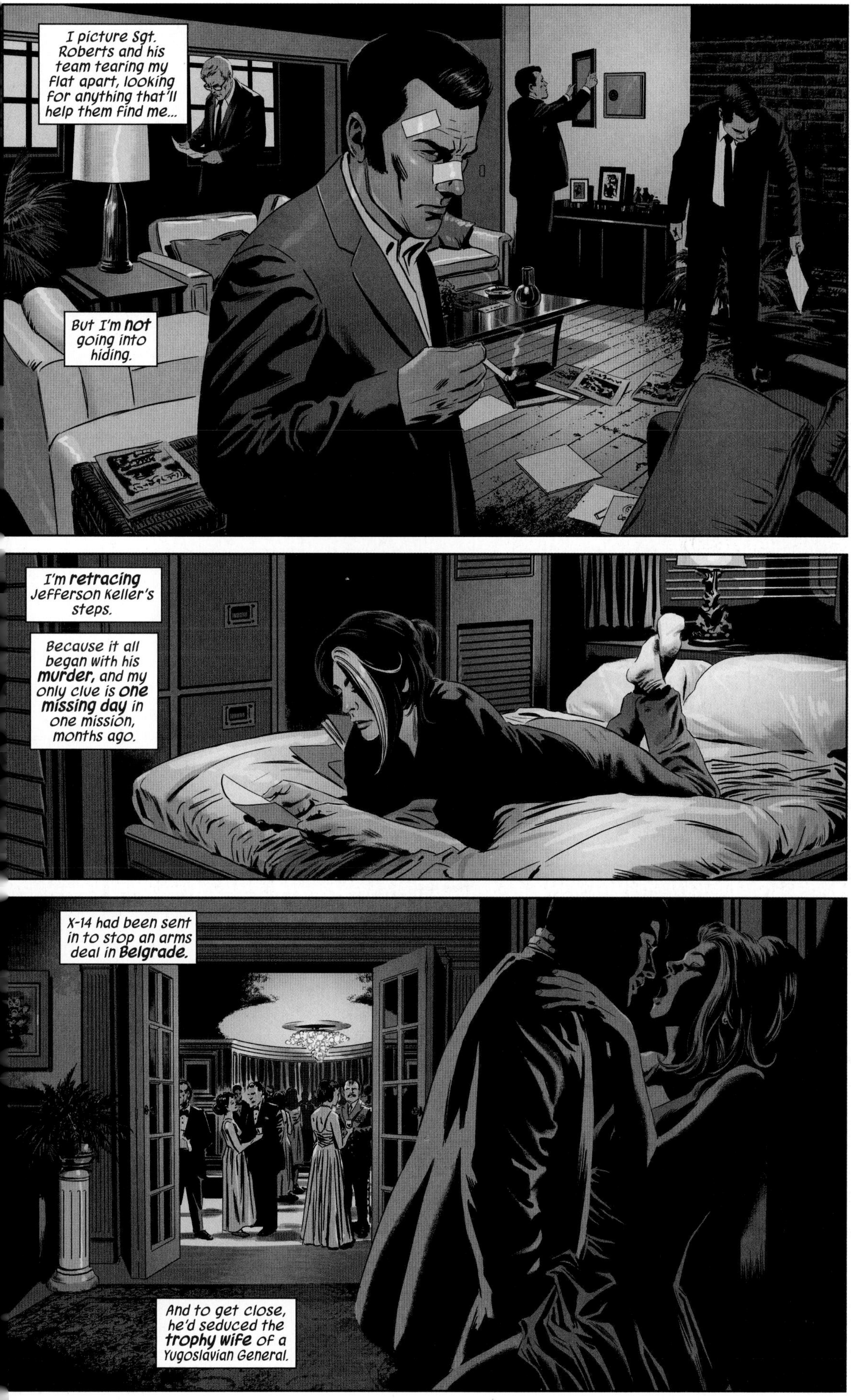

I picture Sgt. Roberts and his team tearing my flat apart, looking for anything that'll help them find me...
But I'm **not** going into hiding.
I'm **retracing** Jefferson Keller's steps.
Because it all began with his **murder,** and my only clue is **one missing day** in one mission, months ago.
X-14 had been sent in to stop an arms deal in **Belgrade.**
And to get close, he'd seduced the **trophy wife** of a Yugoslavian General.

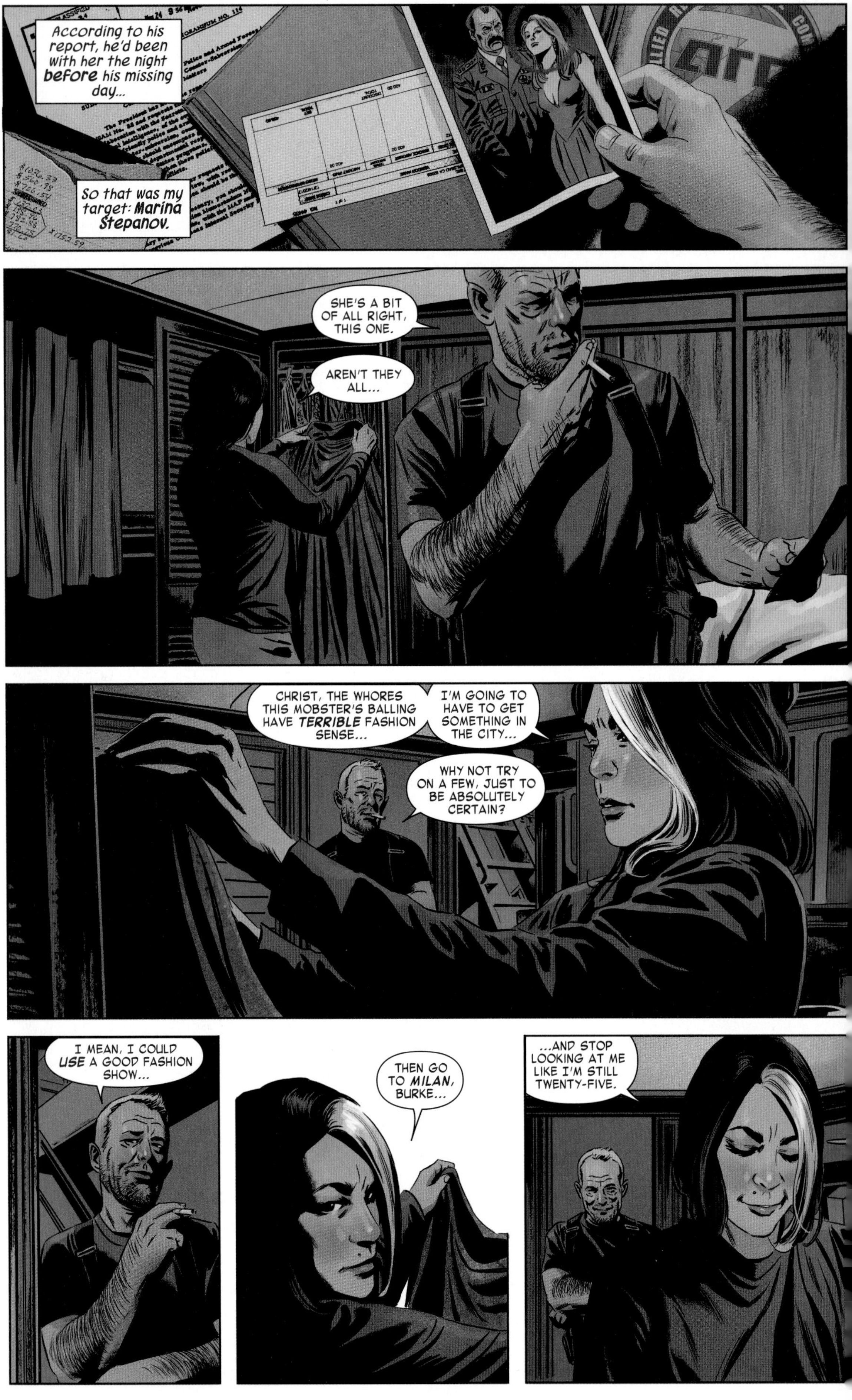
According to his report, he'd been with her the night before his missing day...
So that was my target: Marina Stepanov.
SHE'S A BIT OF ALL RIGHT, THIS ONE.
AREN'T THEY ALL...
CHRIST, THE WHORES THIS MOBSTER'S BALLING HAVE TERRIBLE FASHION SENSE...
I'M GOING TO HAVE TO GET SOMETHING IN THE CITY...
WHY NOT TRY ON A FEW, JUST TO BE ABSOLUTELY CERTAIN?
I MEAN, I COULD USE A GOOD FASHION SHOW...
THEN GO TO MILAN, BURKE...
...AND STOP LOOKING AT ME LIKE I'M STILL TWENTY-FIVE.

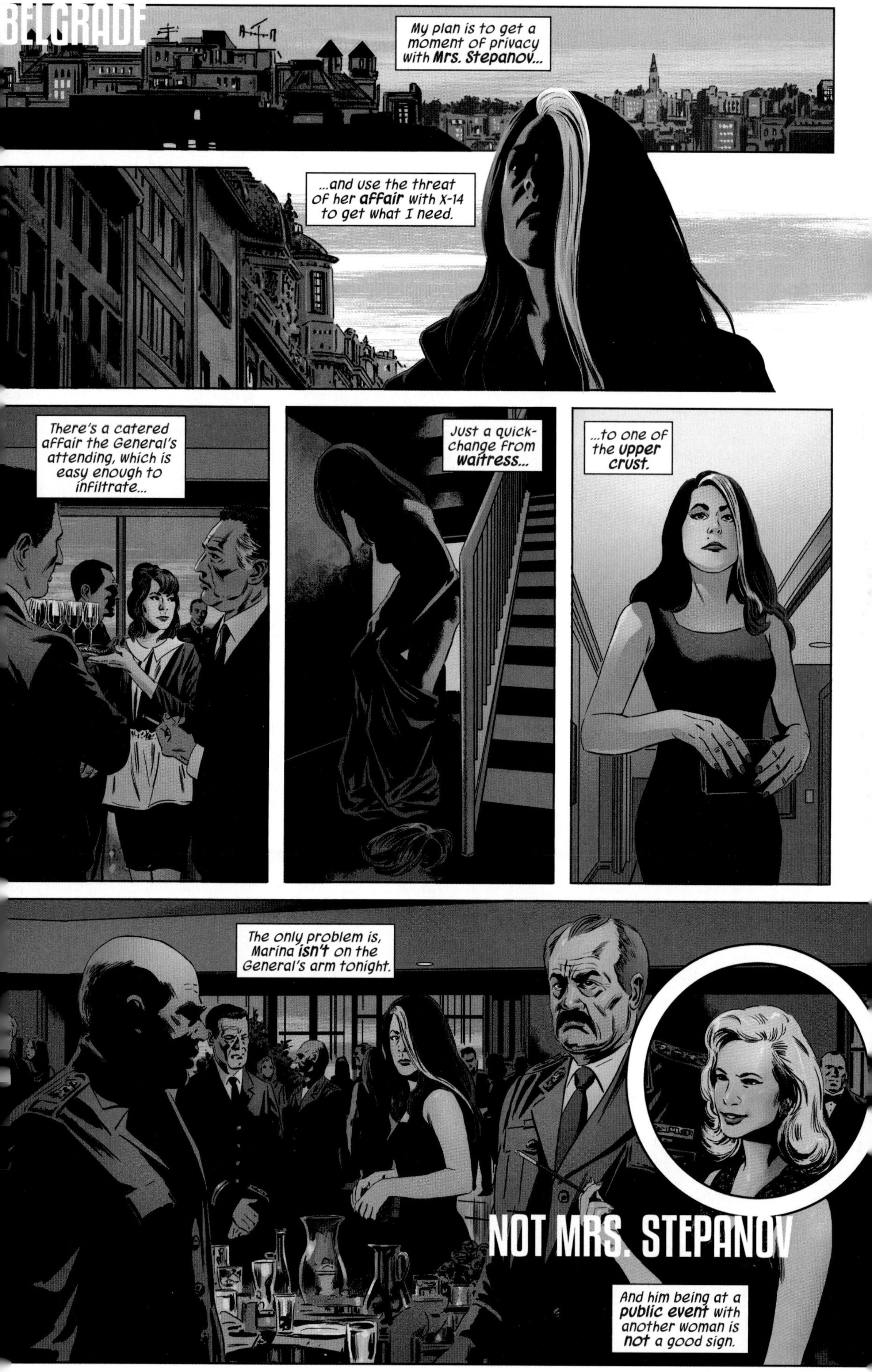
BELGRADE
My plan is to get a moment of privacy with Mrs. Stepanov...
...and use the threat of her affair with X-14 to get what I need.
There's a catered affair the General's attending, which is easy enough to infiltrate...
Just a quick-change from waitress...
...to one of the upper crust.
The only problem is, Marina isn't on the General's arm tonight.
NOT MRS. STEPANOV
And him being at a public event with another woman is not a good sign.

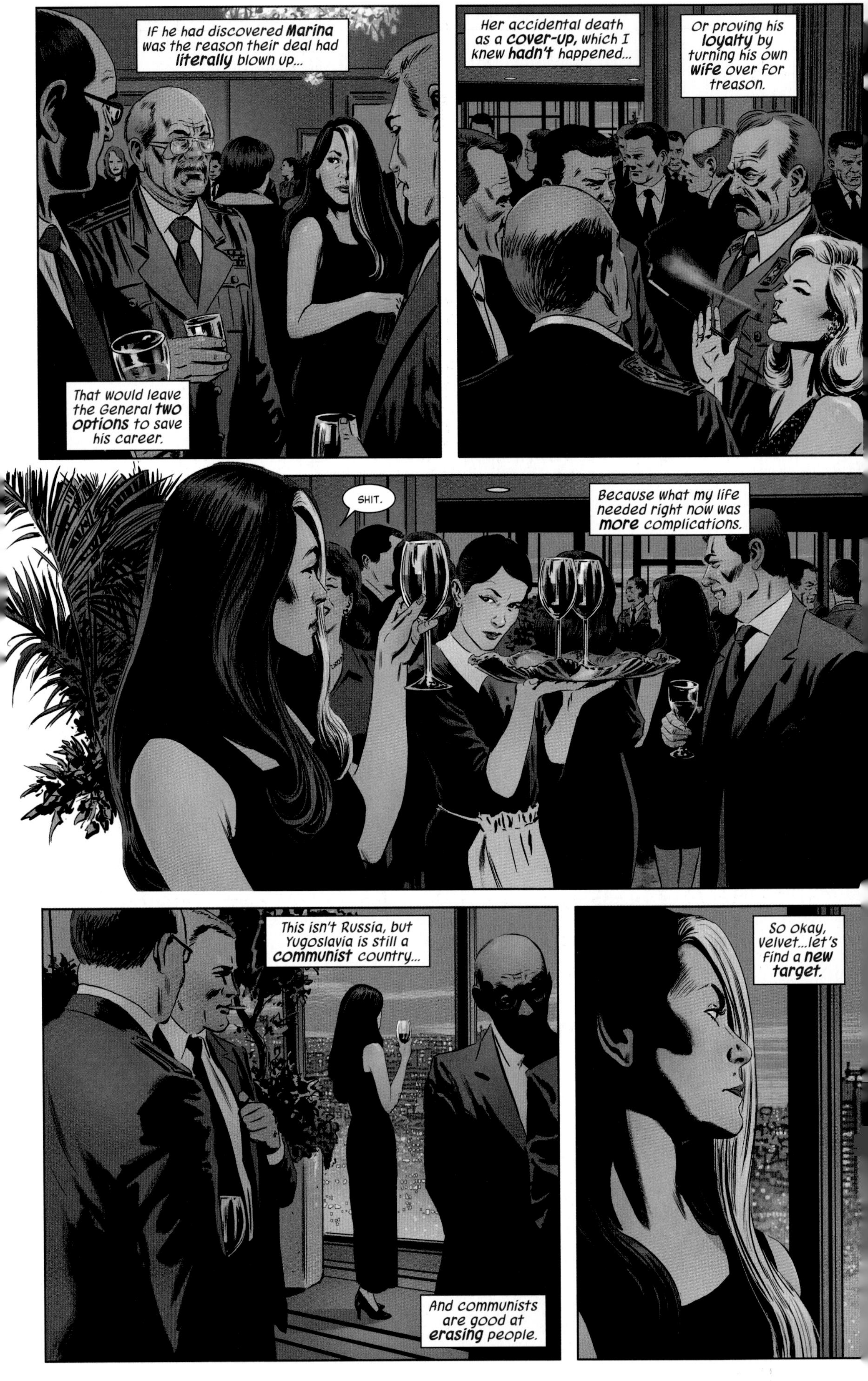

If he had discovered Marina was the reason their deal had literally blown up...
That would leave the General two options to save his career.
Her accidental death as a cover-up, which I knew hadn't happened...
Or proving his loyalty by turning his own wife over for treason.
SHIT.
Because what my life needed right now was more complications.
This isn't Russia, but Yugoslavia is still a communist country...
And communists are good at erasing people.
So okay, Velvet...let's find a new target.

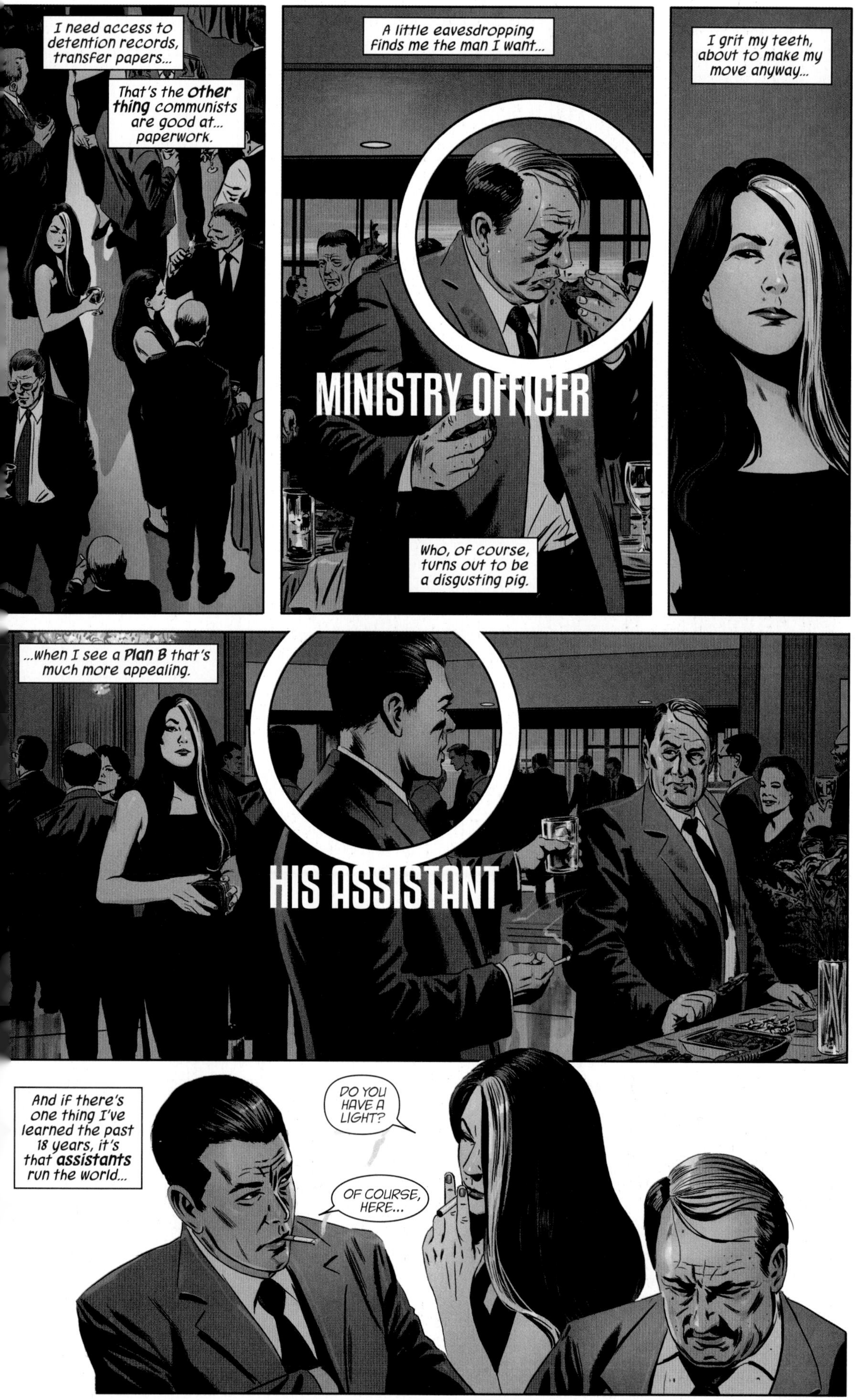
I need access to detention records, transfer papers...
That's the **other thing** communists are good at... paperwork.
A little eavesdropping finds me the man I want...
MINISTRY OFFICER
Who, of course, turns out to be a disgusting pig.
I grit my teeth, about to make my move anyway...
...when I see a **Plan B** that's much more appealing.
HIS ASSISTANT
And if there's one thing I've learned the past 18 years, it's that **assistants** run the world...
DO YOU HAVE A LIGHT?
OF COURSE, HERE...

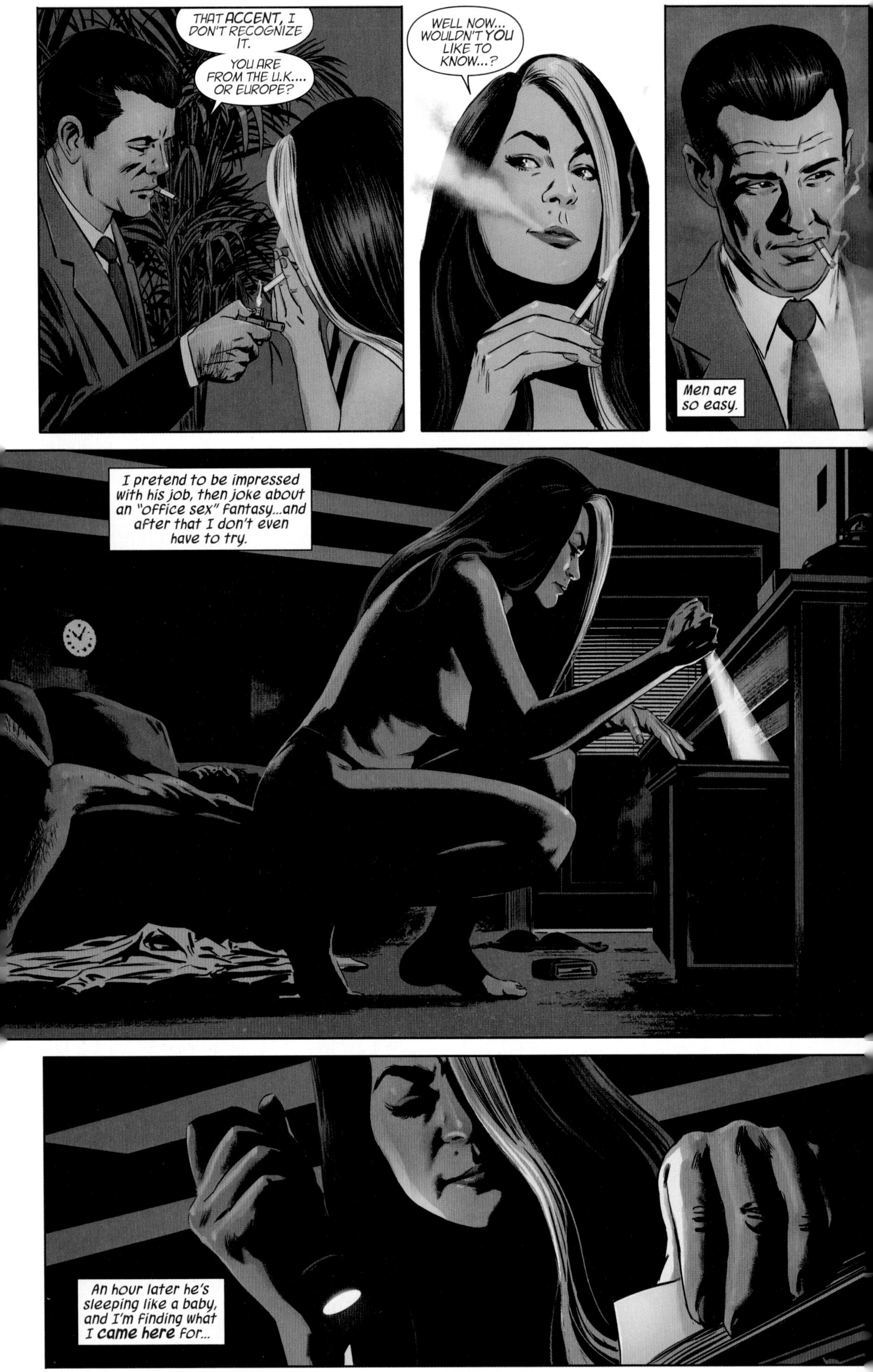
THAT ACCENT, I DON'T RECOGNIZE IT.
YOU ARE FROM THE U.K.... OR EUROPE?
WELL NOW... WOULDN'T YOU LIKE TO KNOW...?
Men are so easy.
I pretend to be impressed with his job, then joke about an "office sex" fantasy...and after that I don't even have to try.
An hour later he's sleeping like a baby, and I'm finding what I came here for...

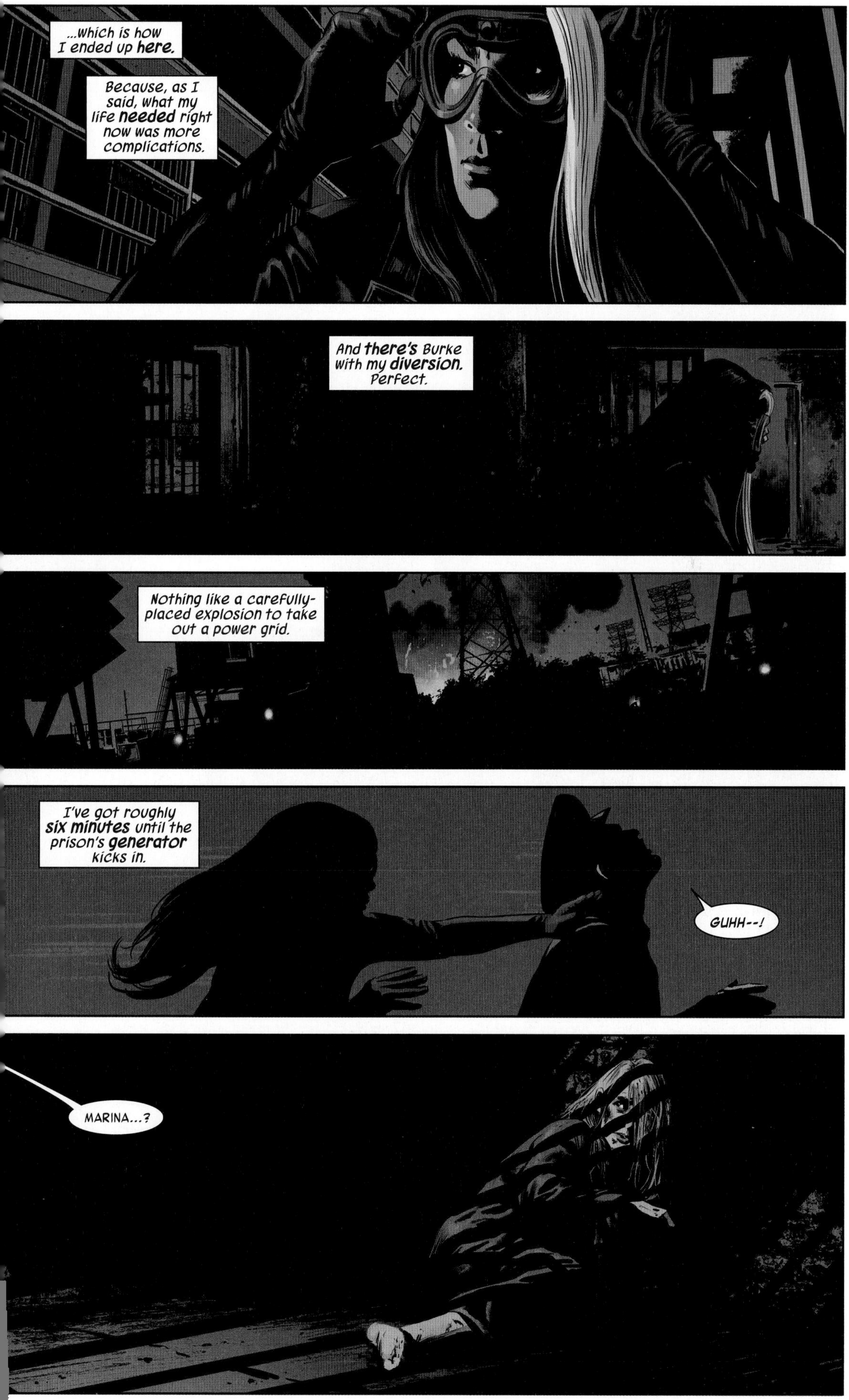
...Which is how I ended up here.
Because, as I said, what my life needed right now was more complications.
And there's Burke with my diversion. Perfect.
Nothing like a carefully-placed explosion to take out a power grid.
I've got roughly six minutes until the prison's generator kicks in.
GUHH--!
MARINA...?

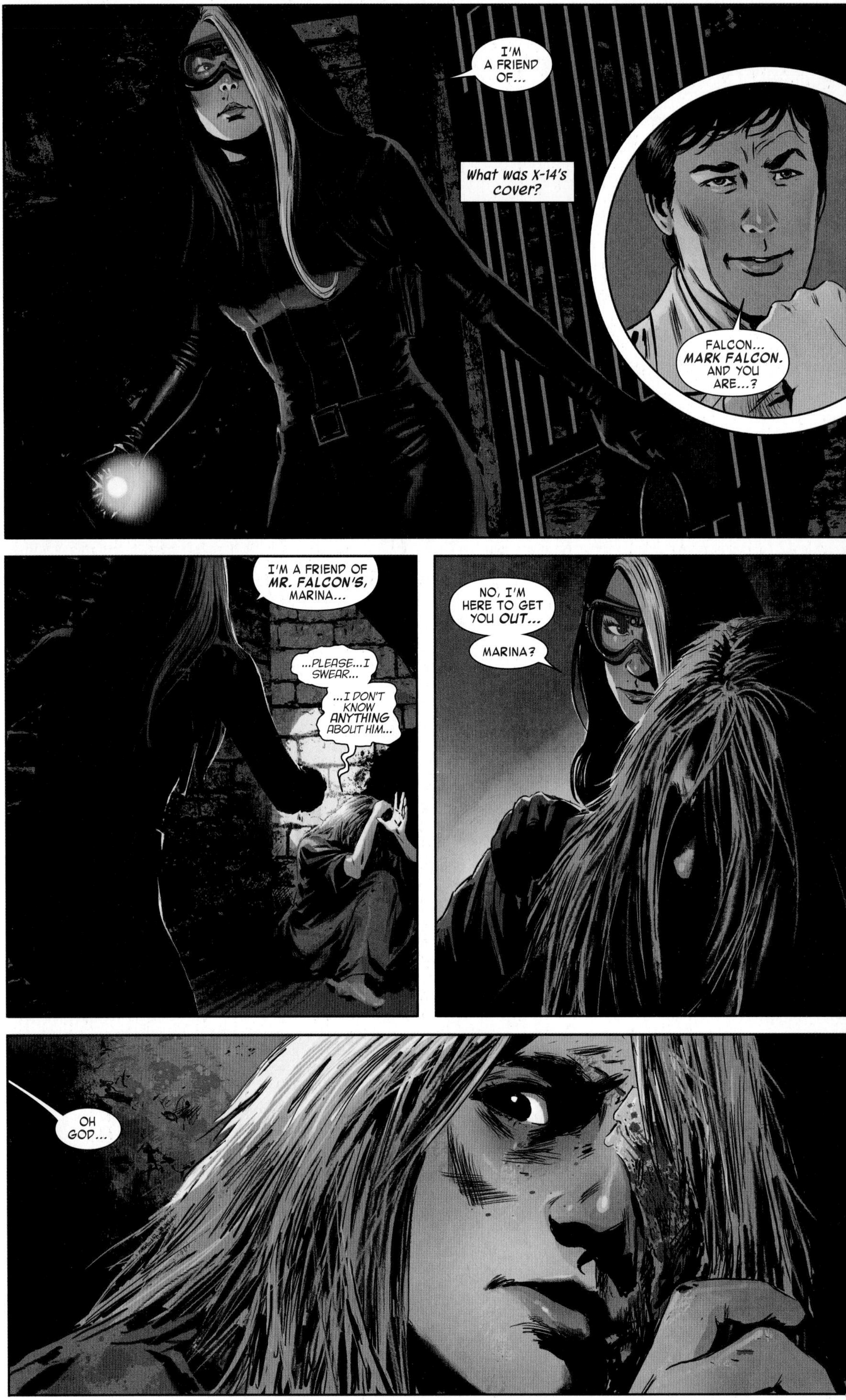

I'M A FRIEND OF...
What was X-14's cover?
FALCON... MARK FALCON. AND YOU ARE...?
I'M A FRIEND OF MR. FALCON'S, MARINA...
...PLEASE...I SWEAR...
...I DON'T KNOW ANYTHING ABOUT HIM...
NO, I'M HERE TO GET YOU OUT...
MARINA?
OH GOD...

Rage boils inside, but I push it back down.

I don't have time for rage.

MARINA, LISTEN TO ME... I NEED YOU TO WALK, *NOW*.

I only have three and a half minutes...

...OKAY...

She's stronger than she looks, thankfully.

I only have to carry her once.

By the time the power's back on, we're halfway down an old sewer line, almost to safety...

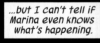

...but I can't tell if Marina even knows what's happening.

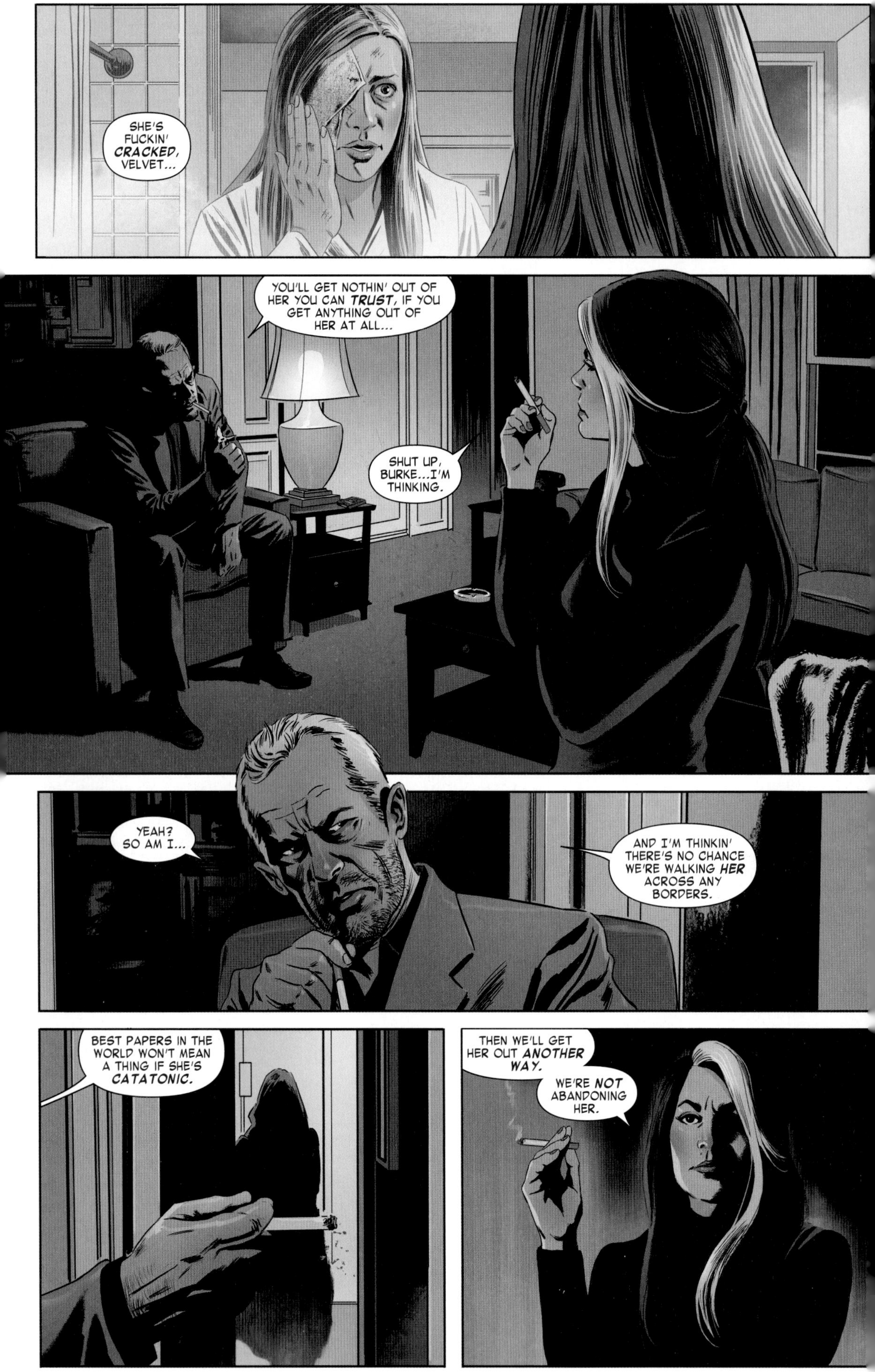
SHE'S FUCKIN' CRACKED, VELVET...
YOU'LL GET NOTHIN' OUT OF HER YOU CAN TRUST, IF YOU GET ANYTHING OUT OF HER AT ALL...
SHUT UP, BURKE...I'M THINKING.
YEAH? SO AM I...
AND I'M THINKIN' THERE'S NO CHANCE WE'RE WALKING HER ACROSS ANY BORDERS.
BEST PAPERS IN THE WORLD WON'T MEAN A THING IF SHE'S CATATONIC.
THEN WE'LL GET HER OUT ANOTHER WAY.
WE'RE NOT ABANDONING HER.

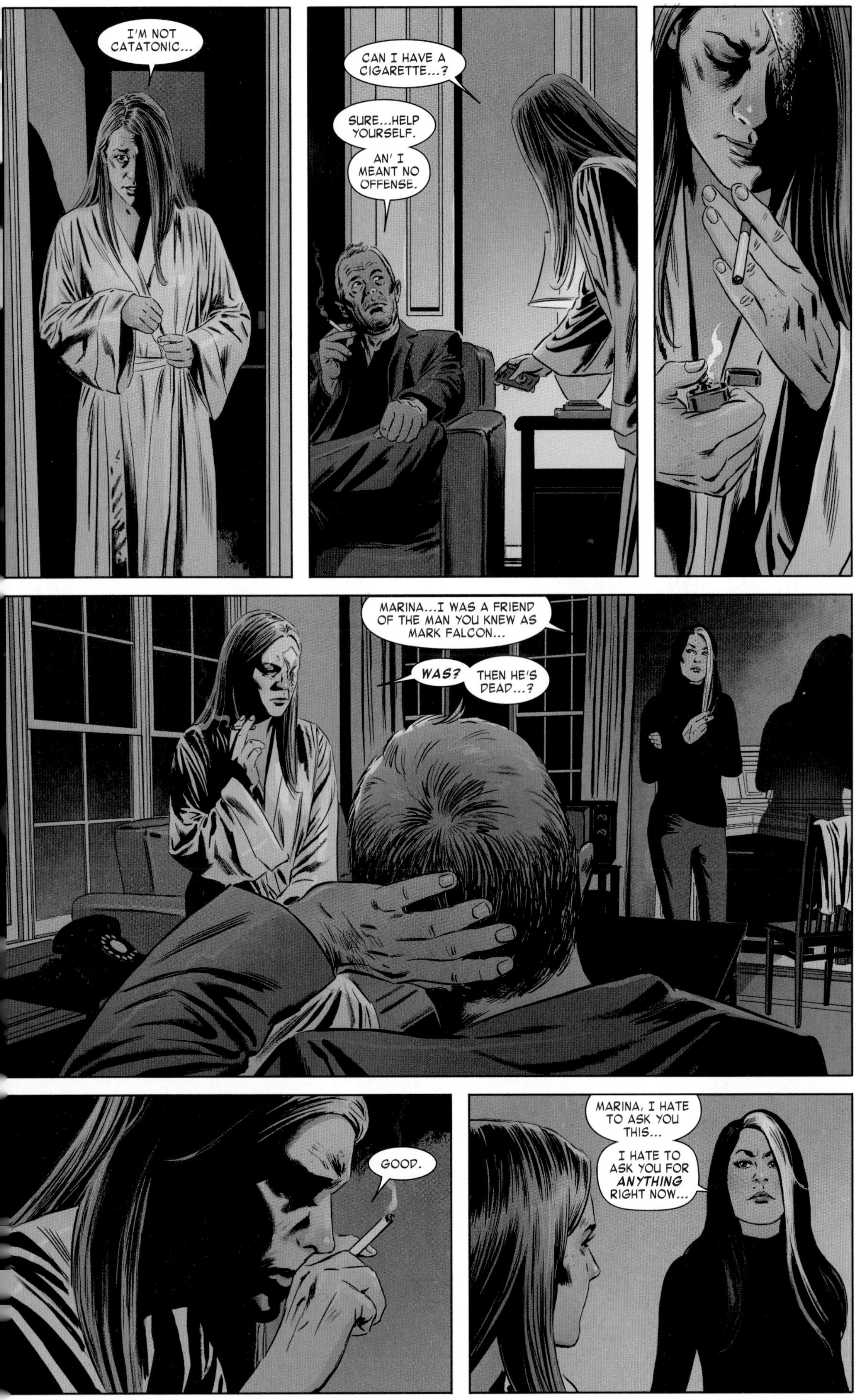
I'M NOT CATATONIC...
CAN I HAVE A CIGARETTE...?
SURE...HELP YOURSELF.
AN' I MEANT NO OFFENSE.
MARINA...I WAS A FRIEND OF THE MAN YOU KNEW AS MARK FALCON...
WAS? THEN HE'S DEAD...?
GOOD.
MARINA, I HATE TO ASK YOU THIS...
I HATE TO ASK YOU FOR ANYTHING RIGHT NOW...

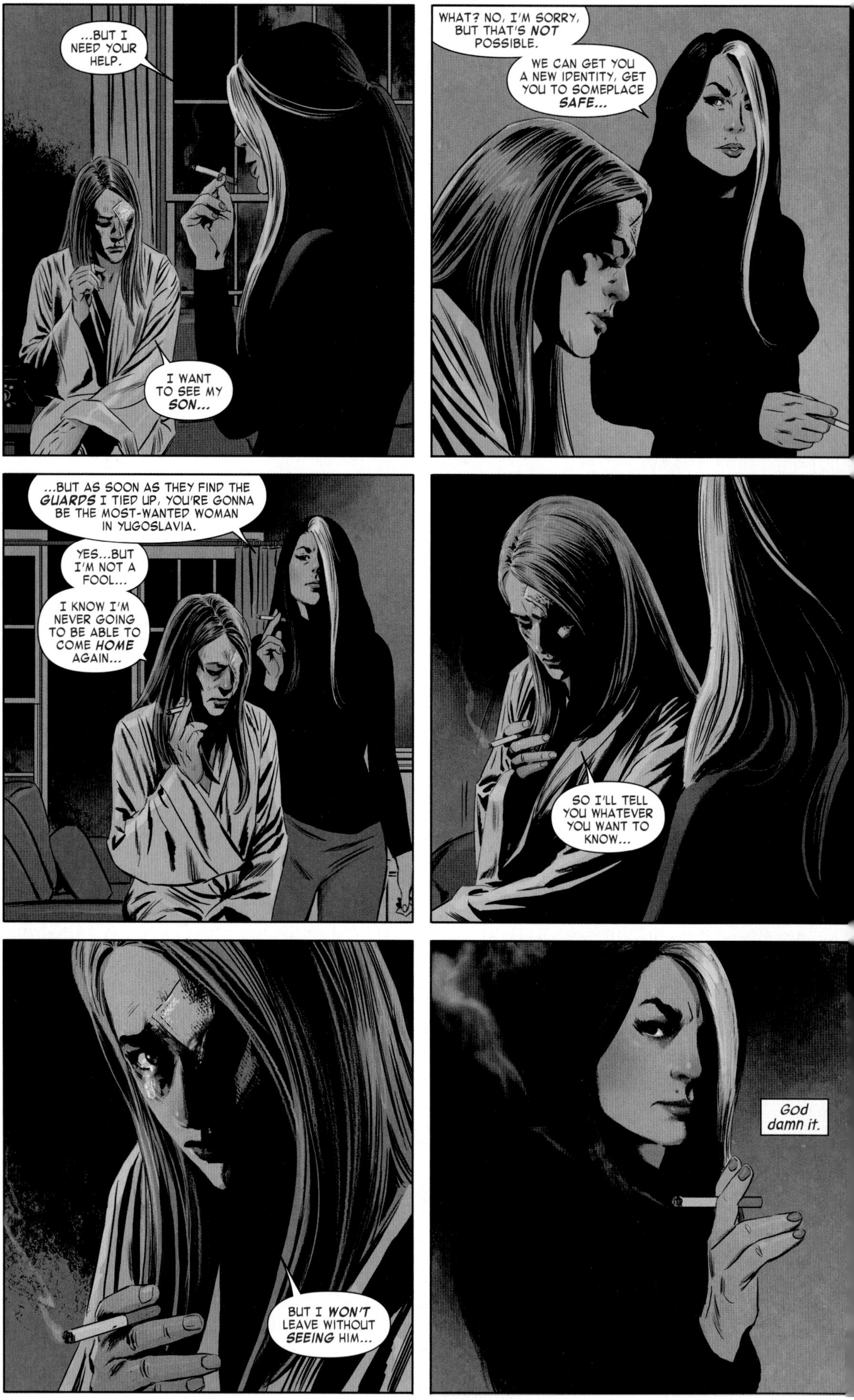
...BUT I NEED YOUR HELP.
I WANT TO SEE MY SON...
WHAT? NO, I'M SORRY, BUT THAT'S NOT POSSIBLE.
WE CAN GET YOU A NEW IDENTITY, GET YOU TO SOMEPLACE SAFE...
...BUT AS SOON AS THEY FIND THE GUARDS I TIED UP, YOU'RE GONNA BE THE MOST-WANTED WOMAN IN YUGOSLAVIA.
YES...BUT I'M NOT A FOOL...
I KNOW I'M NEVER GOING TO BE ABLE TO COME HOME AGAIN...
SO I'LL TELL YOU WHATEVER YOU WANT TO KNOW...
BUT I WON'T LEAVE WITHOUT SEEING HIM...
God damn it.

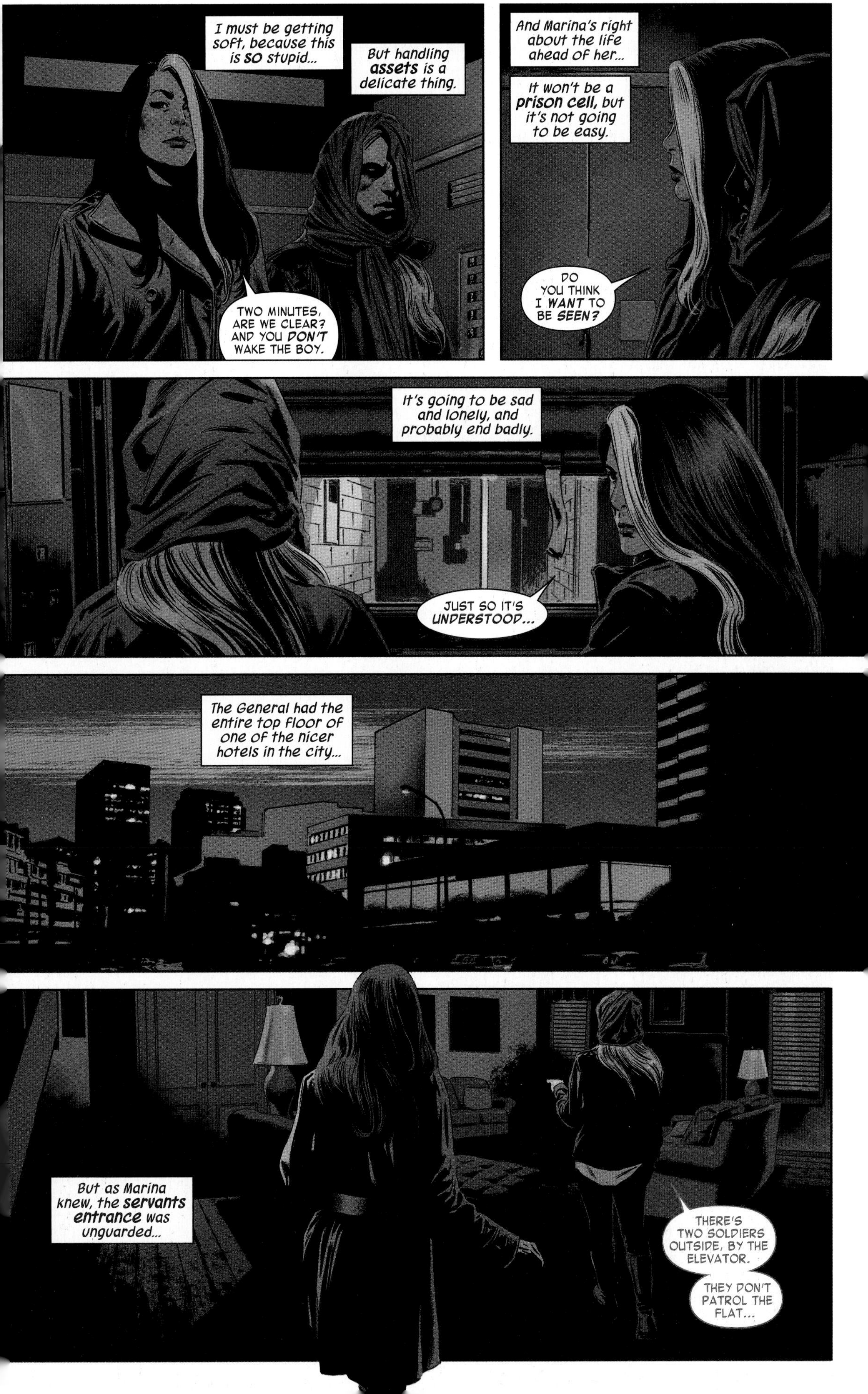

I must be getting soft, because this is SO stupid...
But handling assets is a delicate thing.
TWO MINUTES, ARE WE CLEAR? AND YOU DON'T WAKE THE BOY.
And Marina's right about the life ahead of her...
It won't be a prison cell, but it's not going to be easy.
DO YOU THINK I WANT TO BE SEEN?
It's going to be sad and lonely, and probably end badly.
JUST SO IT'S UNDERSTOOD...
The General had the entire top floor of one of the nicer hotels in the city...
But as Marina knew, the servants entrance was unguarded...
THERE'S TWO SOLDIERS OUTSIDE, BY THE ELEVATOR.
THEY DON'T PATROL THE FLAT...

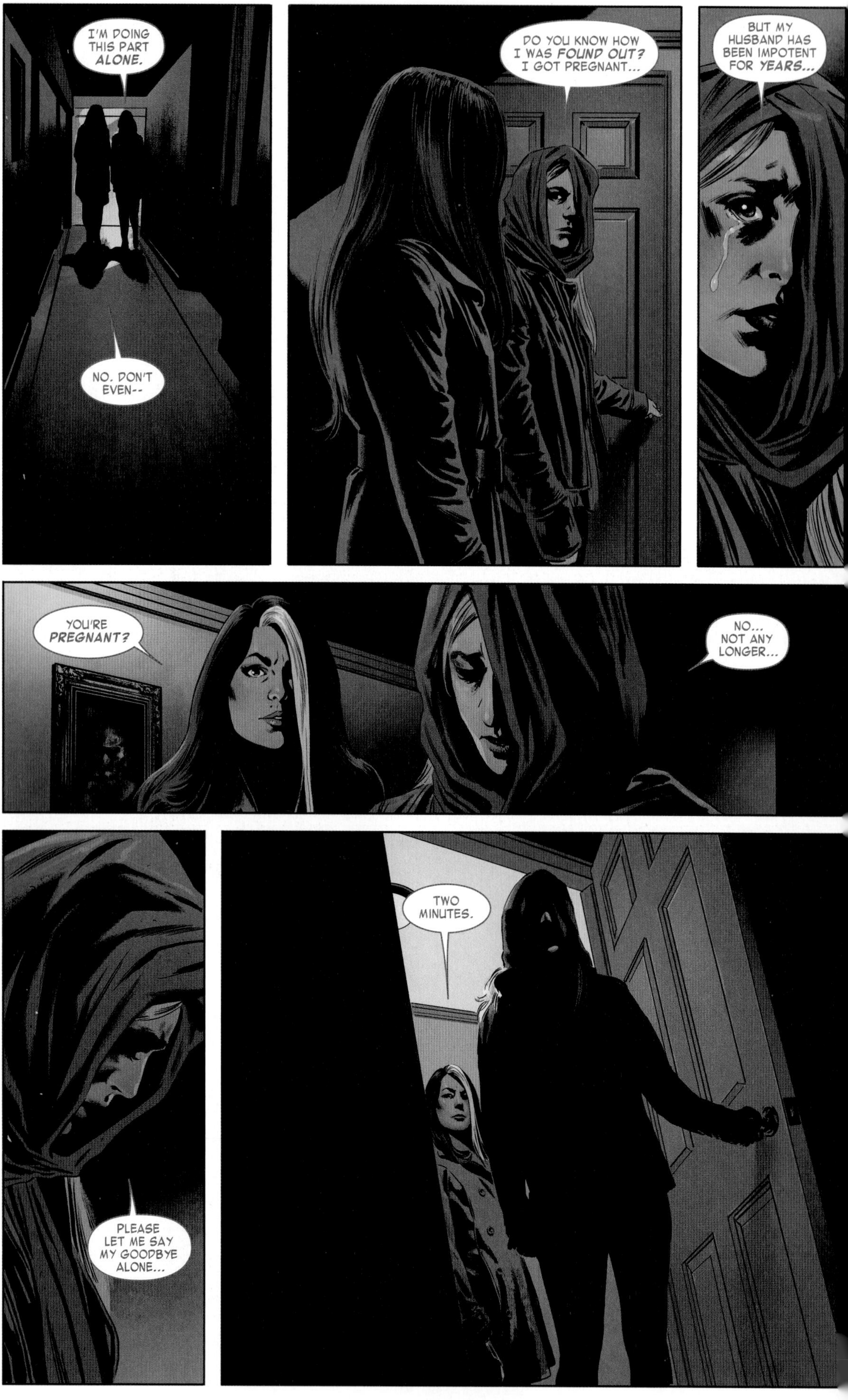
I'M DOING THIS PART *ALONE.*
NO. DON'T EVEN--
DO YOU KNOW HOW I WAS *FOUND OUT?* I GOT PREGNANT...
BUT MY HUSBAND HAS BEEN IMPOTENT FOR *YEARS...*
YOU'RE *PREGNANT?*
NO... NOT ANY LONGER...
PLEASE LET ME SAY MY GOODBYE ALONE...
TWO MINUTES.

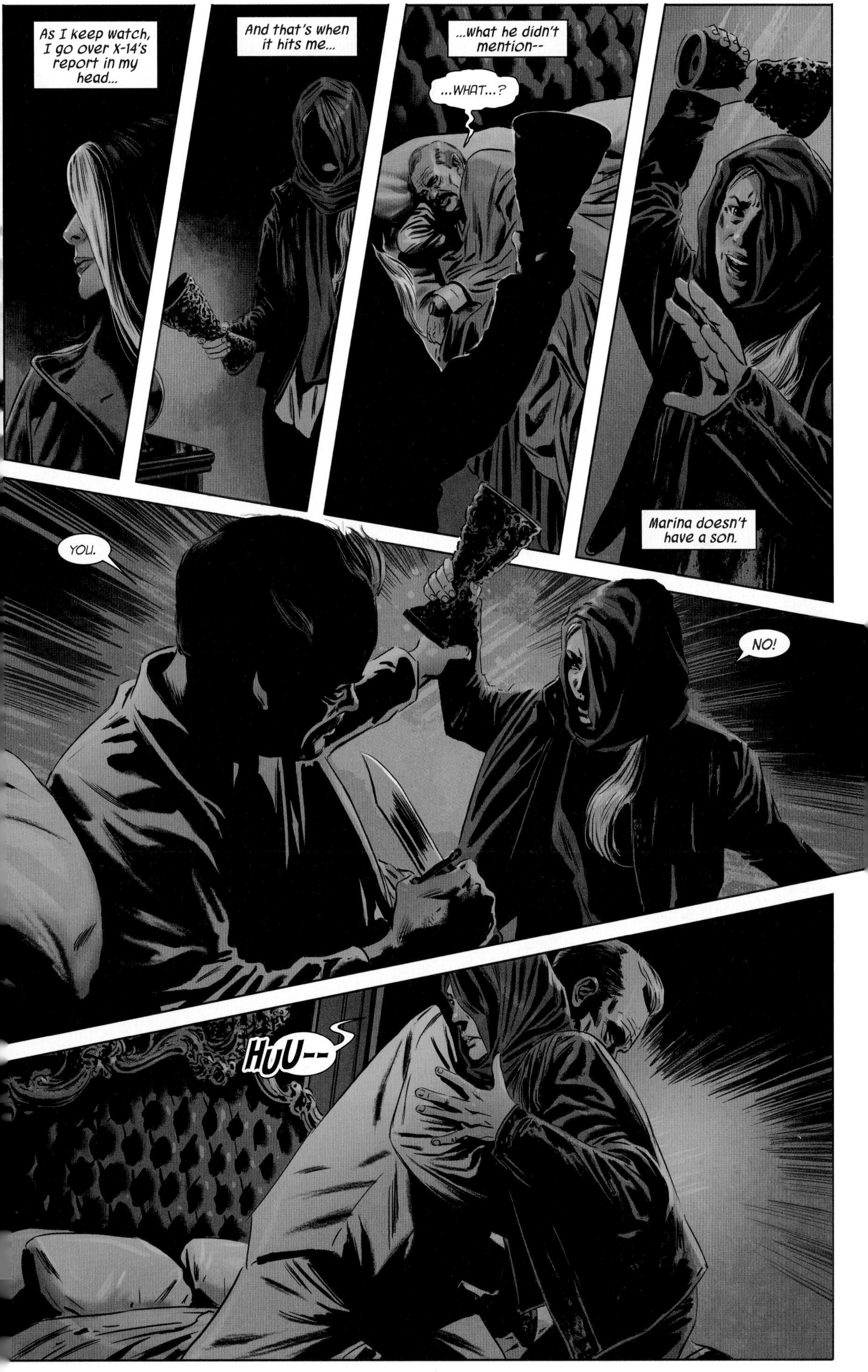
As I keep watch, I go over X-14's report in my head...
And that's when it hits me...
...what he didn't mention--
...WHAT...?
Marina doesn't have a son.
YOU.
NO!
HUU--

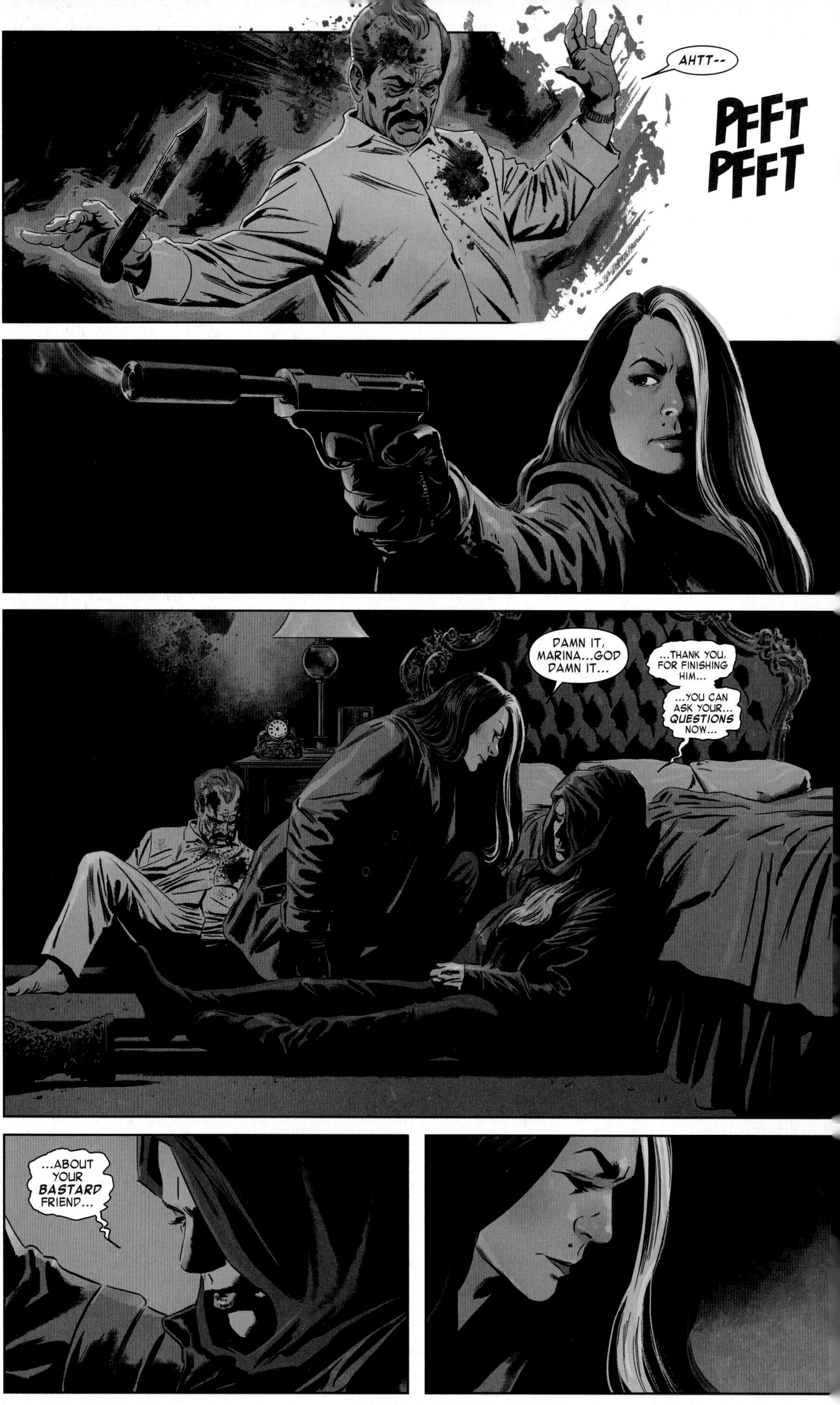
AHTT--
PFFT PFFT
DAMN IT, MARINA...GOD DAMN IT...
...THANK YOU, FOR FINISHING HIM...
...YOU CAN ASK YOUR... QUESTIONS NOW...
...ABOUT YOUR BASTARD FRIEND...

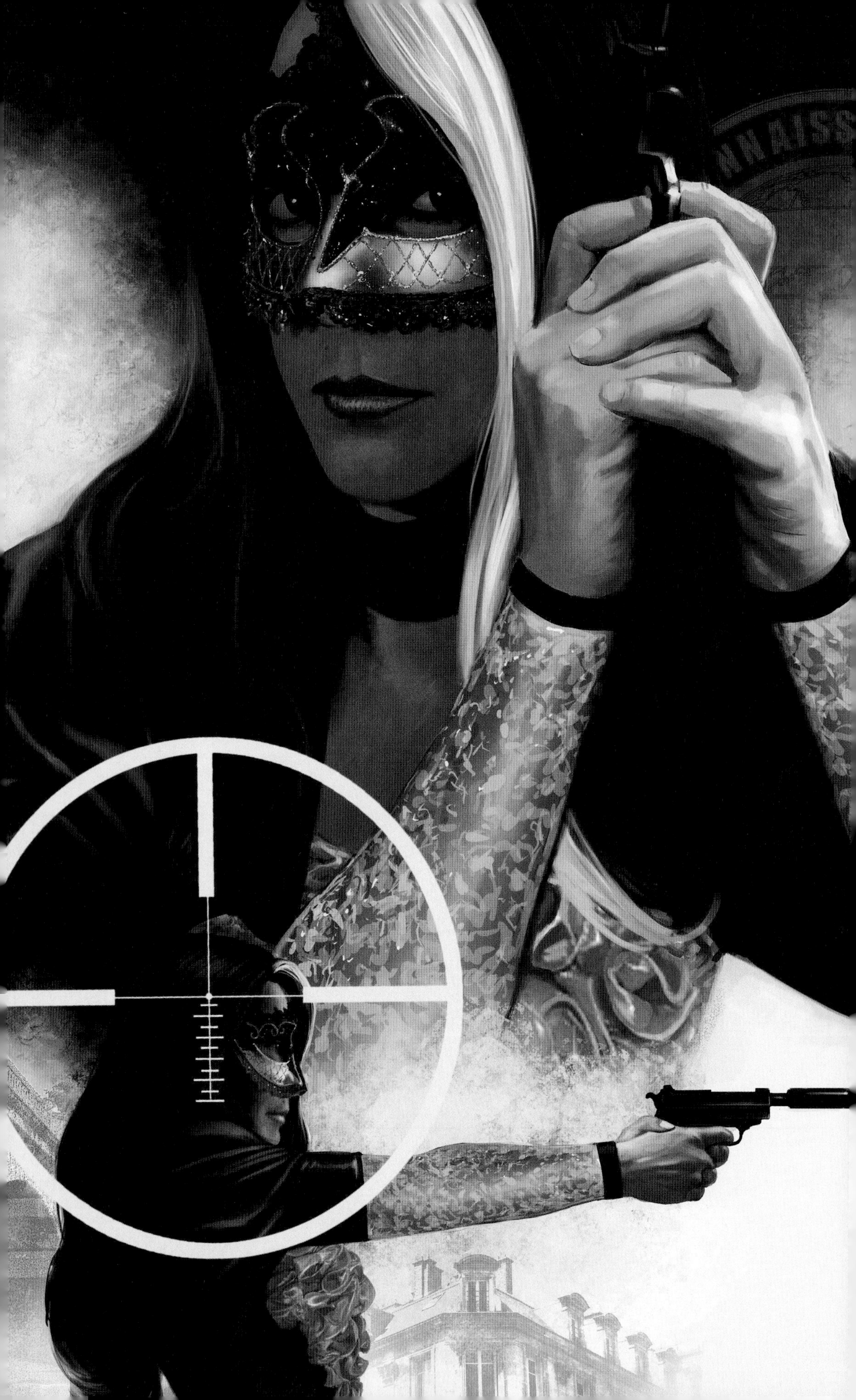

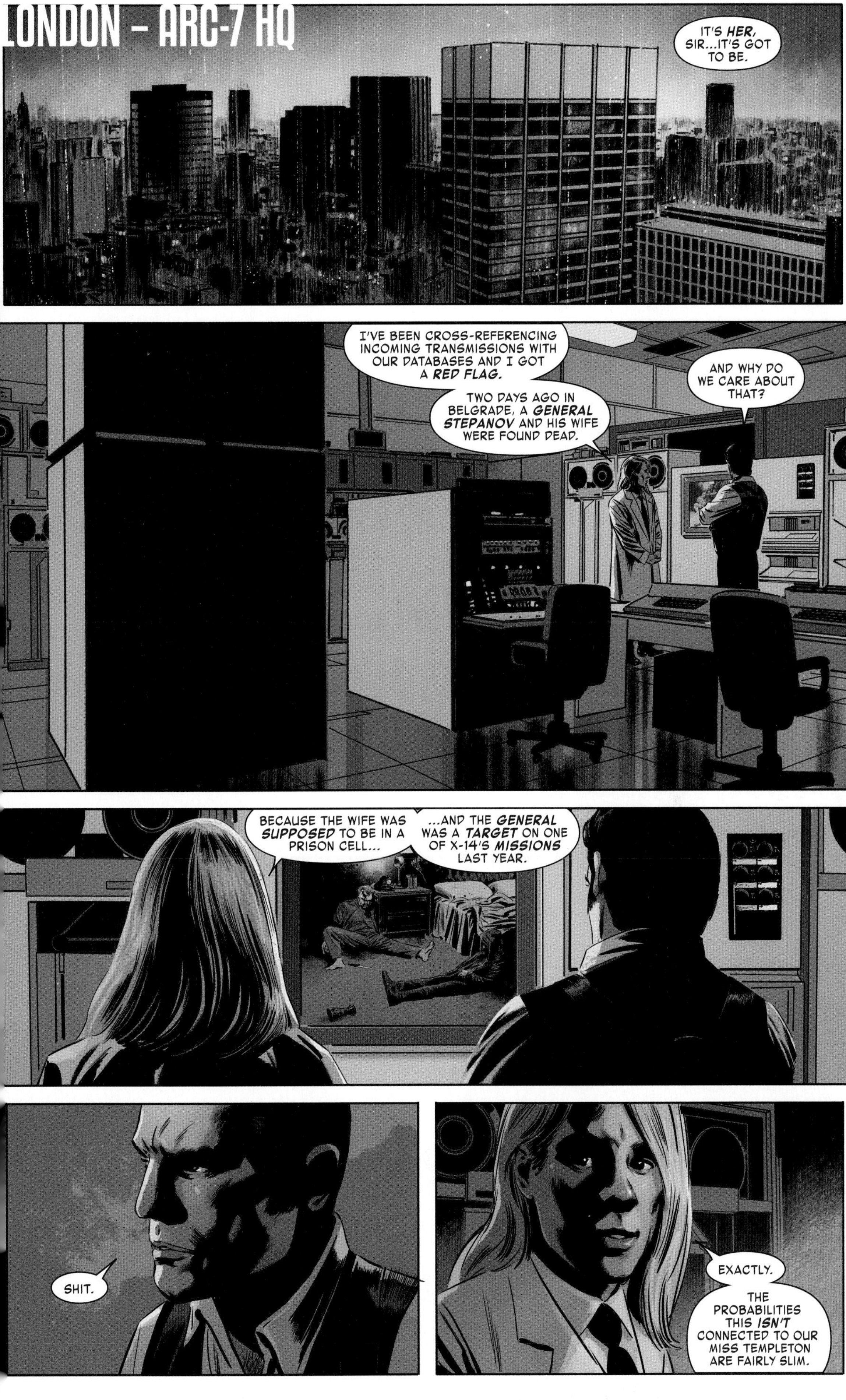
LONDON – ARC-7 HQ
IT'S HER, SIR...IT'S GOT TO BE.
I'VE BEEN CROSS-REFERENCING INCOMING TRANSMISSIONS WITH OUR DATABASES AND I GOT A RED FLAG.
TWO DAYS AGO IN BELGRADE, A GENERAL STEPANOV AND HIS WIFE WERE FOUND DEAD.
AND WHY DO WE CARE ABOUT THAT?
BECAUSE THE WIFE WAS SUPPOSED TO BE IN A PRISON CELL...
...AND THE GENERAL WAS A TARGET ON ONE OF X-14'S MISSIONS LAST YEAR.
SHIT.
EXACTLY.
THE PROBABILITIES THIS ISN'T CONNECTED TO OUR MISS TEMPLETON ARE FAIRLY SLIM.

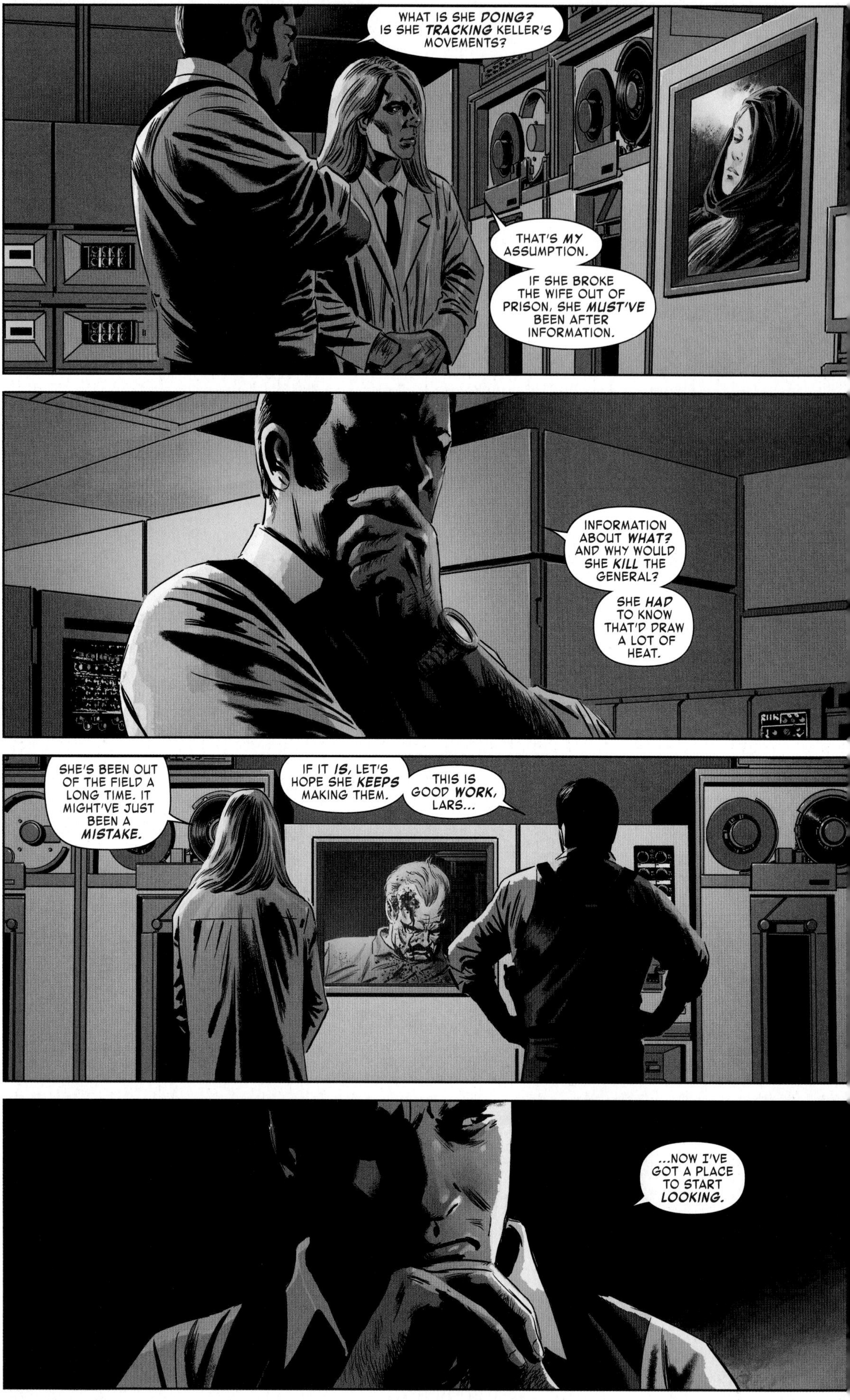
WHAT IS SHE DOING? IS SHE TRACKING KELLER'S MOVEMENTS?
THAT'S MY ASSUMPTION.
IF SHE BROKE THE WIFE OUT OF PRISON, SHE MUST'VE BEEN AFTER INFORMATION.
INFORMATION ABOUT WHAT? AND WHY WOULD SHE KILL THE GENERAL?
SHE HAD TO KNOW THAT'D DRAW A LOT OF HEAT.
SHE'S BEEN OUT OF THE FIELD A LONG TIME. IT MIGHT'VE JUST BEEN A MISTAKE.
IF IT IS, LET'S HOPE SHE KEEPS MAKING THEM.
THIS IS GOOD WORK, LARS...
...NOW I'VE GOT A PLACE TO START LOOKING.

PART FOUR

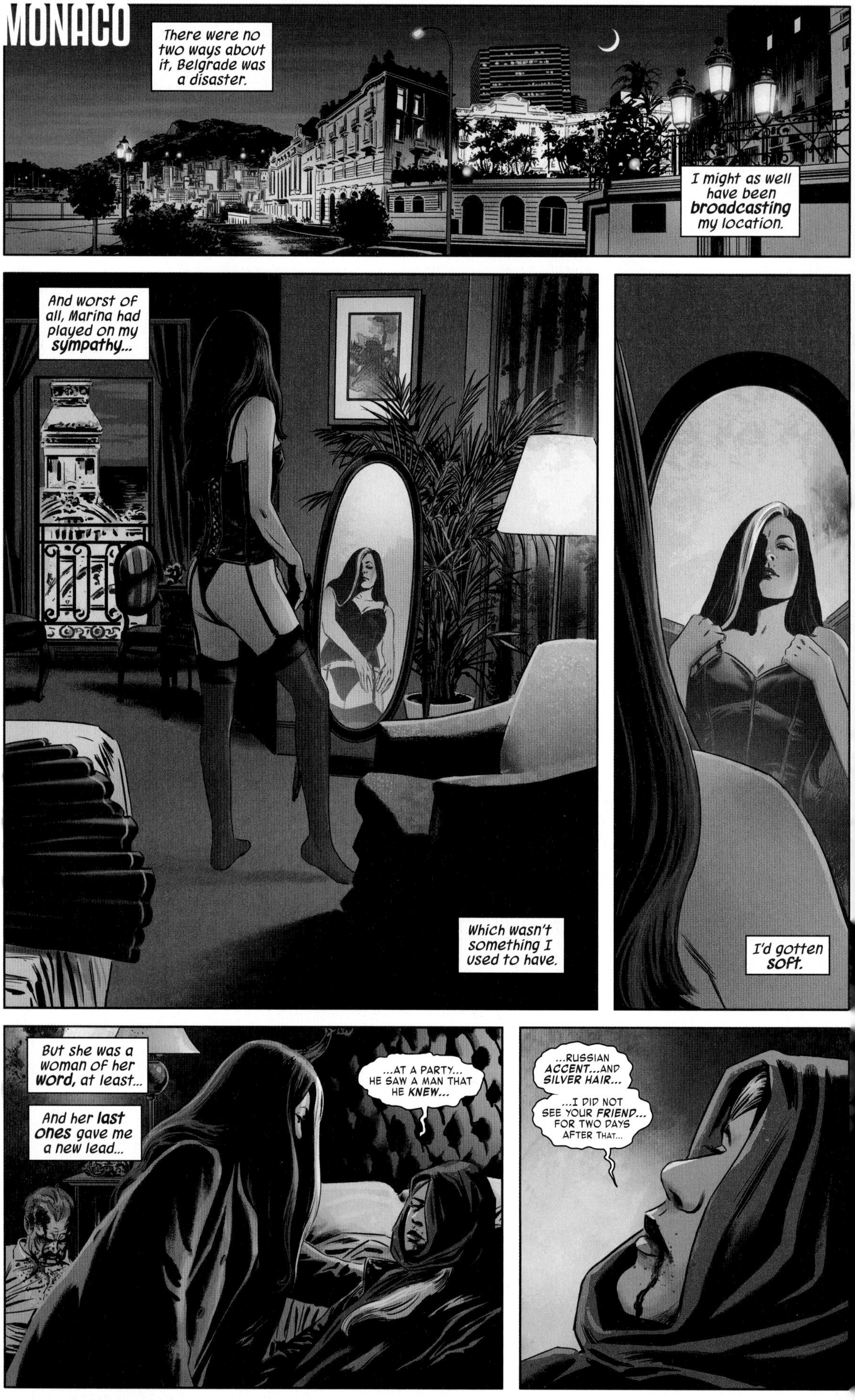
MONACO
There were no two ways about it, Belgrade was a disaster.
I might as well have been broadcasting my location.
And worst of all, Marina had played on my sympathy...
Which wasn't something I used to have.
I'd gotten soft.
But she was a woman of her word, at least...
And her last ones gave me a new lead...
...AT A PARTY... HE SAW A MAN THAT HE KNEW...
...RUSSIAN ACCENT...AND SILVER HAIR...
...I DID NOT SEE YOUR FRIEND... FOR TWO DAYS AFTER THAT...

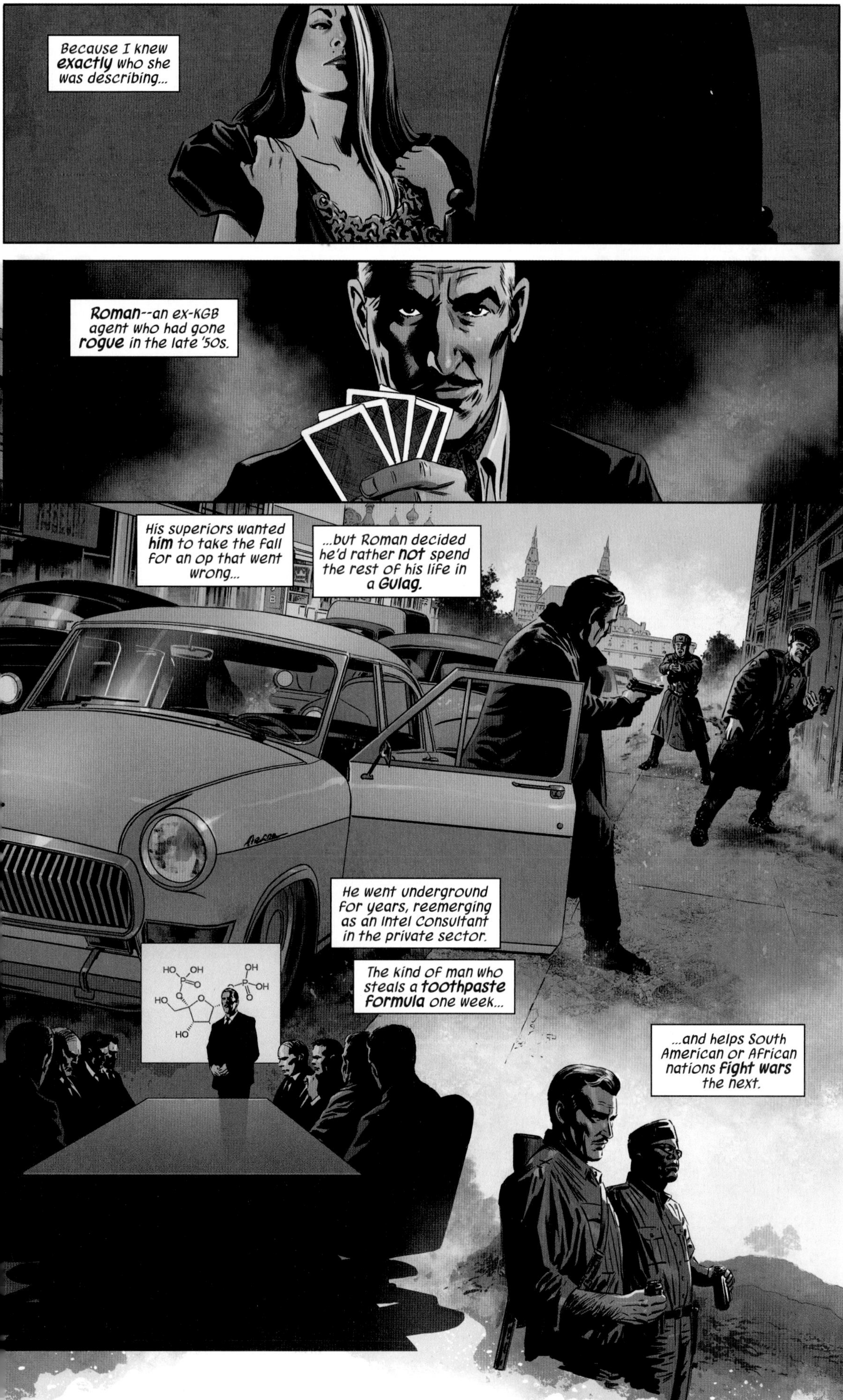

Because I knew exactly who she was describing...
Roman--an ex-KGB agent who had gone rogue in the late '50s.
His superiors wanted him to take the fall for an op that went wrong...
...but Roman decided he'd rather not spend the rest of his life in a Gulag.
He went underground for years, reemerging as an Intel Consultant in the private sector.
The kind of man who steals a toothpaste formula one week...
...and helps South American or African nations fight wars the next.

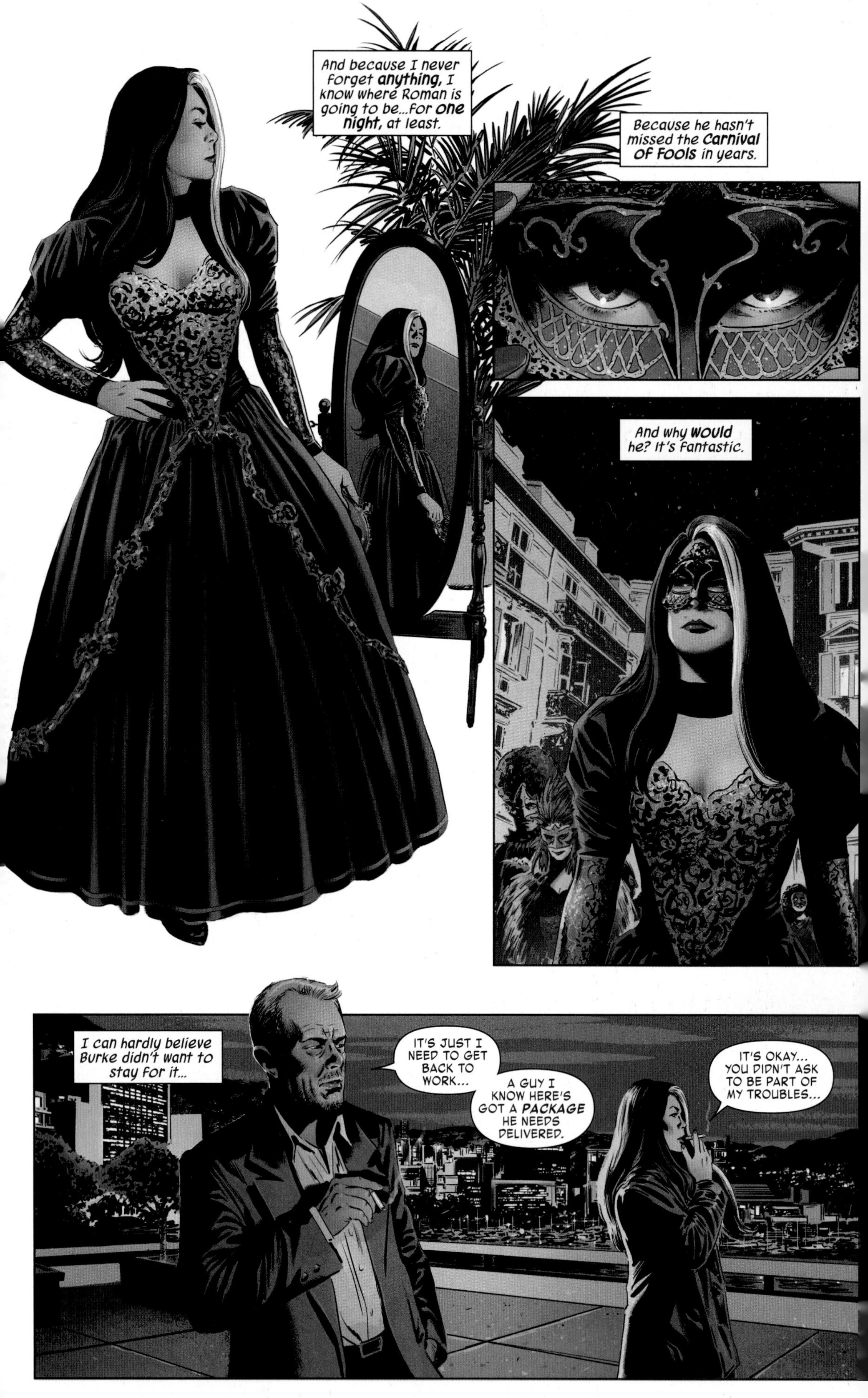

And because I never forget anything, I know where Roman is going to be...For one night, at least.
Because he hasn't missed the Carnival of Fools in years.
And why would he? It's fantastic.
I can hardly believe Burke didn't want to stay for it...
IT'S JUST I NEED TO GET BACK TO WORK...
A GUY I KNOW HERE'S GOT A PACKAGE HE NEEDS DELIVERED.
IT'S OKAY... YOU DIDN'T ASK TO BE PART OF MY TROUBLES...

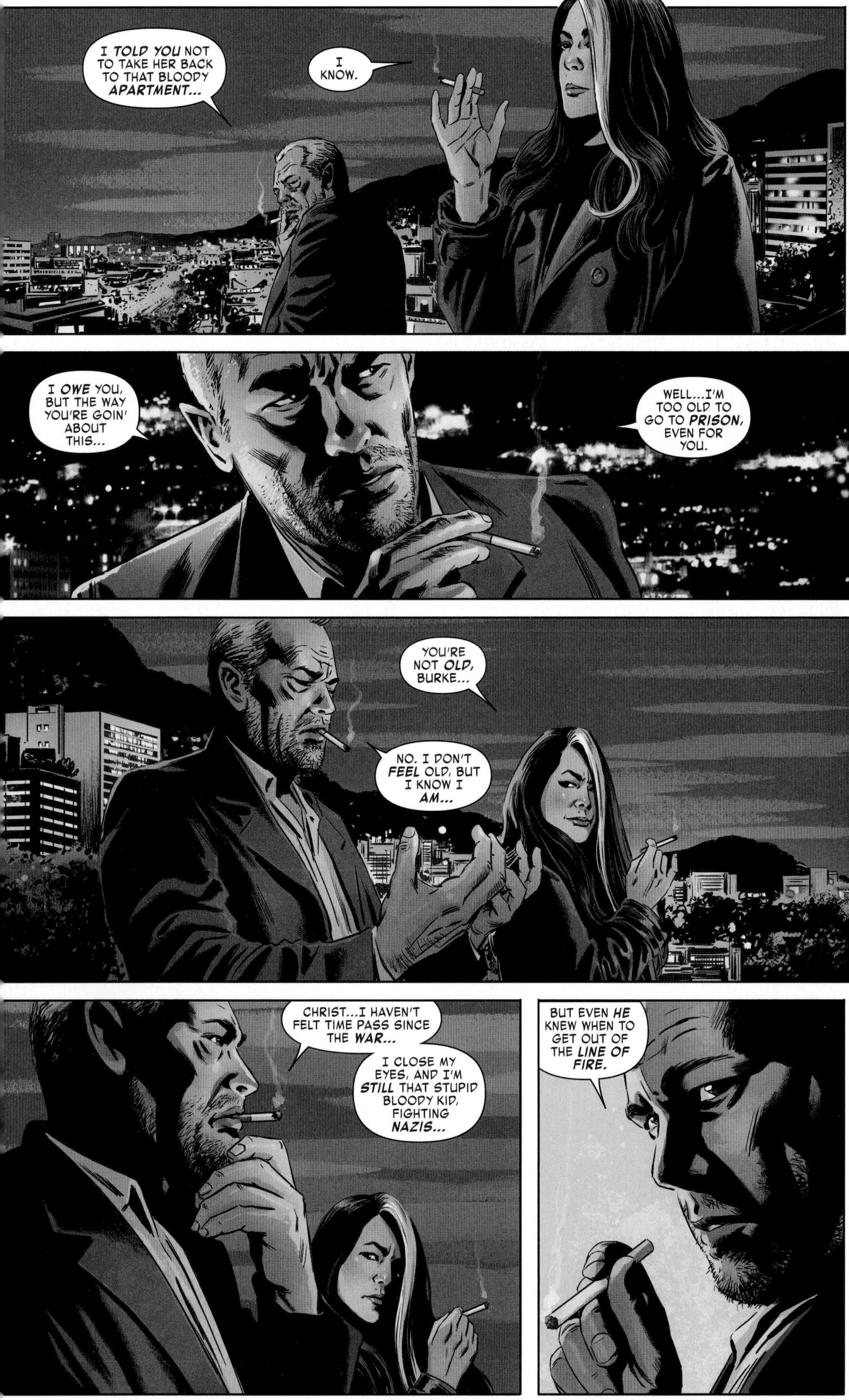
I TOLD YOU NOT TO TAKE HER BACK TO THAT BLOODY APARTMENT...
I KNOW.
I OWE YOU, BUT THE WAY YOU'RE GOIN' ABOUT THIS...
WELL...I'M TOO OLD TO GO TO PRISON, EVEN FOR YOU.
YOU'RE NOT OLD, BURKE...
NO. I DON'T FEEL OLD, BUT I KNOW I AM...
CHRIST...I HAVEN'T FELT TIME PASS SINCE THE WAR...
I CLOSE MY EYES, AND I'M STILL THAT STUPID BLOODY KID, FIGHTING NAZIS...
BUT EVEN HE KNEW WHEN TO GET OUT OF THE LINE OF FIRE.

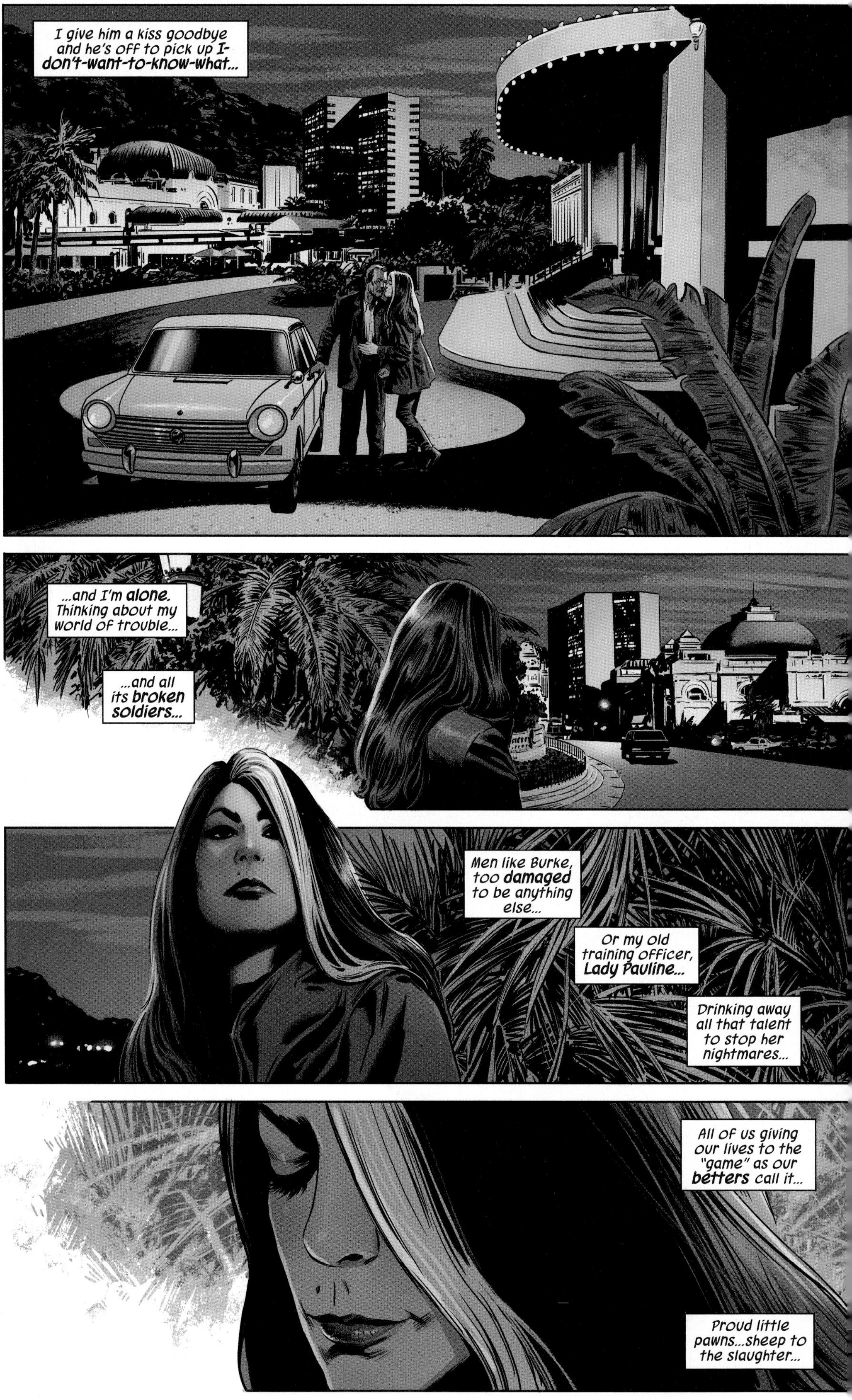
I give him a kiss goodbye and he's off to pick up I-don't-want-to-know-what...
...and I'm alone. Thinking about my world of trouble...
...and all its broken soldiers...
Men like Burke, too damaged to be anything else...
Or my old training officer, Lady Pauline...
Drinking away all that talent to stop her nightmares...
All of us giving our lives to the "game" as our betters call it...
Proud little pawns...sheep to the slaughter...

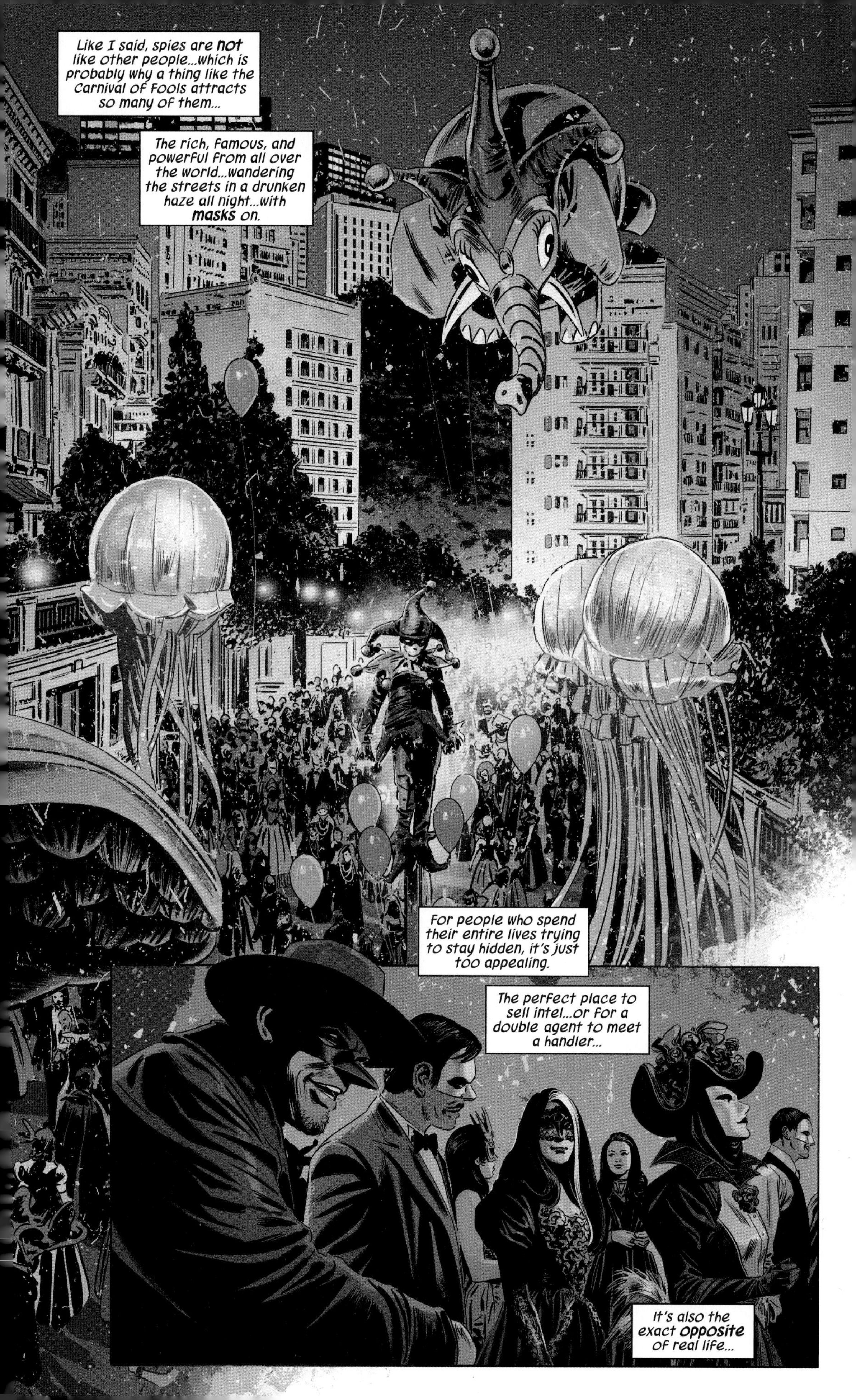

Like I said, spies are **not** like other people...which is probably why a thing like the Carnival of Fools attracts so many of them...
The rich, famous, and powerful from all over the world...wandering the streets in a drunken haze all night...with **masks** on.
For people who spend their entire lives trying to stay hidden, it's just too appealing.
The perfect place to sell intel...or for a double agent to meet a handler...
It's also the exact **opposite** of real life...

...and if spies wanted to be part of real life, they'd never have left it in the first place.

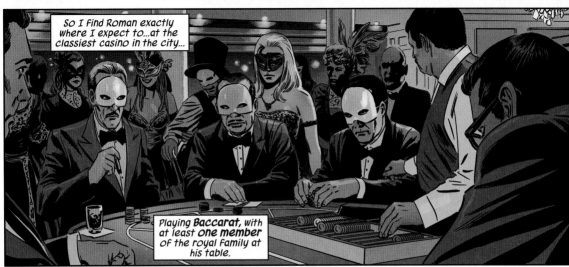

So I find Roman exactly where I expect to...at the classiest casino in the city...

Playing **Baccarat,** with at least **one member** of the royal family at his table.

As far from real life as you could possibly get.

I'LL STAND.

Like most of the world, I have **no idea** how to play Baccarat.

So what do I **do,** then?

I do what I was **trained** to...

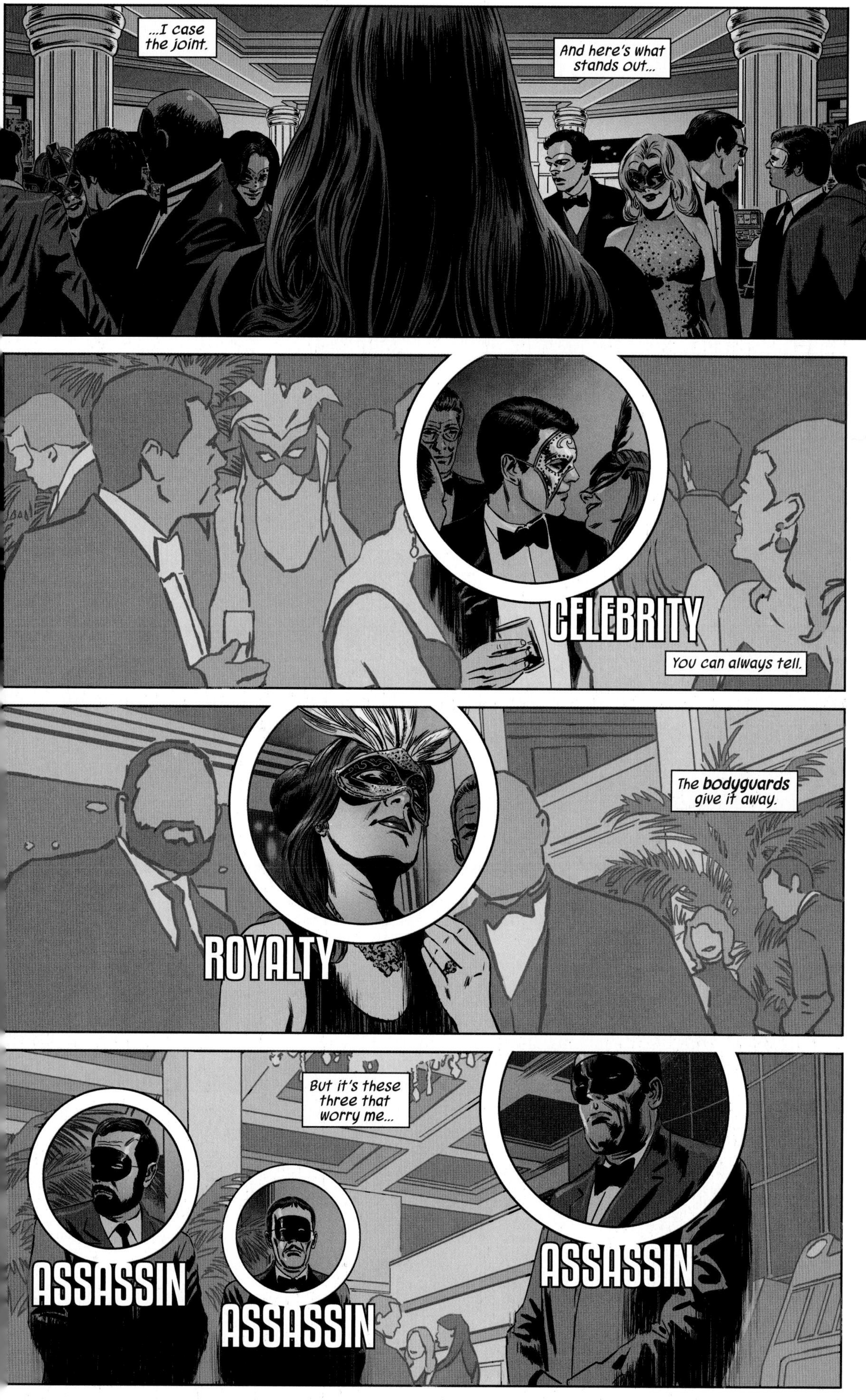

...I case the joint.
And here's what stands out...
CELEBRITY
You can always tell.
ROYALTY
The **bodyguards** give it away.
But it's these three that worry me...
ASSASSIN
ASSASSIN
ASSASSIN

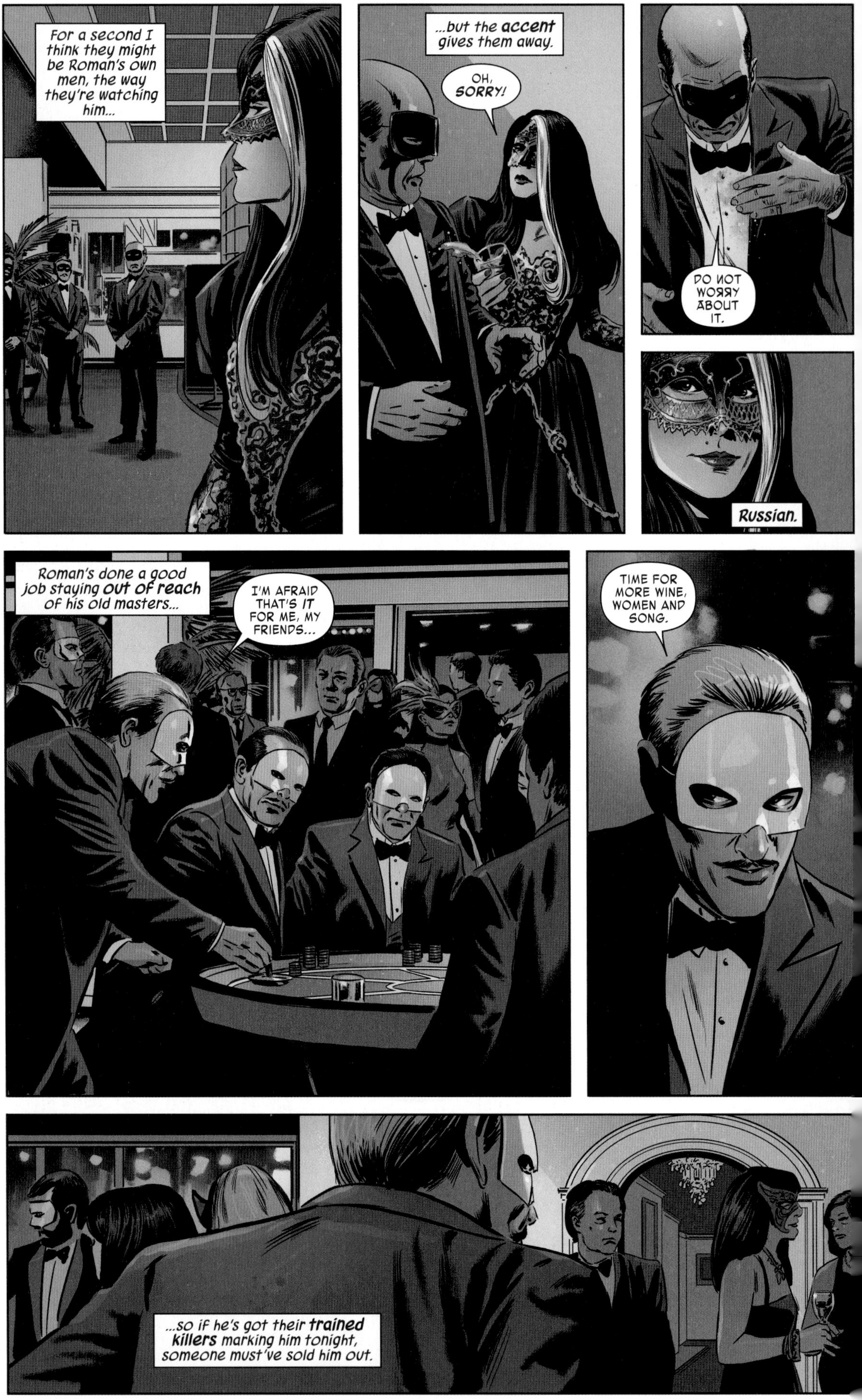
For a second I think they might be Roman's own men, the way they're watching him...
...but the accent gives them away.
OH, SORRY!
DO NOT WORRY ABOUT IT.
Russian.
Roman's done a good job staying out of reach of his old masters...
I'M AFRAID THAT'S IT FOR ME, MY FRIENDS...
TIME FOR MORE WINE, WOMEN AND SONG.
...so if he's got their trained killers marking him tonight, someone must've sold him out.

And I have to wonder, is it because that **someone** knows about his **secret meeting** with X-14?

Have they already figured out what I'm **doing** out here?

Why I was in Belgrade?

TAIRS

GREAT...

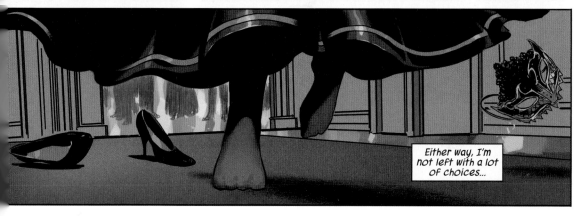

Either way, I'm not left with a lot of choices...

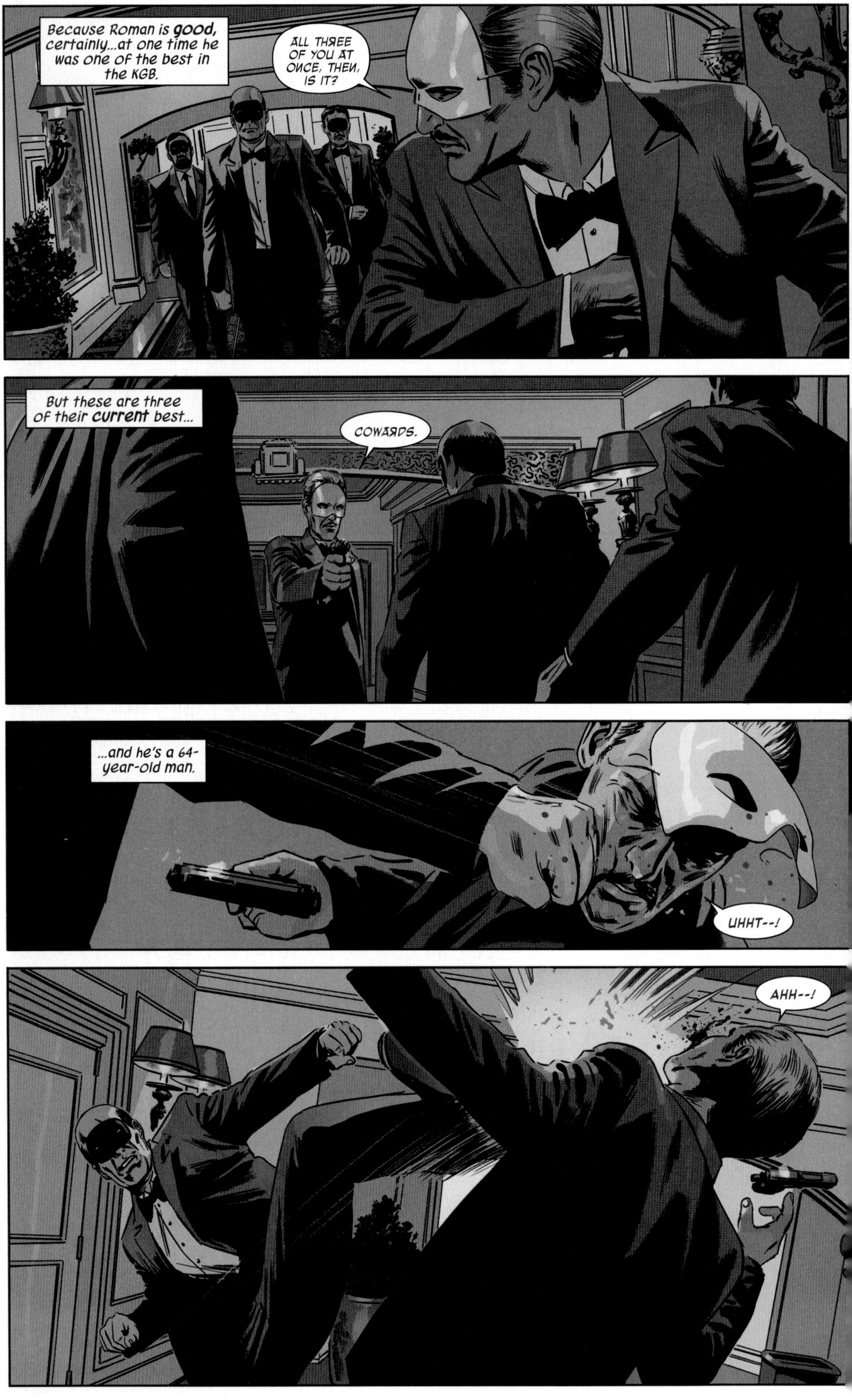

Because Roman is good, certainly...at one time he was one of the best in the KGB.
ALL THREE OF YOU AT ONCE, THEN, IS IT?
But these are three of their current best...
COWARDS.
...and he's a 64-year-old man.
UHHT--!
AHH--!

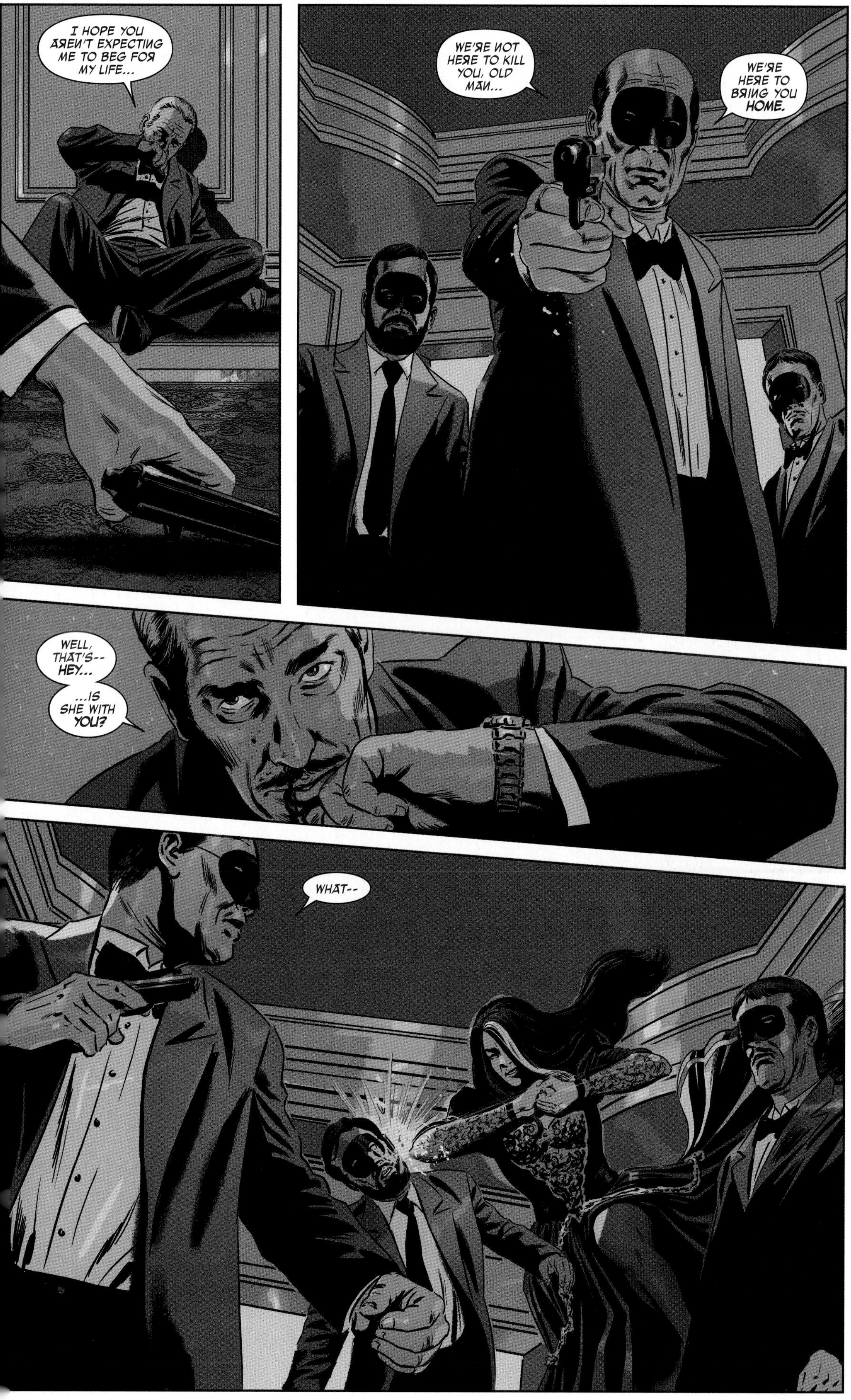
I HOPE YOU AREN'T EXPECTING ME TO BEG FOR MY LIFE...
WE'RE NOT HERE TO KILL YOU, OLD MAN...
WE'RE HERE TO BRING YOU HOME.
WELL, THAT'S-- HEY...
...IS SHE WITH YOU?
WHAT--

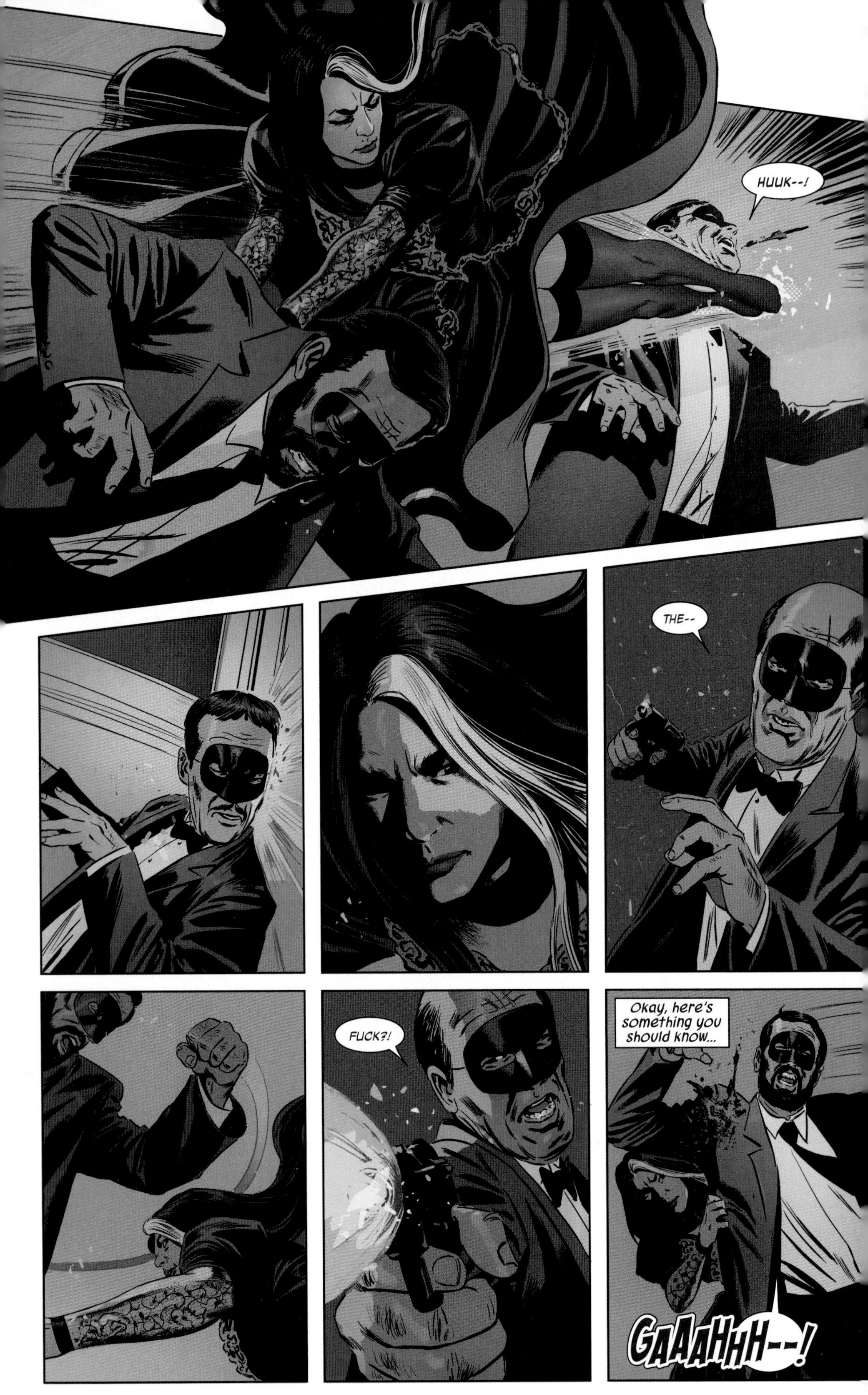
HUUK--!
THE--
FUCK?!
Okay, here's something you should know...
GAAAHHH--!

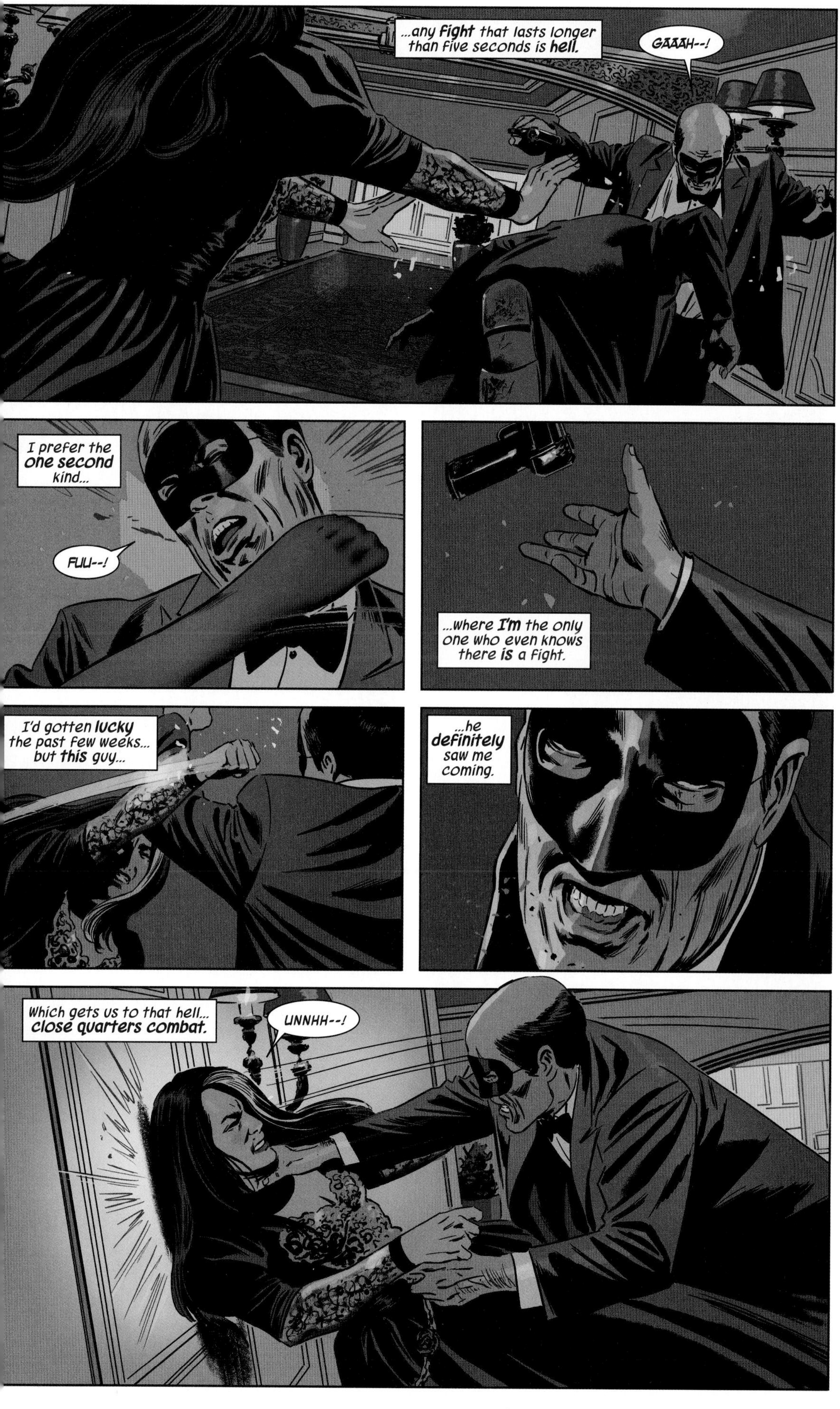
...any fight that lasts longer than five seconds is hell.
GAAAH--!
I prefer the one second kind...
FUU--!
...where I'm the only one who even knows there is a fight.
I'd gotten lucky the past few weeks... but this guy...
...he definitely saw me coming.
Which gets us to that hell... close quarters combat.
UNNHH--!

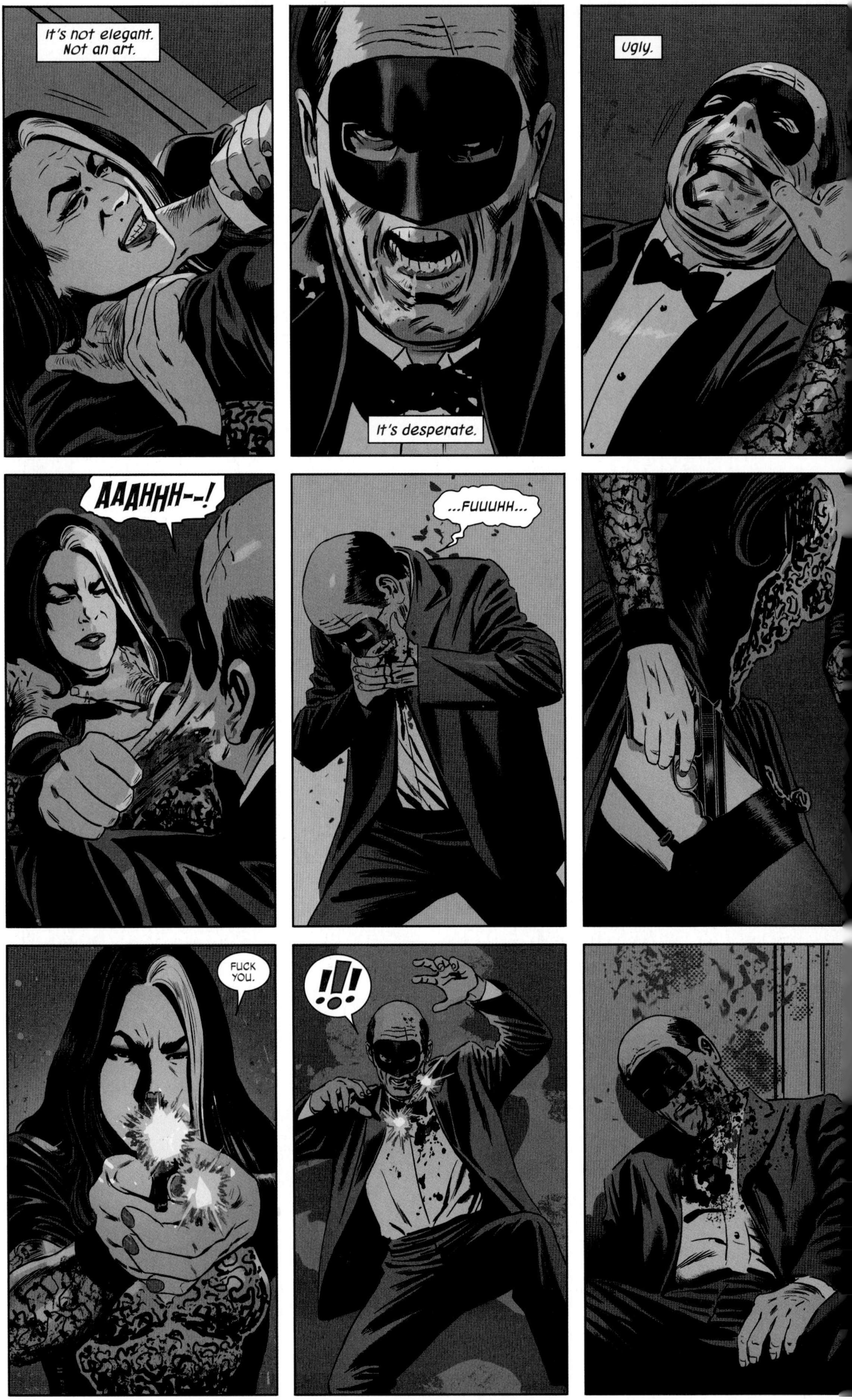
It's not elegant. Not an art.
It's desperate.
Ugly.
AAAHHH--!
...FUUUHH...
FUCK YOU.
!!!

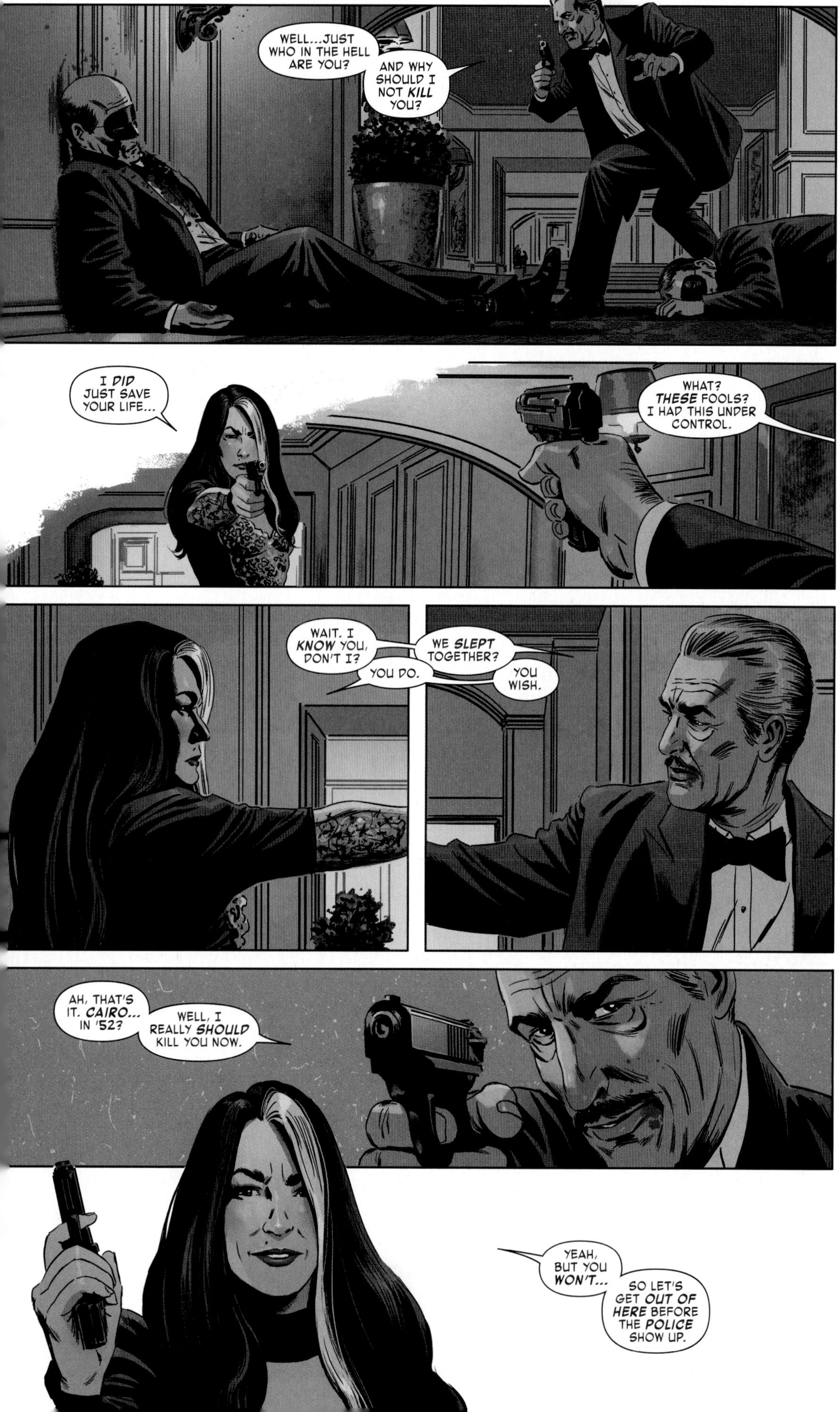
WELL...JUST WHO IN THE HELL ARE YOU?
AND WHY SHOULD I NOT KILL YOU?
I DID JUST SAVE YOUR LIFE...
WHAT? THESE FOOLS? I HAD THIS UNDER CONTROL.
WAIT. I KNOW YOU, DON'T I?
WE SLEPT TOGETHER?
YOU DO.
YOU WISH.
AH, THAT'S IT. CAIRO... IN '52?
WELL, I REALLY SHOULD KILL YOU NOW.
YEAH, BUT YOU WON'T...
SO LET'S GET OUT OF HERE BEFORE THE POLICE SHOW UP.

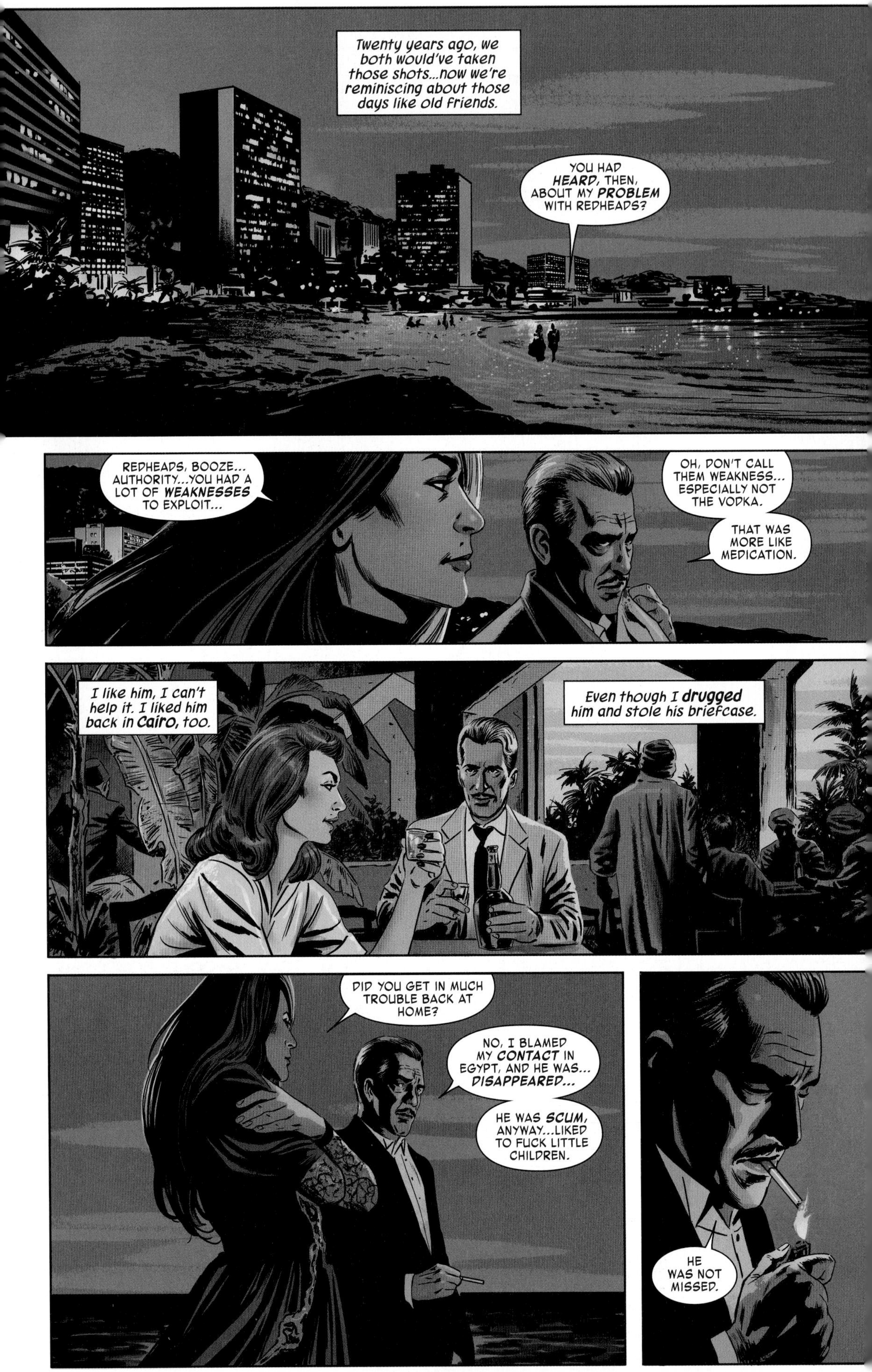
Twenty years ago, we both would've taken those shots...now we're reminiscing about those days like old friends.
YOU HAD HEARD, THEN, ABOUT MY PROBLEM WITH REDHEADS?
REDHEADS, BOOZE... AUTHORITY...YOU HAD A LOT OF WEAKNESSES TO EXPLOIT...
OH, DON'T CALL THEM WEAKNESS... ESPECIALLY NOT THE VODKA.
THAT WAS MORE LIKE MEDICATION.
I like him, I can't help it. I liked him back in Cairo, too.
Even though I drugged him and stole his briefcase.
DID YOU GET IN MUCH TROUBLE BACK AT HOME?
NO, I BLAMED MY CONTACT IN EGYPT, AND HE WAS... DISAPPEARED...
HE WAS SCUM, ANYWAY...LIKED TO FUCK LITTLE CHILDREN.
HE WAS NOT MISSED.

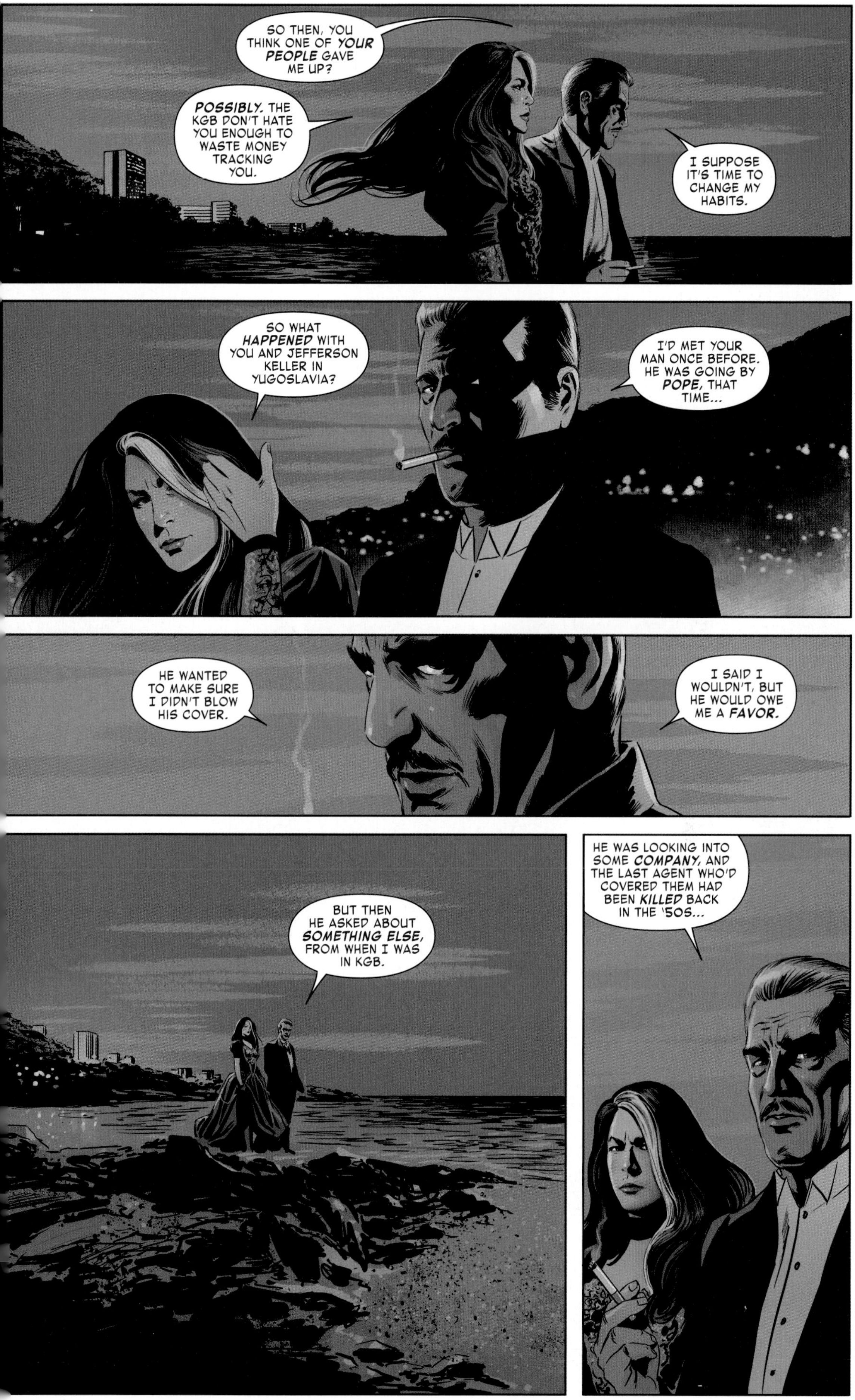
SO THEN, YOU THINK ONE OF YOUR PEOPLE GAVE ME UP?
POSSIBLY. THE KGB DON'T HATE YOU ENOUGH TO WASTE MONEY TRACKING YOU.
I SUPPOSE IT'S TIME TO CHANGE MY HABITS.
SO WHAT HAPPENED WITH YOU AND JEFFERSON KELLER IN YUGOSLAVIA?
I'D MET YOUR MAN ONCE BEFORE. HE WAS GOING BY POPE, THAT TIME...
HE WANTED TO MAKE SURE I DIDN'T BLOW HIS COVER.
I SAID I WOULDN'T, BUT HE WOULD OWE ME A FAVOR.
BUT THEN HE ASKED ABOUT SOMETHING ELSE, FROM WHEN I WAS IN KGB.
HE WAS LOOKING INTO SOME COMPANY, AND THE LAST AGENT WHO'D COVERED THEM HAD BEEN KILLED BACK IN THE '50S...

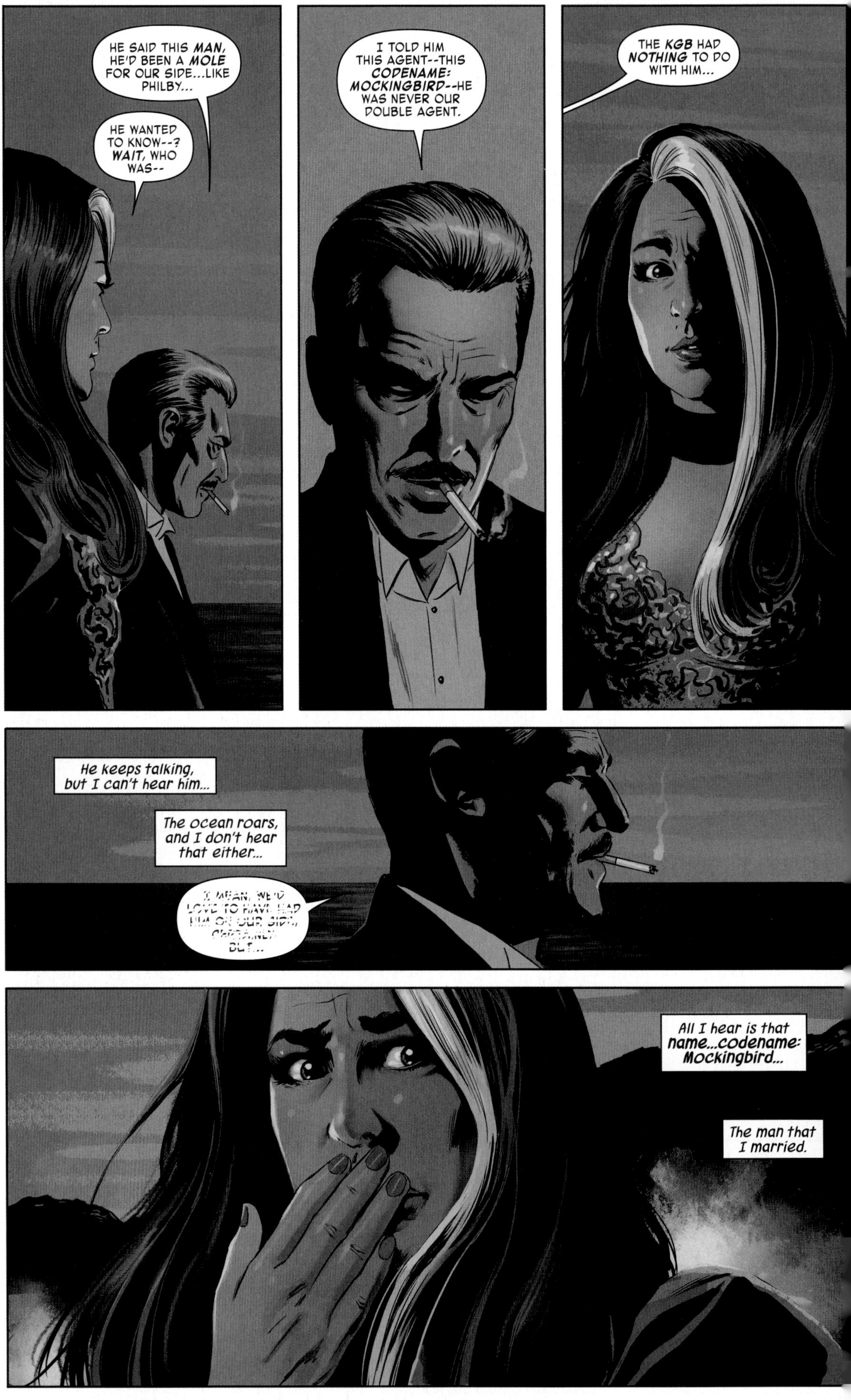

HE SAID THIS MAN, HE'D BEEN A MOLE FOR OUR SIDE...LIKE PHILBY...
HE WANTED TO KNOW--? WAIT, WHO WAS--
I TOLD HIM THIS AGENT--THIS CODENAME: MOCKINGBIRD--HE WAS NEVER OUR DOUBLE AGENT.
THE KGB HAD NOTHING TO DO WITH HIM...
He keeps talking, but I can't hear him...
The ocean roars, and I don't hear that either...
I MEAN, WE'D LOVE TO HAVE HAD HIM ON OUR SIDE, CERTAINLY. BUT...
All I hear is that name...codename: Mockingbird...
The man that I married.

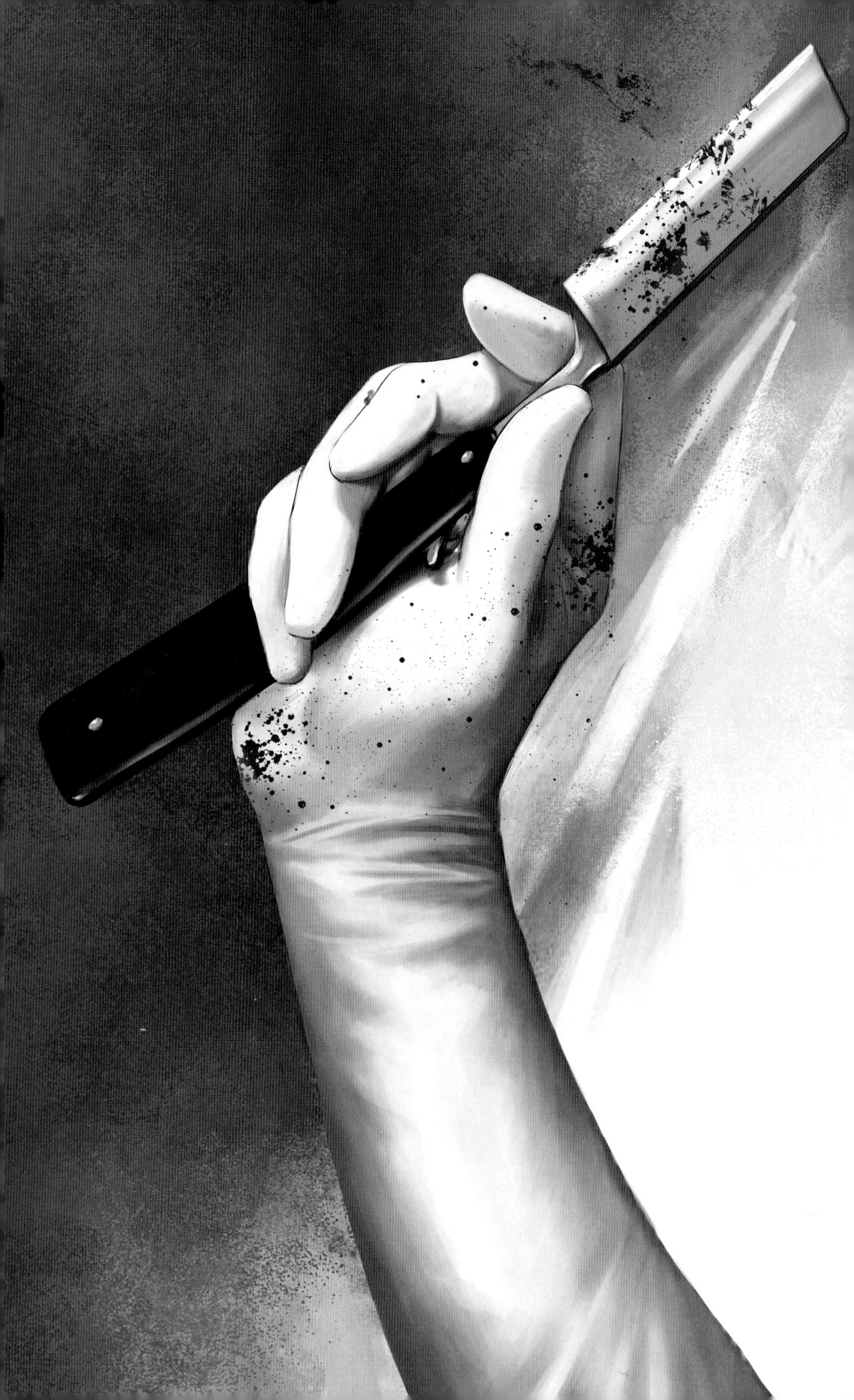

THE BAHAMAS – 1956

WHAT ABOUT THAT ONE?

STOP, RICHARD... I'M *NOT* PLAYING.

OH C'MON, V... IT'S OBVIOUS HE'S IN ADVERTISING.

WHY IS IT *OBVIOUS*?

THE WAY HE'S GAZING AT THE OCEAN... LIKE HE'S TRYING TO PICTURE HOW OTHER PEOPLE MIGHT SEE IT.

PSSH...YOU'RE REACHING.

AND I THOUGHT WE AGREED TO *LEAVE* ALL THAT AT THE OFFICE...

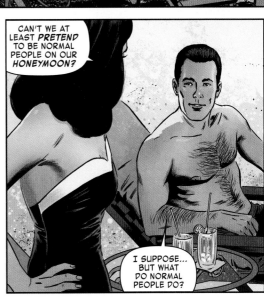

CAN'T WE AT LEAST *PRETEND* TO BE NORMAL PEOPLE ON OUR *HONEYMOON*?

I SUPPOSE... BUT WHAT DO NORMAL PEOPLE DO?

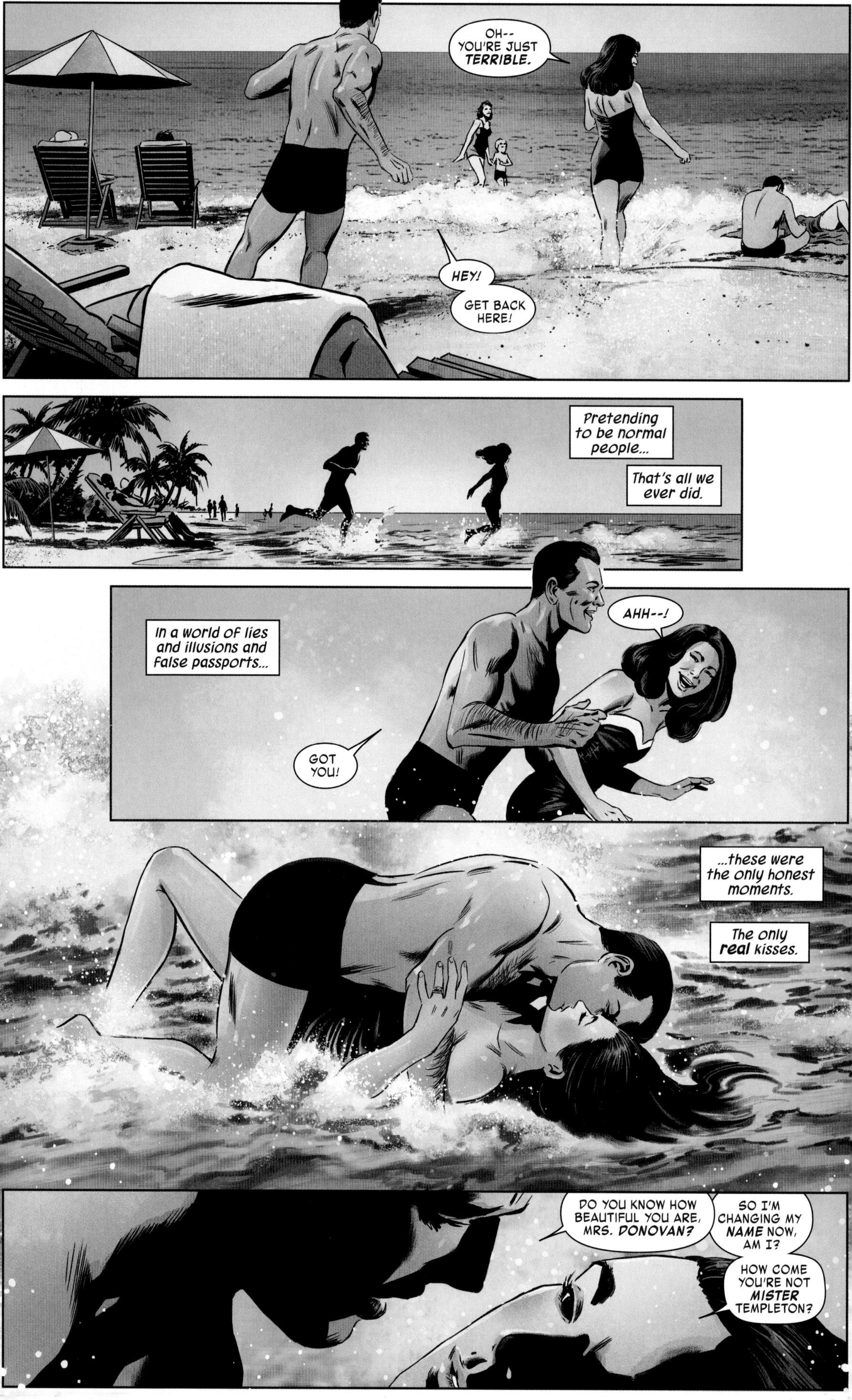

OH-- YOU'RE JUST TERRIBLE.
HEY!
GET BACK HERE!
Pretending to be normal people...
That's all we ever did.
In a world of lies and illusions and false passports...
AHH--!
GOT YOU!
...these were the only honest moments.
The only real kisses.
DO YOU KNOW HOW BEAUTIFUL YOU ARE, MRS. DONOVAN?
SO I'M CHANGING MY NAME NOW, AM I?
HOW COME YOU'RE NOT MISTER TEMPLETON?

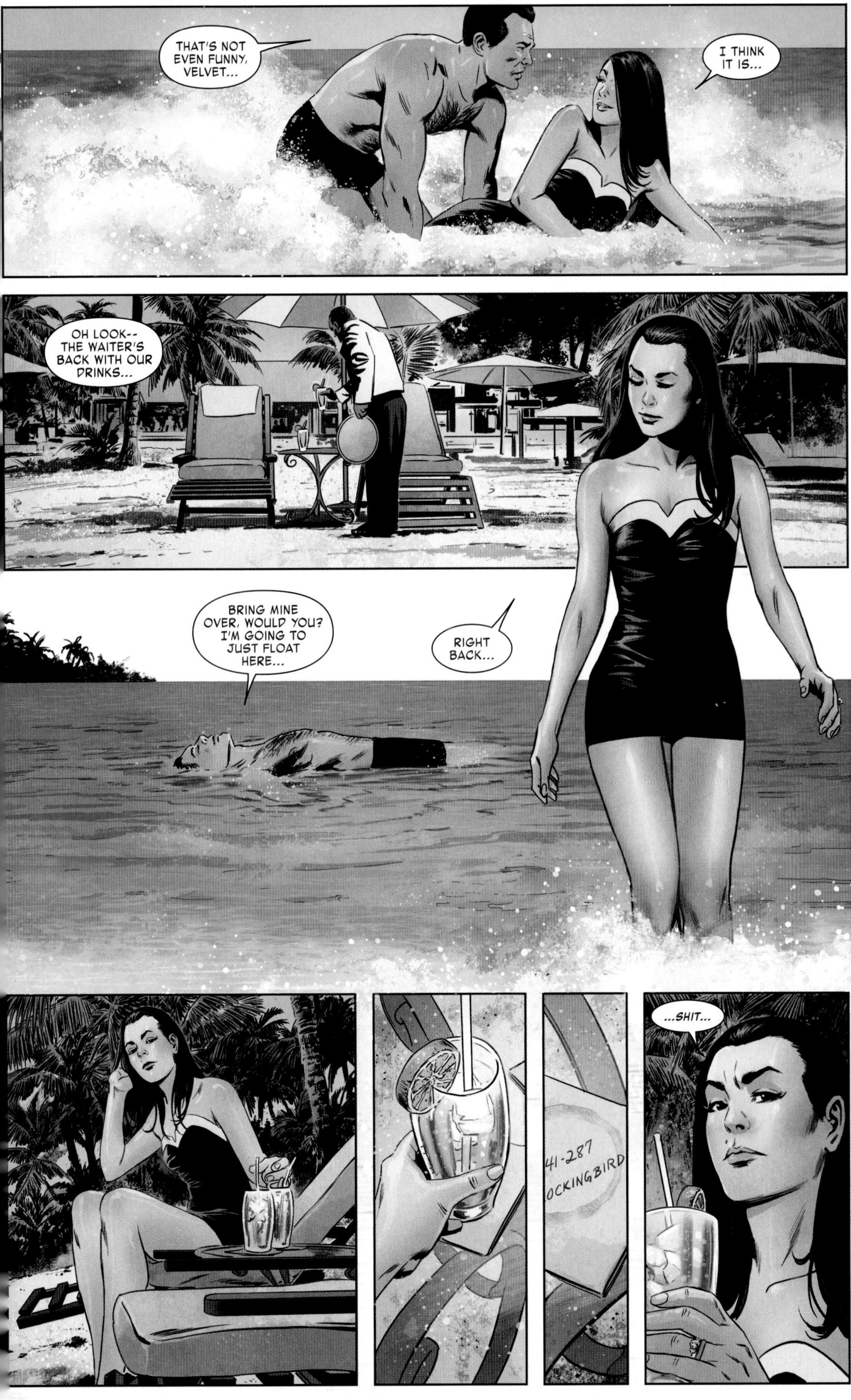
THAT'S NOT EVEN FUNNY, VELVET...
I THINK IT IS...
OH LOOK-- THE WAITER'S BACK WITH OUR DRINKS...
BRING MINE OVER, WOULD YOU? I'M GOING TO JUST FLOAT HERE...
RIGHT BACK...
41-287
OCKINGBIRD
...SHIT...

PART FIVE

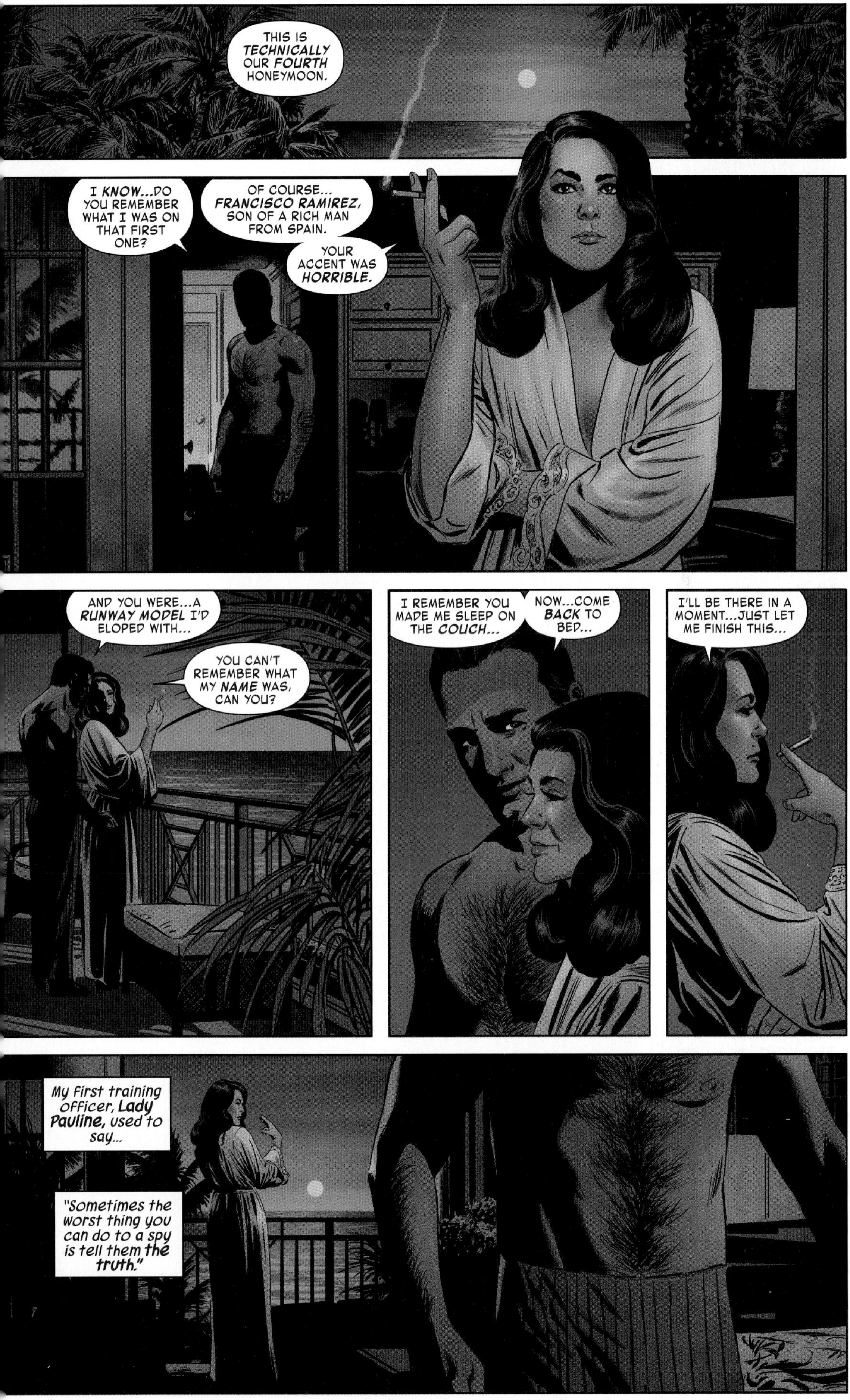
THIS IS TECHNICALLY OUR FOURTH HONEYMOON.
I KNOW...DO YOU REMEMBER WHAT I WAS ON THAT FIRST ONE?
OF COURSE... FRANCISCO RAMIREZ, SON OF A RICH MAN FROM SPAIN.
YOUR ACCENT WAS HORRIBLE.
AND YOU WERE...A RUNWAY MODEL I'D ELOPED WITH...
YOU CAN'T REMEMBER WHAT MY NAME WAS, CAN YOU?
I REMEMBER YOU MADE ME SLEEP ON THE COUCH...
NOW...COME BACK TO BED...
I'LL BE THERE IN A MOMENT...JUST LET ME FINISH THIS...
My first training officer, Lady Pauline, used to say...
"Sometimes the worst thing you can do to a spy is tell them the truth."

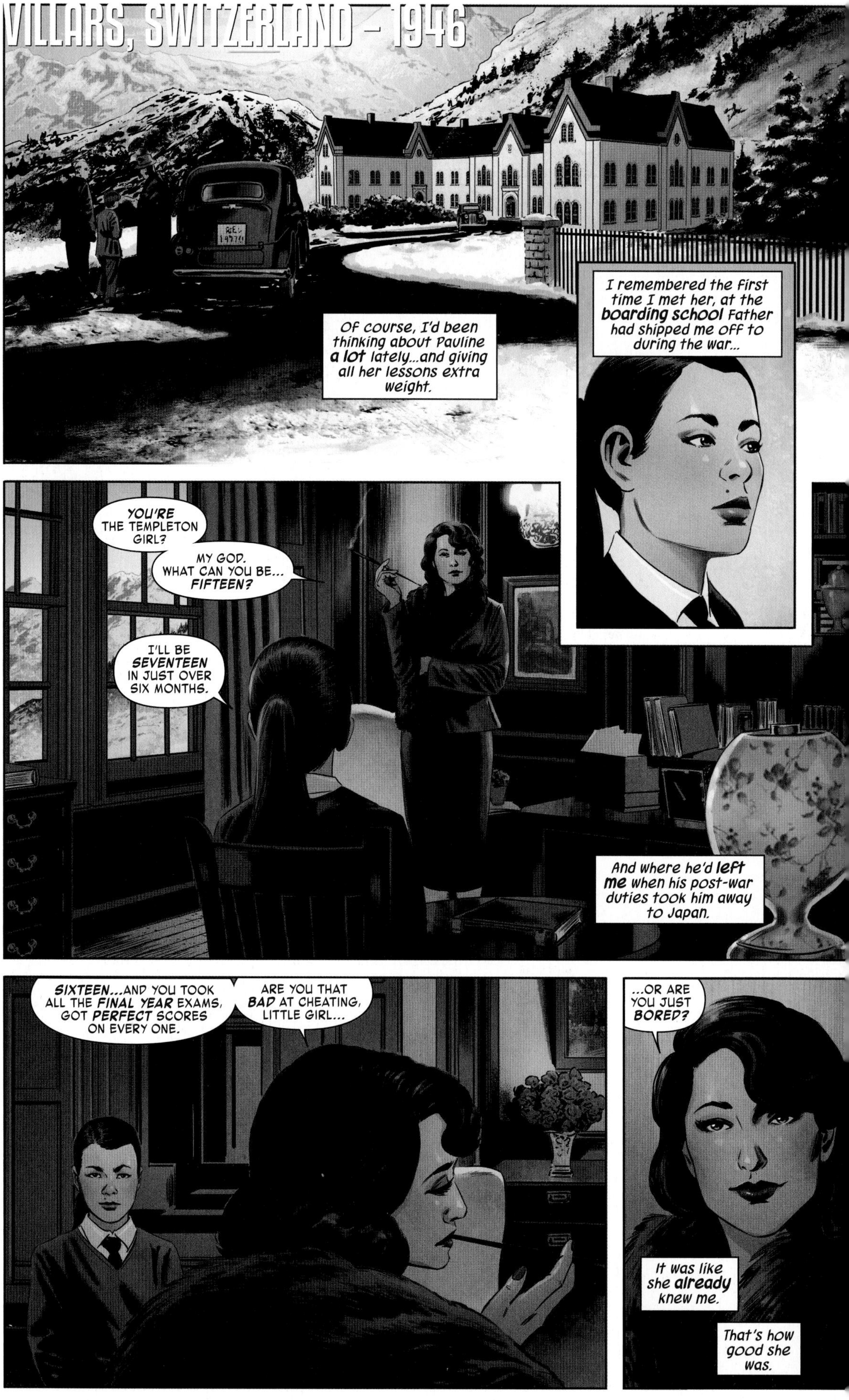
VILLARS, SWITZERLAND – 1946
Of course, I'd been thinking about Pauline a lot lately...and giving all her lessons extra weight.
I remembered the first time I met her, at the boarding school Father had shipped me off to during the war...
YOU'RE THE TEMPLETON GIRL?
MY GOD. WHAT CAN YOU BE... FIFTEEN?
I'LL BE SEVENTEEN IN JUST OVER SIX MONTHS.
And where he'd left me when his post-war duties took him away to Japan.
SIXTEEN...AND YOU TOOK ALL THE FINAL YEAR EXAMS, GOT PERFECT SCORES ON EVERY ONE.
ARE YOU THAT BAD AT CHEATING, LITTLE GIRL...
...OR ARE YOU JUST BORED?
It was like she already knew me.
That's how good she was.

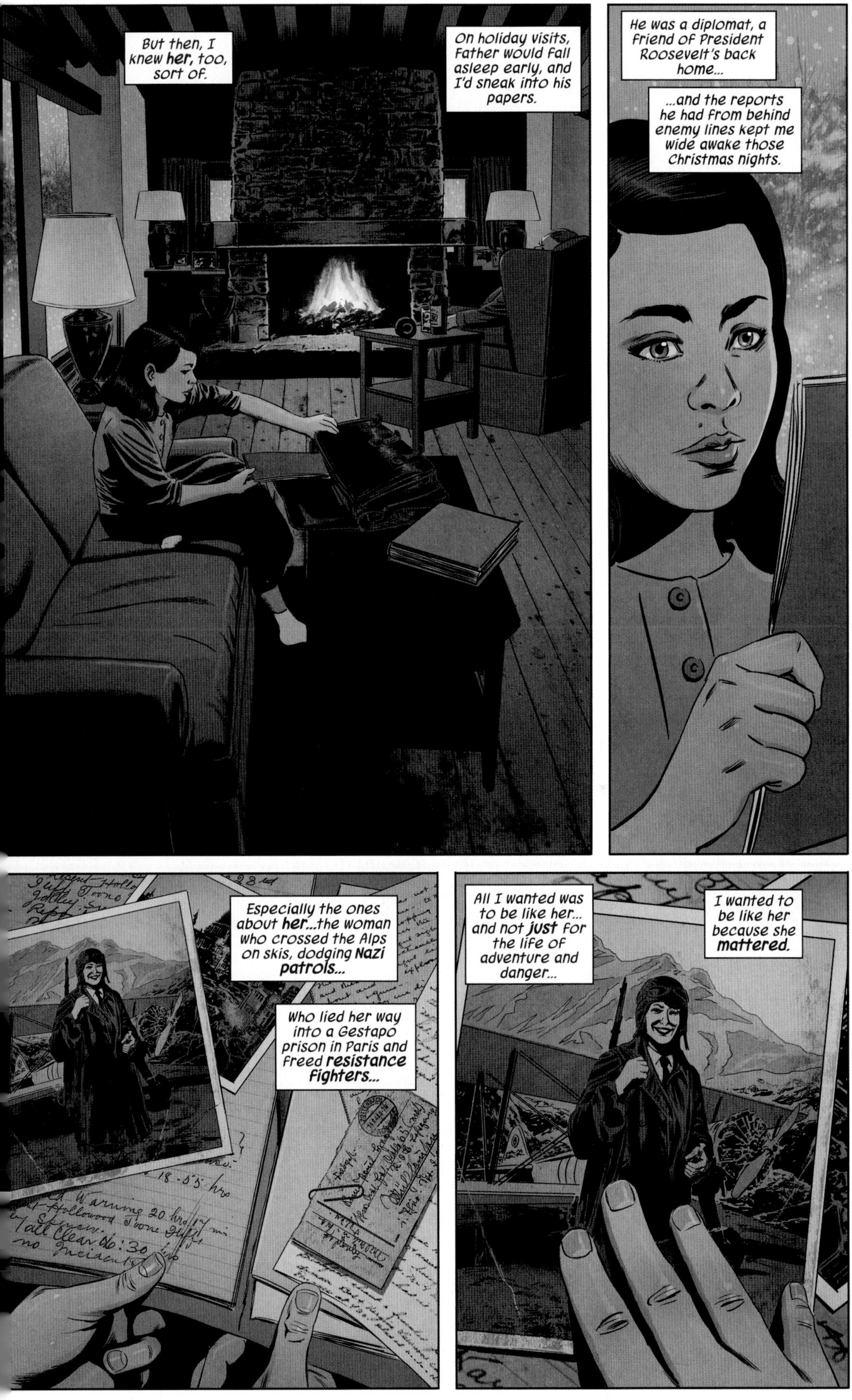
But then, I knew her, too, sort of.
On holiday visits, Father would fall asleep early, and I'd sneak into his papers.
He was a diplomat, a friend of President Roosevelt's back home...
...and the reports he had from behind enemy lines kept me wide awake those Christmas nights.
Especially the ones about her...the woman who crossed the Alps on skis, dodging Nazi patrols...
Who lied her way into a Gestapo prison in Paris and freed resistance fighters...
All I wanted was to be like her... and not just for the life of adventure and danger...
I wanted to be like her because she mattered.

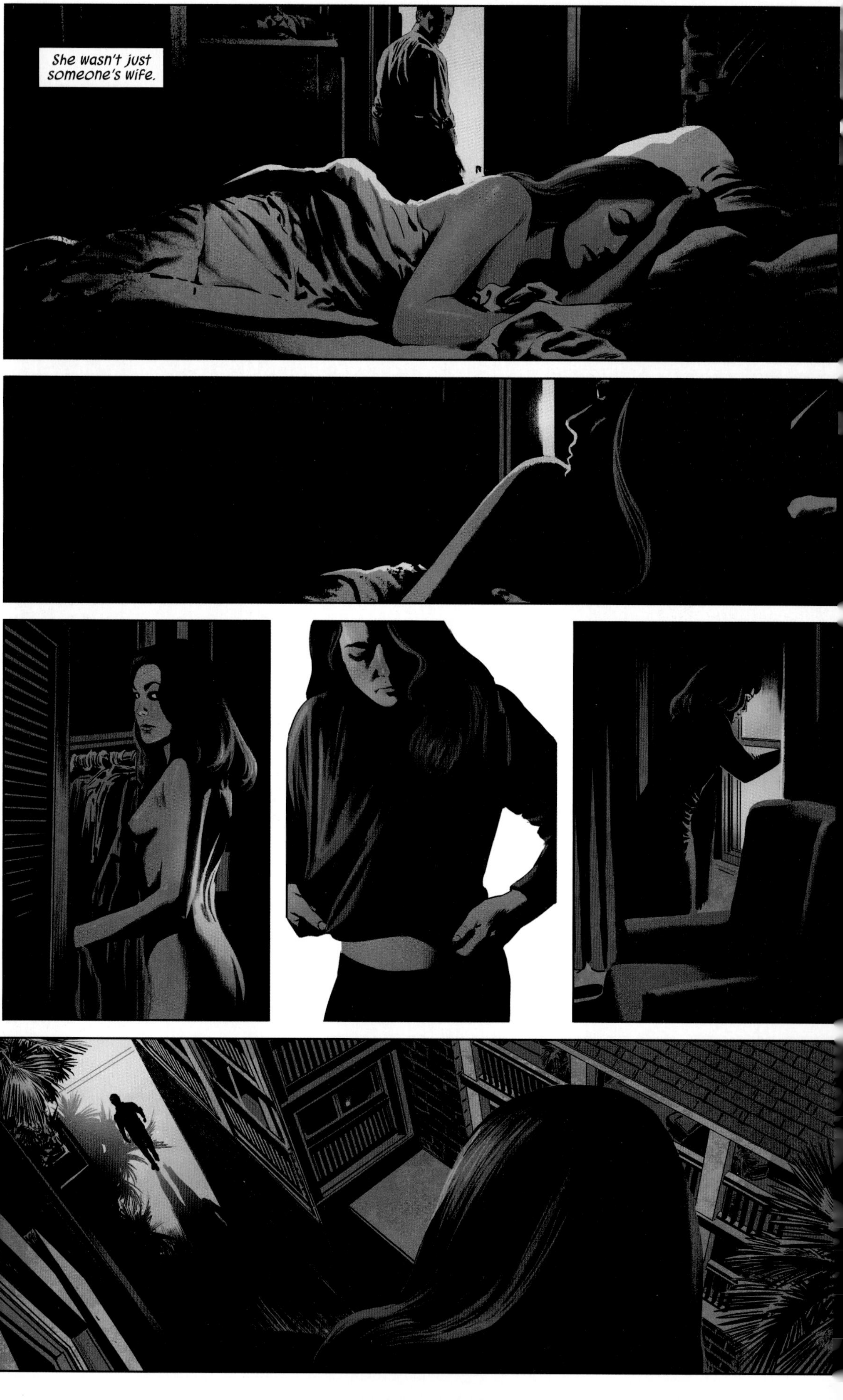
She wasn't just someone's wife.

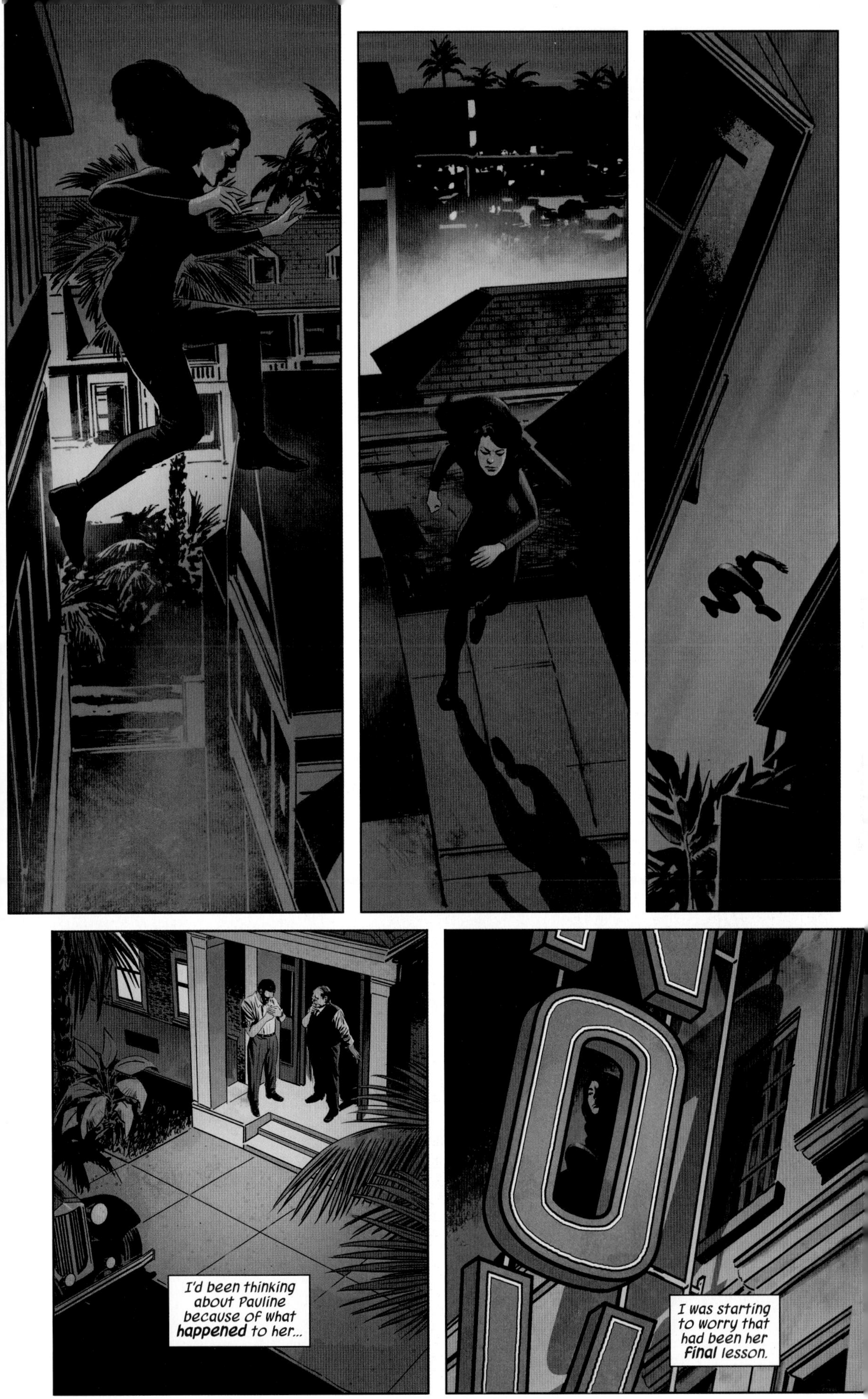
I'd been thinking about Pauline because of what happened to her...
I was starting to worry that had been her final lesson.

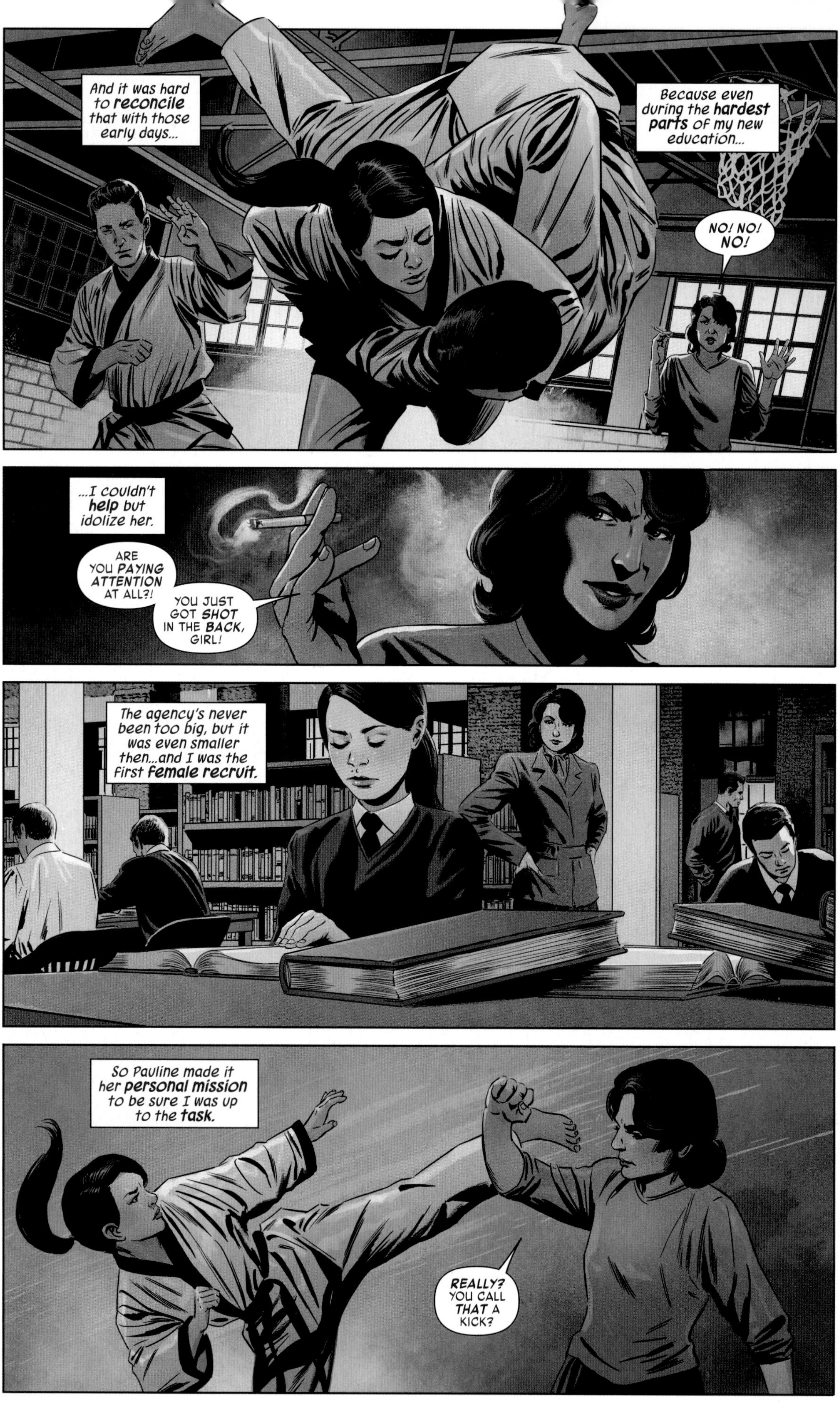
And it was hard to reconcile that with those early days...
Because even during the hardest parts of my new education...
NO! NO! NO!
...I couldn't help but idolize her.
ARE YOU PAYING ATTENTION AT ALL?!
YOU JUST GOT SHOT IN THE BACK, GIRL!
The agency's never been too big, but it was even smaller then...and I was the first female recruit.
So Pauline made it her personal mission to be sure I was up to the task.
REALLY? YOU CALL THAT A KICK?

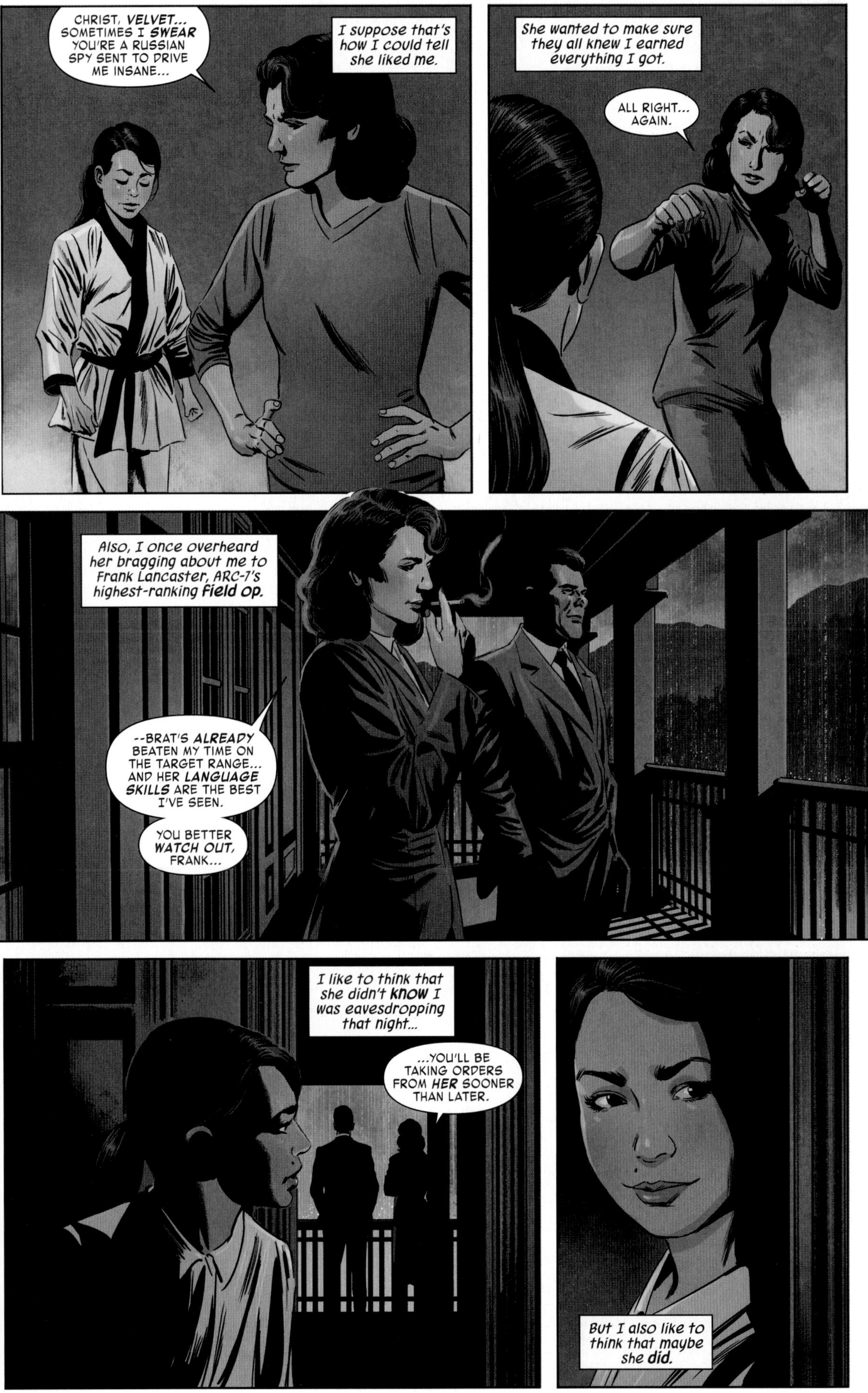
CHRIST, VELVET... SOMETIMES I SWEAR YOU'RE A RUSSIAN SPY SENT TO DRIVE ME INSANE...
I suppose that's how I could tell she liked me.
She wanted to make sure they all knew I earned everything I got.
ALL RIGHT... AGAIN.
Also, I once overheard her bragging about me to Frank Lancaster, ARC-7's highest-ranking field op.
--BRAT'S ALREADY BEATEN MY TIME ON THE TARGET RANGE... AND HER LANGUAGE SKILLS ARE THE BEST I'VE SEEN.
YOU BETTER WATCH OUT, FRANK...
I like to think that she didn't KNOW I was eavesdropping that night...
...YOU'LL BE TAKING ORDERS FROM HER SOONER THAN LATER.
But I also like to think that maybe she did.

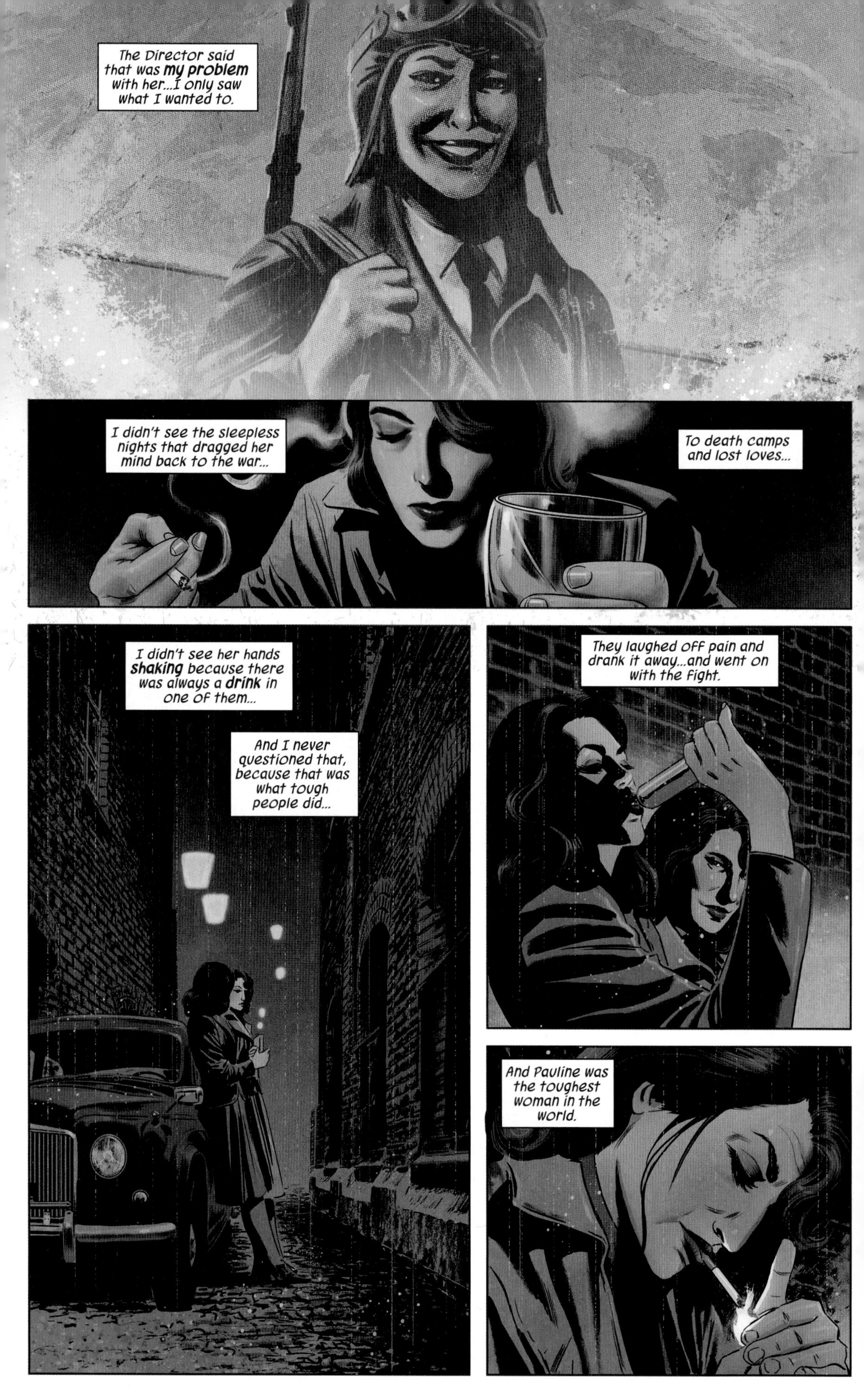
The Director said that was **my problem** with her...I only saw what I wanted to.
I didn't see the sleepless nights that dragged her mind back to the war...
To death camps and lost loves...
I didn't see her hands **shaking** because there was always a **drink** in one of them...
And I never questioned that, because that was what tough people did...
They laughed off pain and drank it away...and went on with the fight.
And Pauline was the toughest woman in the world.

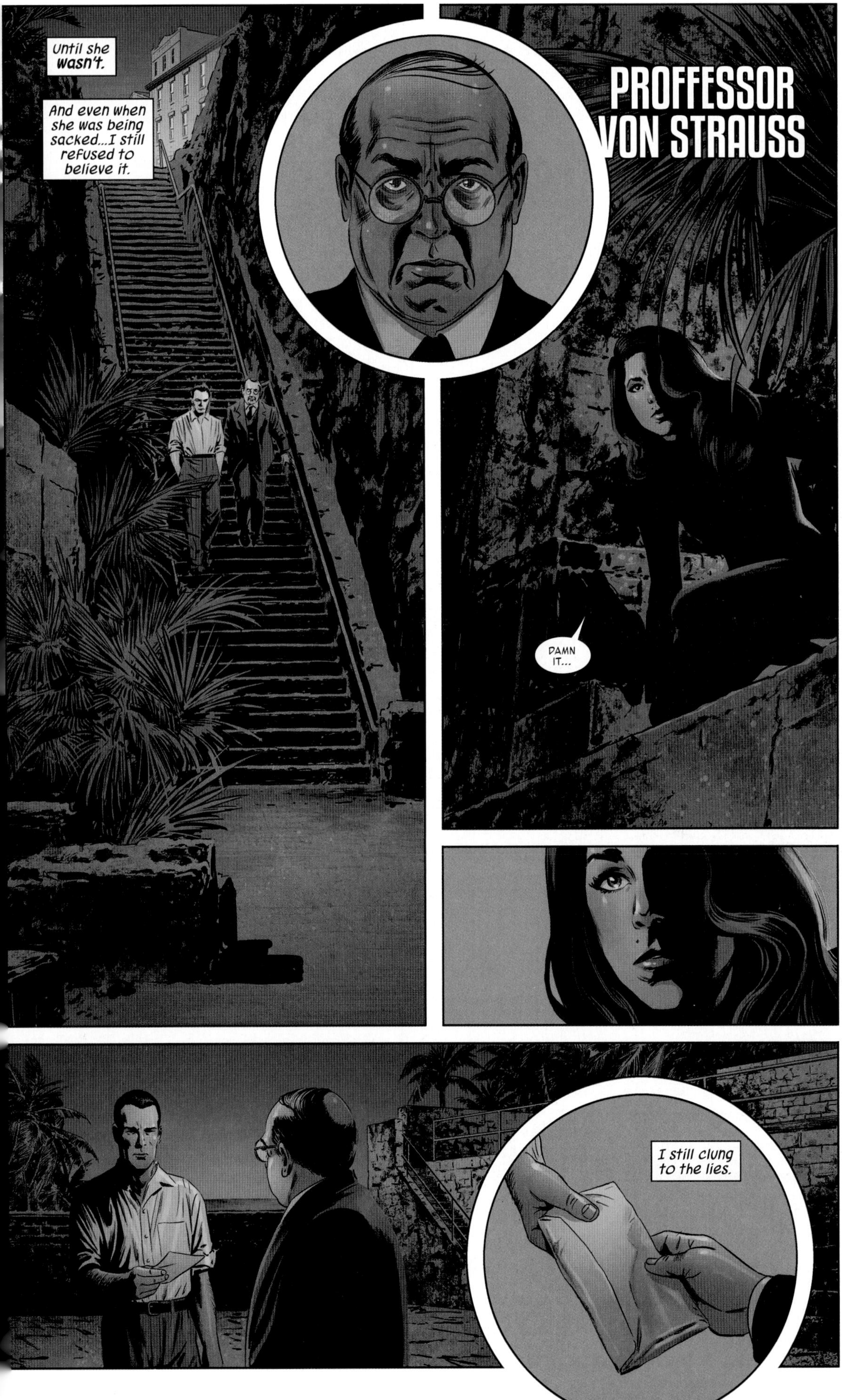
Until she wasn't.
And even when she was being sacked...I still refused to believe it.
PROFFESSOR VON STRAUSS
DAMN IT...
I still clung to the lies.

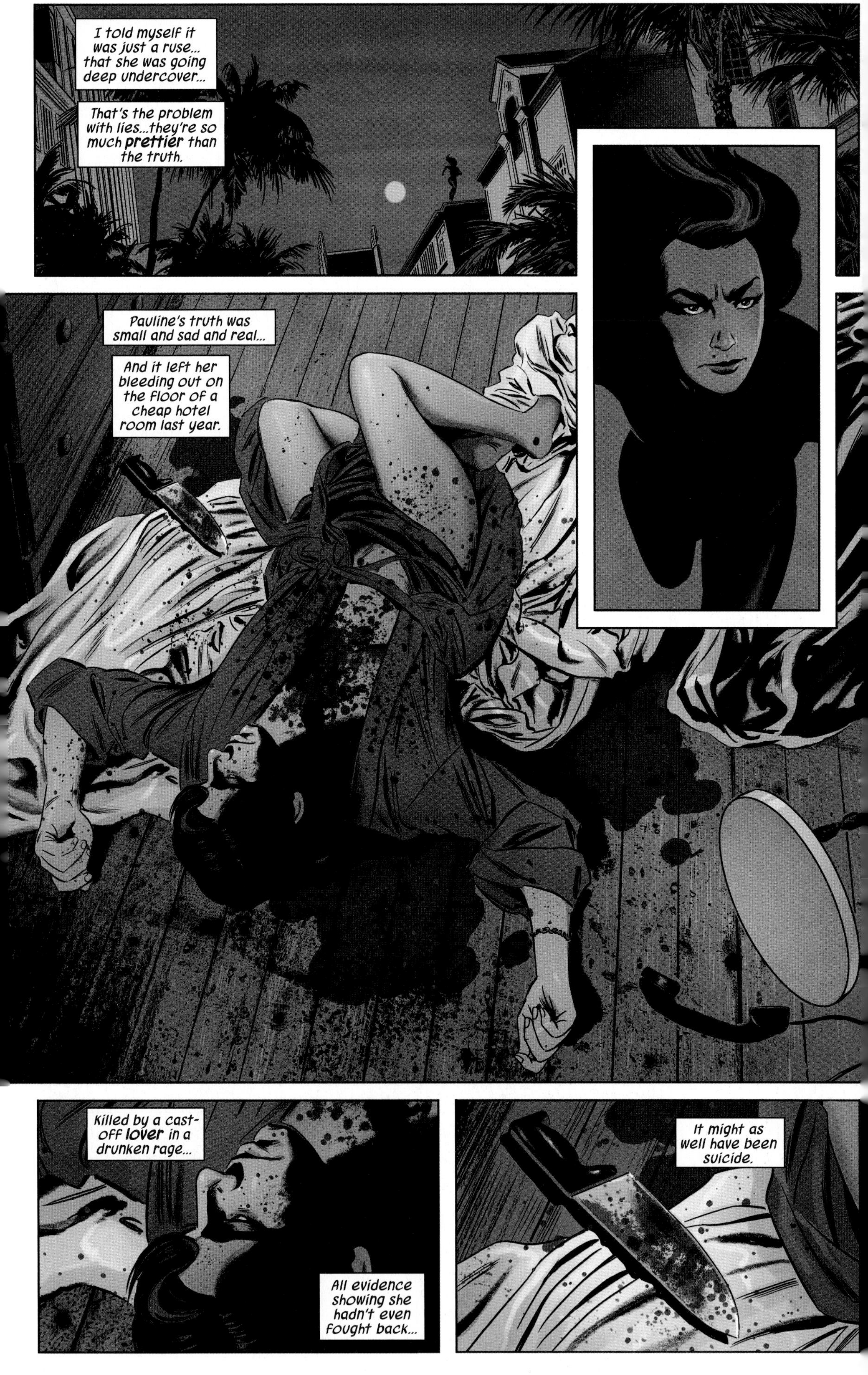
I told myself it was just a ruse... that she was going deep undercover...
That's the problem with lies...they're so much prettier than the truth.
Pauline's truth was small and sad and real...
And it left her bleeding out on the floor of a cheap hotel room last year.
Killed by a cast-off lover in a drunken rage...
All evidence showing she hadn't even fought back...
It might as well have been suicide.

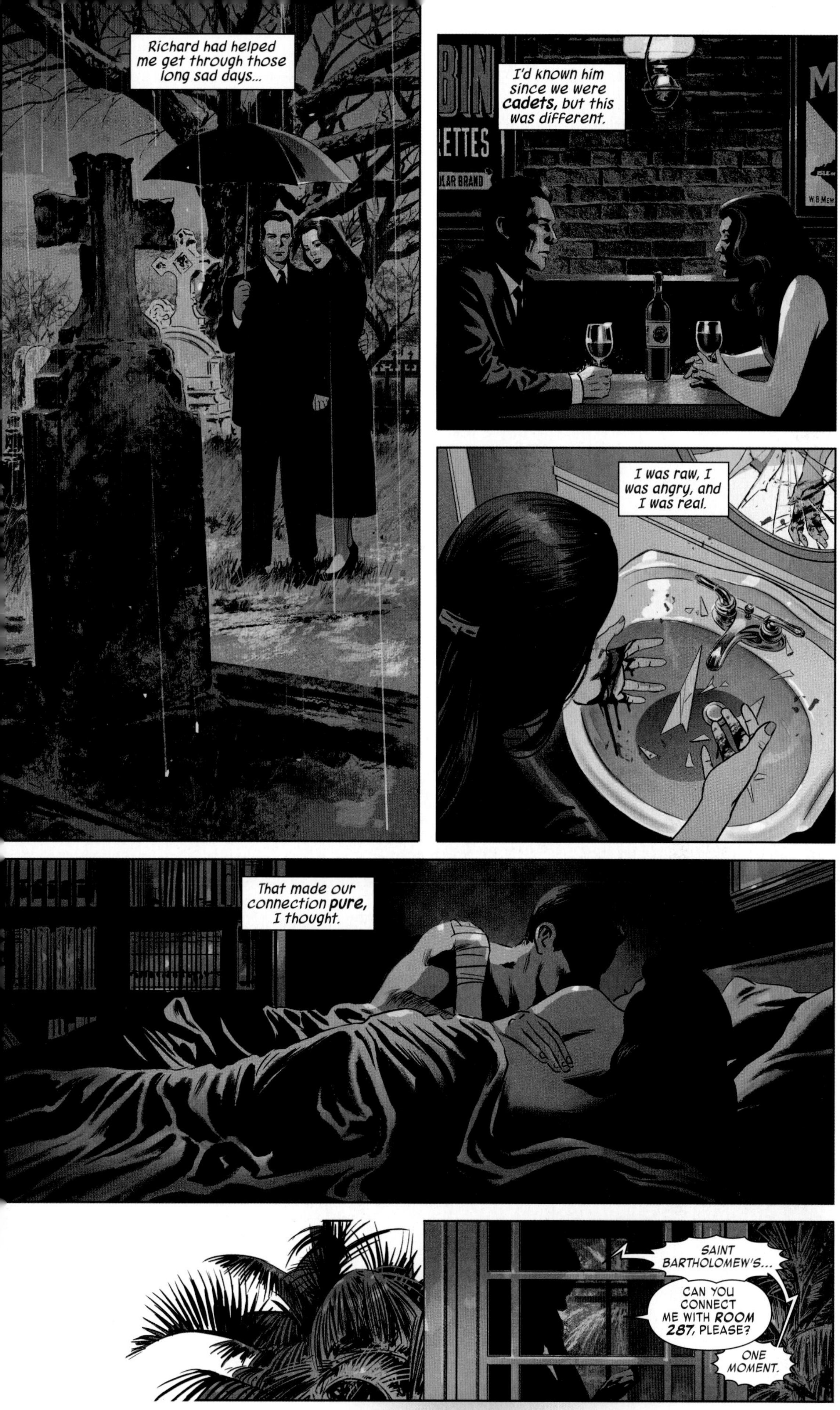
Richard had helped me get through those long sad days...
I'd known him since we were **cadets,** but this was different.
I was raw, I was angry, and I was real.
That made our connection **pure,** I thought.
SAINT BARTHOLOMEW'S...
CAN YOU CONNECT ME WITH **ROOM 287,** PLEASE?
ONE MOMENT.

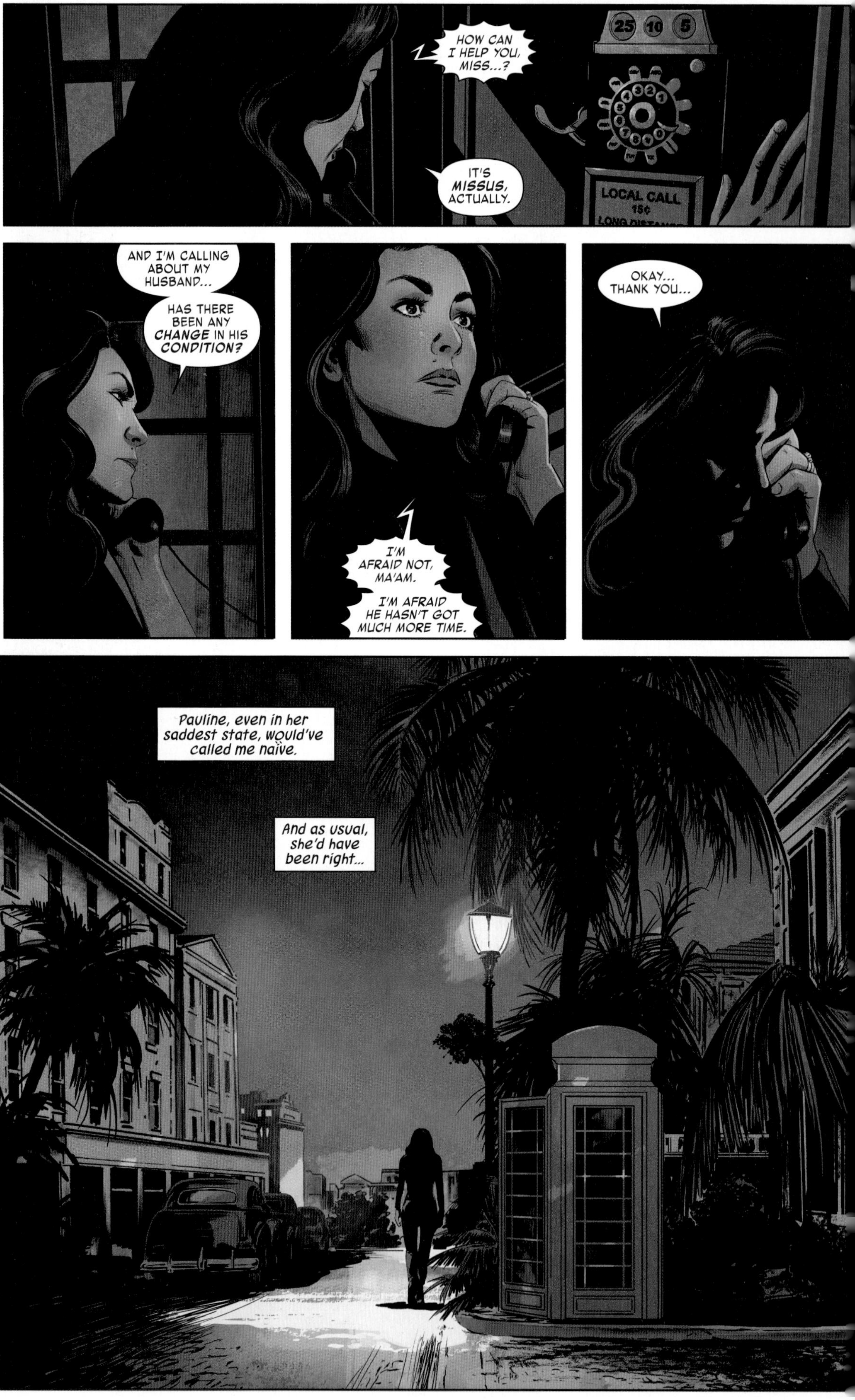

25 10 5
HOW CAN I HELP YOU, MISS...?
IT'S MISSUS, ACTUALLY.
LOCAL CALL 15¢
AND I'M CALLING ABOUT MY HUSBAND...
HAS THERE BEEN ANY CHANGE IN HIS CONDITION?
I'M AFRAID NOT, MA'AM.
I'M AFRAID HE HASN'T GOT MUCH MORE TIME.
OKAY... THANK YOU...
Pauline, even in her saddest state, would've called me naïve.
And as usual, she'd have been right...

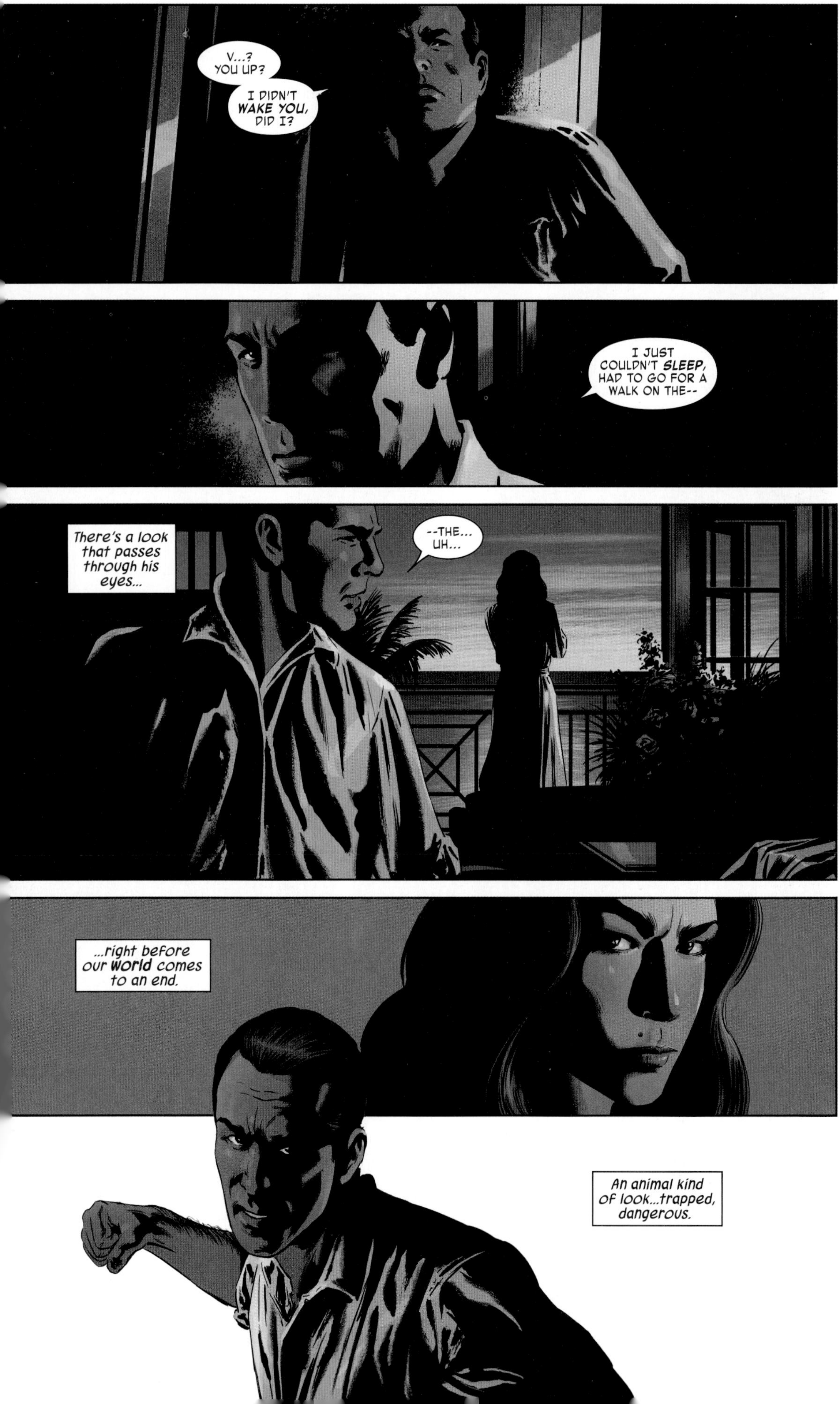
V...? YOU UP?
I DIDN'T WAKE YOU, DID I?
I JUST COULDN'T SLEEP, HAD TO GO FOR A WALK ON THE--
There's a look that passes through his eyes...
--THE... UH...
...right before our world comes to an end.
An animal kind of look...trapped, dangerous.

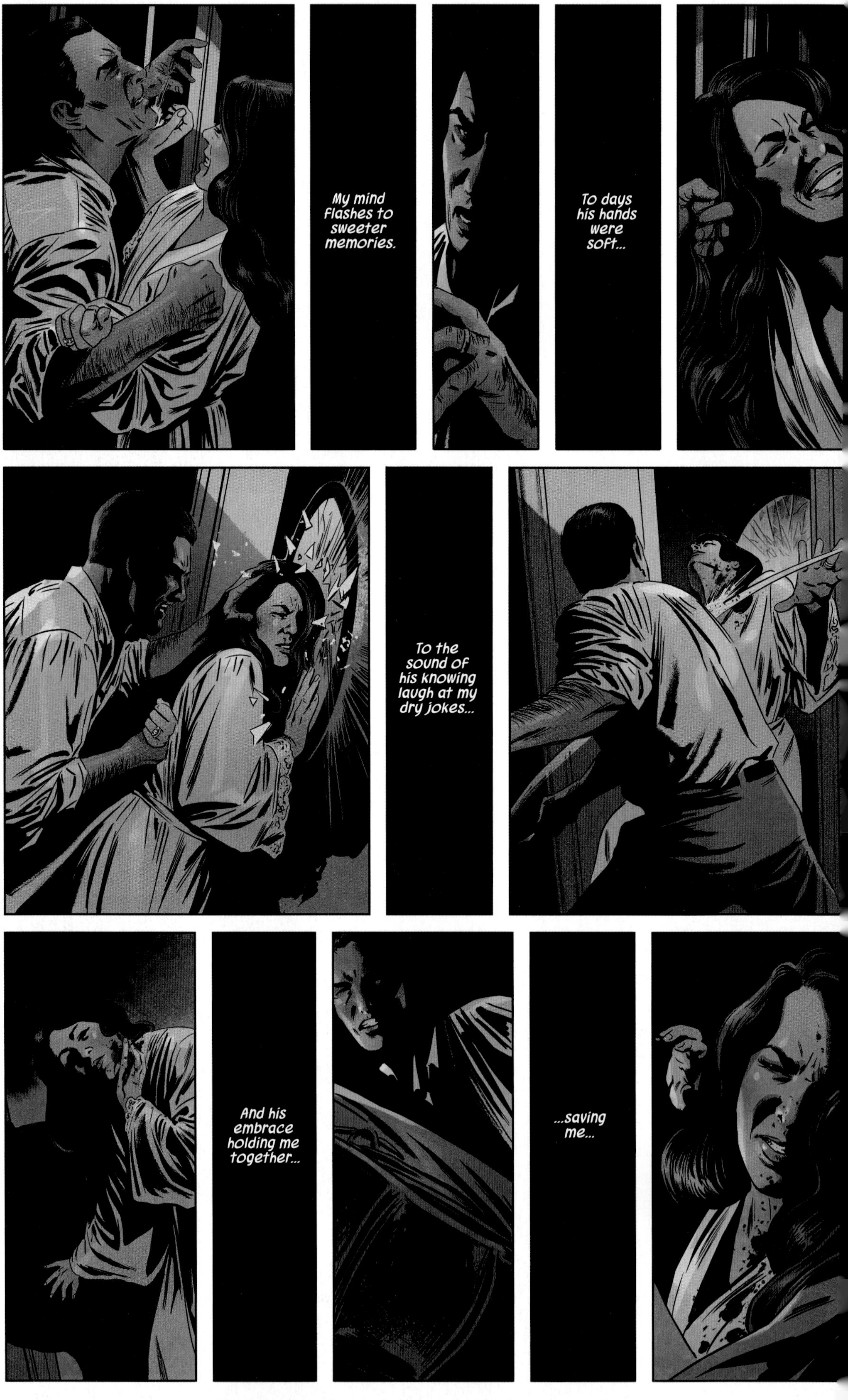
My mind flashes to sweeter memories.
To days his hands were soft...
To the sound of his knowing laugh at my dry jokes...
And his embrace holding me together...
...saving me...

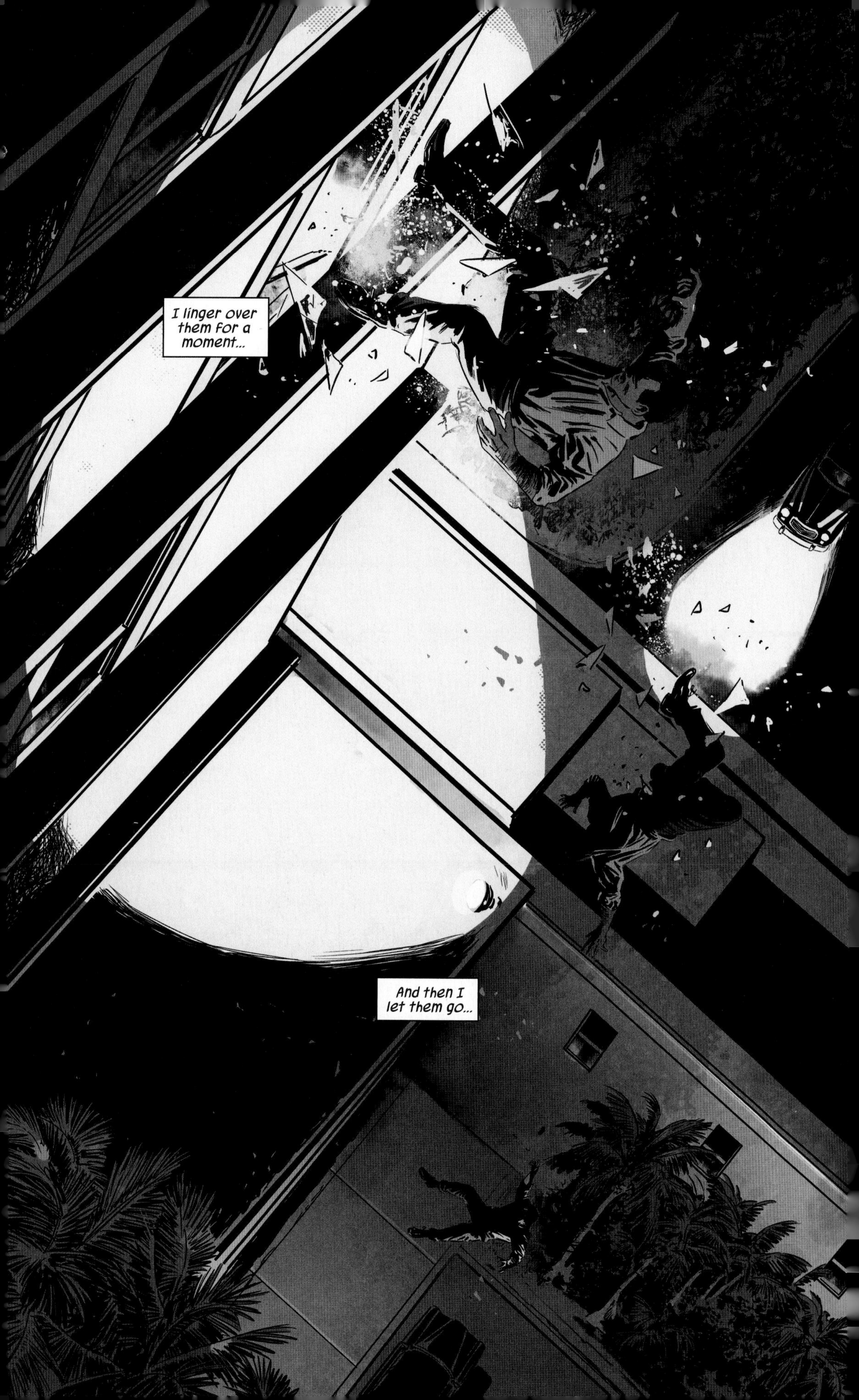
I linger over them for a moment...
And then I let them go...

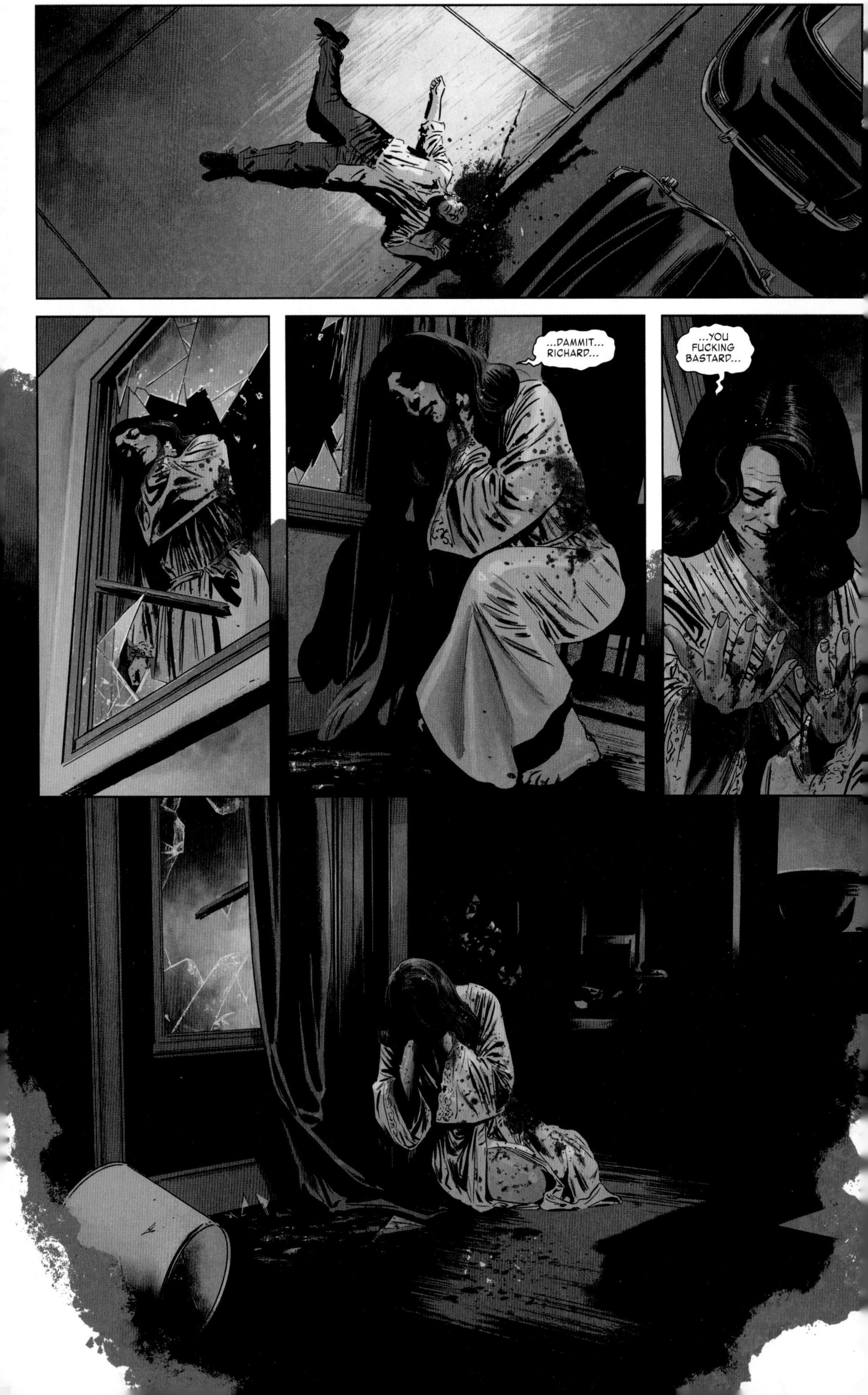
...DAMMIT... RICHARD...
...YOU FUCKING BASTARD...

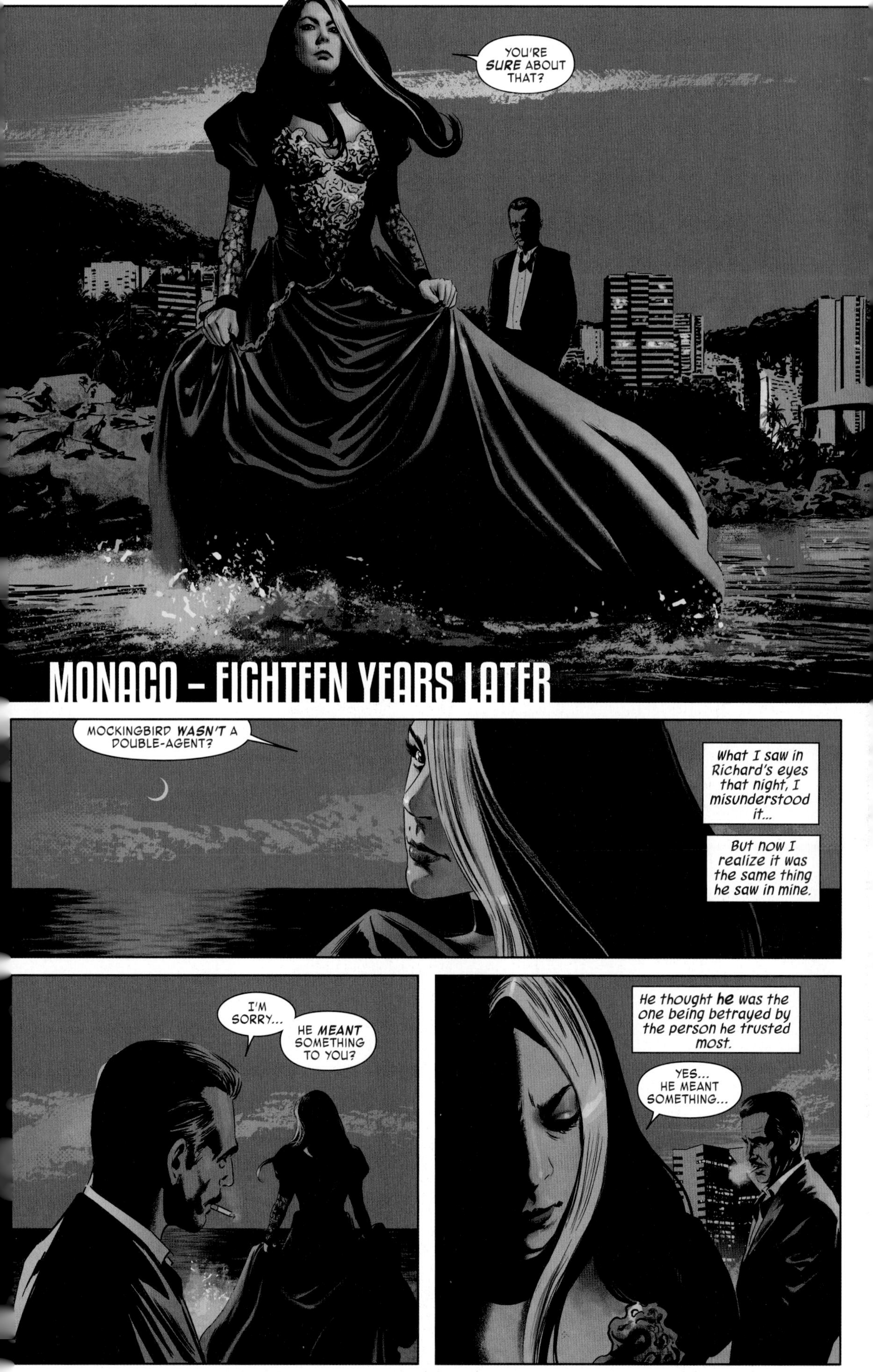
YOU'RE SURE ABOUT THAT?
MONACO – EIGHTEEN YEARS LATER
MOCKINGBIRD WASN'T A DOUBLE-AGENT?
What I saw in Richard's eyes that night, I misunderstood it...
But now I realize it was the same thing he saw in mine.
I'M SORRY...
HE MEANT SOMETHING TO YOU?
He thought he was the one being betrayed by the person he trusted most.
YES... HE MEANT SOMETHING...

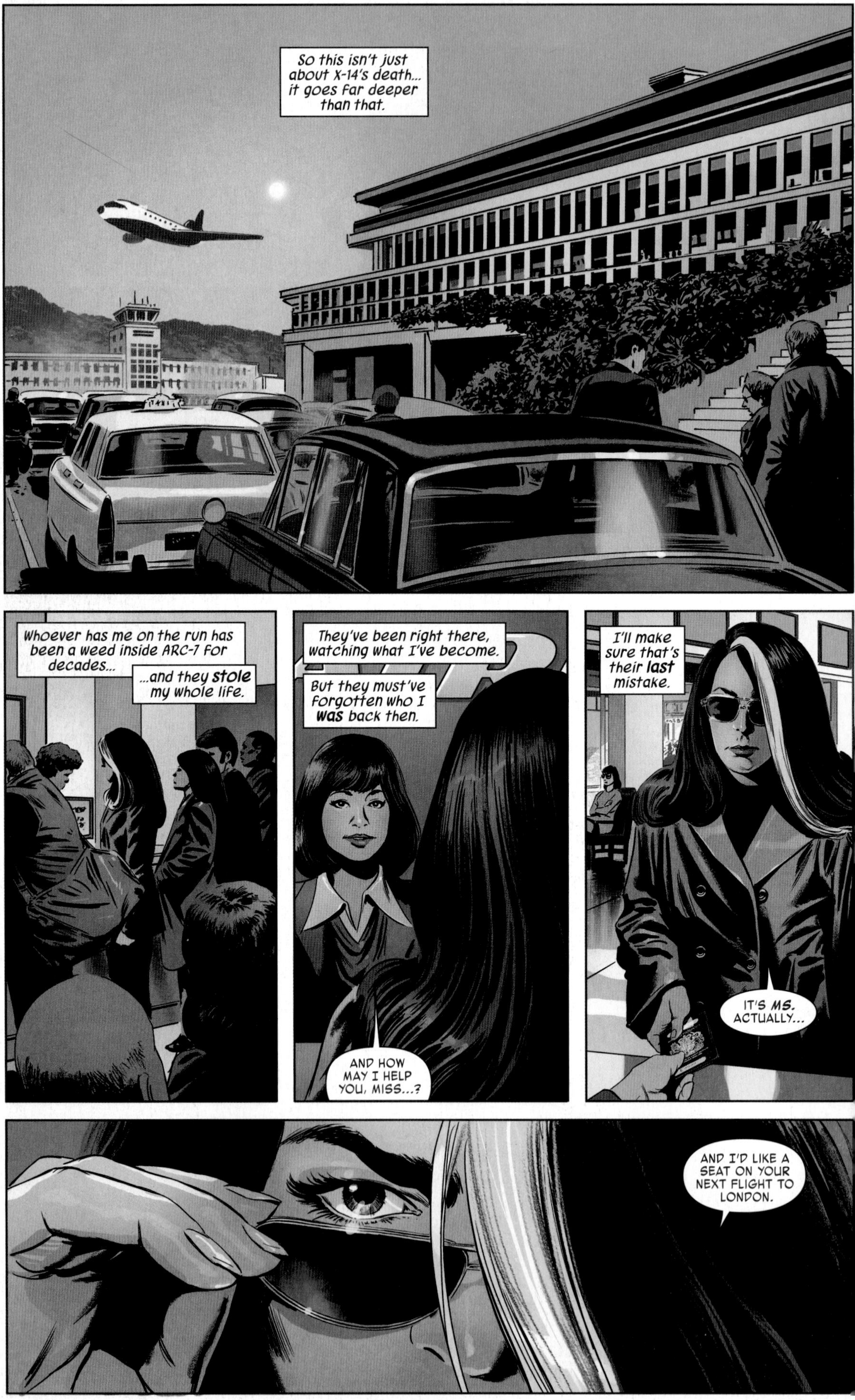
So this isn't just about X-14's death... it goes far deeper than that.
Whoever has me on the run has been a weed inside ARC-7 for decades...
...and they stole my whole life.
They've been right there, watching what I've become.
But they must've forgotten who I was back then.
AND HOW MAY I HELP YOU, MISS...?
I'll make sure that's their last mistake.
IT'S MS. ACTUALLY...
AND I'D LIKE A SEAT ON YOUR NEXT FLIGHT TO LONDON.

TO BE CONTINUED